Dear Peggy,
it was a pleasure
I hope you enjoy the book.
All the best,
[signature]

FROM ORPHAN
TO
HIGH-FLYER

A SPOKEN AUTOBIOGRAPHY

DENIS ELLIOTT AND PHILIP MARTIN

Denis Elliott during his post-war RAF service
For more photos, please visit
www.fromorphantohighflyer.com

ISBN 978-1-8384330-0-0

CONTENTS

INTRODUCTION

Although the idea for this book didn't come to me until April 2018, its roots can be found many years in the past.

I first met Denis at the age of ten, when he had decided to bring his decades of driving to a close. Following this decision, he subsequently sold his car to my mother after a mutual friend put the two of them in touch, knowing that the specifications of the car that Denis was selling matched what my mother was looking to acquire.

A friendship between us did not instantly blossom. In fact, my earliest memory of Denis is of him rebuffing my offer to play a game of chess with him. Fortunately, a friendship between my mother and Denis did form, and from then on whenever a Sunday lunch was cooked Denis was one of the invited guests.

As I entered my teenage years a strong interest in history was born within me, and it was then that I began to ask him questions and realised what calibre of a man was sat around our table. He is a man who has witnessed and experienced so much in his life, who came from and lived through an era that, although studied around the world, is so hard to comprehend for the post-Second World War generations. The Second World War defined Denis's generation: spanning the globe, it remains the largest conflict in human history. It was fought in every environment imaginable: from the jungles of Burma to the deserts of North Africa, the plains of Russia, across Europe and in the oceans of the world. In the towns and cities of multiple continents and in many other fields, both rural and urban, sweltering and freezing, humid and arid. This was a war in which ideologies clashed, empires died, borders changed and tens of millions died. This war, the likes of which we as humans will hopefully never experience again, irreversibly changed the world.

Denis is a man who left his adolescent years and entered adulthood as the war progressed. He bore witness to German aircraft in the skies above Britain. He is someone who experienced the daily life of rationing and blackouts, and as a pilot flew many iconic aircraft in numerous countries around the world. He experienced things that people now read about as taking place in a bygone era with little in common with the modern world. To have him sat with me answering my questions and telling me about his experiences was more than worth its weight in gold, to put it mildly.

What really opened the door that exposed me to it all took place over the course of a Sunday lunch when I was seventeen. Denis asked me if I would be willing to help him maintain his rather large garden, as it was beginning to become too much for him. It was an offer I gladly accepted.

From then on, a new world opened up to me. I would go to his house almost every Saturday, and once work was finished, if there was any to do, we would sit and talk. I would steer the conversation to his RAF service, which he was all too happy to tell me about. It was during this time that I first bore witness to his wonderfully preserved log books. Combing through them with awe and fascination and seeing the written entries of the various operations and exercises that he had told me about was wonderful, as was my pointing out a specific entry, asking him what happened and then listening as he recounted the event with such a high level of detail and eloquence.

As my friendship with Denis reached new heights, so did his friendship with my mother. What started out as the occasional lunch on Sunday soon grew to shopping twice a week and days out, with Sunday lunch becoming a permanent fixture.

Despite all of this, writing a book with Denis about his life never crossed my mind. Besides, he had told me on several occasions during casual conversation that there had been people who wanted to interview him regarding his wartime service, to be used in publications, but that he was just not interested.

The real catalyst for this book came in April 2018, when Denis became very ill. It culminated in a fall and a subsequent stay in hospital. I visited Denis every day, which resulted in me having a lot of time to think about things during the drive to and from the hospital. It came to my mind what an injustice it was that a man who had fought in the biggest conflict that the human race has seen had not recorded his story. It seemed a great shame not to have some record of a man who has lived such an incredible life, whose memory is still unbelievably sharp and who still possesses all of his log books and other records. These stories need to be available to the wider public.

To me, there has always been a huge value in personal stories. Whilst it is always worth studying a battle or an operation in terms of the numbers involved, troop movements and other tactical perspectives, the personal stories of individuals who took part in the battle or event adds another dimension to the account. The personal touch of an individual story offers a unique, emotional depth. It takes the reader right into the heart of whatever battle or event they are reading about.

I didn't expect him to say yes to my proposal of writing a book about his life. Denis has never been one to openly boast about his RAF service or to go on parade or attend events. There is always a humble tone whenever he talks about his life, and time in the RAF; to him, his experiences have been nothing special. Denis is also quite a private man, so I doubted that he would want to share his stories with the world. Still, I had to try, knowing what would be lost if his life story remained locked away within his mind.

One afternoon, Denis was sitting up in his hospital bed and appeared to be in good spirits. After a few minutes of conversing, I told him that I wished to propose something to him. I explained the idea of the book to him, and how we could help to further shine a light onto the war in the Far East and especially onto the flying side of it. I told him this is something that isn't always thought about and that it would be a nice tribute to the men he fought alongside. I suggested that lessons could be passed on to current and future generations, that it would be a wonderful legacy for him and that for both of us 2018 would be quite a symbolic year, being both the hundredth anniversary of the RAF and the centenary of the end of the First World War. I then explained my ideas on how the book could be structured and formatted, but I assured him that these were just suggestions and that he could change any of my ideas if he wished.

He thought about it and then told me that we should do it, which caught me by surprise. During the rest of Denis's stay in hospital we discussed chapter ideas, topics to cover and everything that one can talk about in relation to creating a book. Before long, we were both looking forward to getting started.

Once Denis was out of hospital and settled into his new home, we began, in the first week of May 2018. Although it was unfamiliar territory for both of us, we quickly found a rhythm and got into the swing of things, bouncing ideas off one another as we discussed Denis's life from childhood until the fall which resulted in the idea for this book. As we spoke, I really saw how sharp Denis's mind was; it would work at such a quick pace as he recounted childhood stories in an effortless manner, remembering the smallest detail, some of which happened over ninety years ago.

Fortunately, his rich memory not only applied to his childhood but also to every other period of his life. He would speak in a soft tone, his emotional state reflecting the story which he was recounting. Denis would always recollect the part of his life that we were talking about in acute detail, though the mood would reflect the topic at hand. A sombre, sad atmosphere would descend as Denis, sometimes shedding tears, described his childhood. Yet he would spring to life with laughter and quick energy as he shared his tales of flying across the world. To witness this incredible human being delve into the depths of his past with such honesty and energy, while always being very polite and open, has been the greatest honour of my life.

Over the course of the summer of 2018, we worked most days and were making good progress. In late August, however, Denis had another fall but miraculously didn't break anything, and he came away from it unscathed. The accident was something we hardly spoke about, but from then on we began working seven days a week, from September until December of that year, when the first draft was finished. Then came the lengthy, but essential, task of editing, inserting additions and polishing. During the whole process, Denis's enthusiasm and seemingly boundless reserves of energy were a sight to behold. For hours he recounted stories, or read through what we had written, or suggested new ideas, without seeming to fade at all. There were times when I was tired after many hours of working, and Denis would look at me with a twinkle in his eye and ask me if I wanted to continue, which we would.

Denis's enthusiasm continued throughout 2019, 2020 and 2021, as this book was revised and amended. During this time, we discovered new information from various other sources, including copies of the records of the squadrons on which Denis served, much of which we felt would enhance the book. Together, we worked on adding these new pieces of information into the relevant sections. Also, memories and stories that had not been recalled during our original conversations also came to Denis's mind, which he wanted to include. However, in the spring of 2021, the events surrounding the biggest mystery of Denis's life was also solved, the mystery of what had happened with his biological parents and the events surrounding him being sent to an orphanage. How Denis came to know the truth was because contact was re-established with Ann Soo, the daughter of Daisy, Denis's foster sister, and during the period in which they had lost touch, Ann had discovered what had happened with Denis's biological family after coming into contact with Denis's biological half-niece, Laura Hardin. After Denis and I initiated contact with Laura, she provided us with a lot information regarding Denis's biological family; much of this new information has been added to the book.

This book is written in a Question and Answer format - my question followed by Denis's response. We adopted this style to ensure that, except for reasonable edits, Denis's words appear exactly as he said them, without having to be filtered and adjusted by me or anyone else. Our desire is that the reader will feel as though they are sitting there with us, listening to it all. From a personal perspective, it is also my hope that the reader will see what a truly wonderful and remarkable man Denis is and the unbelievable life that he has lived.

Denis and I would like to thank everyone who read this book and provided feedback to us during its various stages, and those who helped us in various other ways, but we would especially like to express our gratitude to Matt Poole. An aviation historian and expert on RAF Liberator squadrons in the Far East, Matt spent countless hours cross-referencing this book to his archives and sending us his views and suggestions.

We would also like to thank Jonathan Laverick, a British aviation historian living in Botswana (formerly Bechuanaland), for helping us clarify the story which Denis speaks about in Chapter Four. Jonathan wrote a book, *The Kalahari Killings*, about the events surrounding the horrific murders; we are very grateful for his time and expertise.

During the entire process of writing and completing this book, Denis had the final say on everything and has also read and approved this final version.

It is our hope that we have managed to construct this book in such a way that the reader can fully appreciate the incredible life that Denis has lived and will be able to gain value from it. We also hope that this book will help to shine more of a light on the war in the Far East, that we have successfully added to the collective knowledge of modern history and that lessons can be learnt. Denis never banned any topic from being spoken about during our conversations, so if any questions or topics are missing from this book it is only due to my shortcomings in formulating and asking the right questions.

We would be happy to hear from any reader who may be able to provide us with information relative to Denis's story, for consideration for future editions.

Philip Martin
December 2018
March 2021
May 2021

CHAPTER ONE

A BRUTAL CHILDHOOD

*Denis's biological family, life in the orphanage,
foster parents and strict schools*

**It is said that the formative years of someone's life have a strong
influence on the person they become. Your formative years were
largely spent in an orphanage in West Norwood, London. So it's
quite plausible to say that your life could have turned out very
differently.**
Yes, had I been with my own parents it would have been different.
A prime example of that is when I was a child. I was watching
my friends play cricket, and one of them called over to ask me
if I wanted to join them. I replied that it was best if I didn't, or
otherwise my mother would scold me. His response was, 'She's not
your mother, you're only fostered.' It's little things like that which
can add up and have a negative effect on a child.

I was born in Croydon and spent most of my childhood being
brought up by foster parents, firstly in Orpington, Kent, and then in
Farnborough, a small village on the outskirts of Orpington.

Under what circumstances did you have to go into an orphanage?
My first memory is of me sitting on my mother's lap; I must have
been around two-and-a-half. We were both looking at the fire, and
I asked her what the sparks were, and she told me that the sparks
represented people going to church. Her name was Violet Kimber;
she was born in 1891.

It's only recently that I have finally learnt the truth about my
biological family, but still, I am not entirely sure of the exact reason
why I was sent into an orphanage; I always assumed it was because
my mother had an illness like cancer that she knew was going to kill
her. I never knew anything about my father, Walter Kimber, though
I now know that he was born in 1885 and passed away in 1951.

However, what I have recently discovered is that after I was born, my father left my mother and started another family with a different woman, leaving my mother to look after me, my two brothers and one sister. I had an older brother, who like my father was named Walter Kimber. He was eleven years older than me as he was born in 1913; I have no recollection of him and, until recently, didn't even know that I had a brother named Walter. He passed away in 2001. Then there was my sister Doris Elliott, she was nine years older than me as she was born in 1915; I only have very faint memories of her. I only recently found out that we had the same last name, and I didn't even find out that we were related until after the war when Daisy, my foster sister, informed me that the woman I knew as the 'egg lady' (because she looked after chickens and sold eggs) was Harold's sister. I took that to mean she was my half-sister because I assumed that her last name was 'Kimber', the same as my brother, Harold Kimber, who I believed was my half-brother due to our different surnames. Harold was four years older than me as he was born in 1920; he passed away on the 7th of November 1941 while serving with the Merchant Navy. I have some strong memories of him as we were in the same orphanage and were with the same foster parents, my first set of foster parents, for a few weeks.

Why my father put the surname of 'Elliott' on both mine and my sister's birth certificates, and why the surnames of both my mother and father appear as 'Elliott' on my birth certificate, is a mystery to me. But going back to my mother, she eventually met another man and started a family with him. He either didn't want to take care of me and my three siblings or couldn't afford to, the result being that Harold and I were put in an orphanage; I don't know where Walter and Doris went. But I now know that during the war, Doris met a man who was in the Canadian forces; they married and moved to Canada in 1945. She passed away in 1969. My mother passed away in 1975.

But I remember my mother visiting me twice while I was in the orphanage. The first time she brought us pears, the second time toffees. During her visits we would converse in the courtyard with my brother Harold, who was in the junior house. The orphanage was split into three tiers: infants, juniors and seniors. One was an infant until reaching the age of five and starting school, then one was transferred to the juniors, and then if my memory is correct, on turning twelve or thirteen, one was moved into the seniors. However, I never went into the seniors, as I left the orphanage when I was seven.

Growing up in an orphanage in the 1920s when British society still had similarities and links to the Victorian era must have been hard. Could you describe what memories you have of the orphanage?

My main memories are of how strict and regimented day-to-day life was. I was too young to go to school when I first arrived, which was when I was around three-and-a-half years old. One has to remember that in those days one didn't start school until the age of five.

The place was run by females who we had to call 'Sisters', and they were rather cruel people, always ready with a ruler to rap you over the knuckles if you did anything wrong, which your own parents would never do.

So, it was a very rigid, very disciplinarian type of upbringing? I guess it lacked love, the individual connection that every child needs?

Very much so. It was a junior version, if you like, of an army regiment. It was run on very strict lines. No affection, love or anything like that was shown to me or any of the other boys. There were quite a few of us, all around the same age, with the oldest being around seven. But even so, there was always a lingering fear in the air of being punished for doing something wrong, for committing an infraction of some kind.

As a result of living in such an environment, did you boys band together and become close? What was the relationship like between you all?

Between us, there was no difficulty at all. We were in it together, and it wasn't just the one dormitory, there were two, so there was a fair number of us all in it together. We all got on quite well.

A few of us started school at the same time; I still remember that school. I was five years old, so it was after the summer of 1929. It had a very tiny playground, and there was only one master (teacher). The philosophy of education there was learning by rote, in other words, by repetition. I remember that we were given a piece of chalk and a frame inlaid with slate, upon which I learnt how to write the alphabet, my name, birthday, various words and things like that. I was in that school for two years, until I was seven. At that point, I moved in with the first foster parents and that included a change of school.

I remember that a group of us were walking back to the orphanage from school one day during the winter, and we were scraping ice out of the gutter by the road and eating it. It was on that occasion that one of the boys was killed. He was trying to scrape ice out of the gutter when he was hit by a car. His head smashed against the corner of the curb, which split his head open, exposing his brain, which was grey. Being five years old, I didn't know what colour a brain was; at the time I didn't even realise it was a brain. Five years old and having to witness something like that... I can still picture that incident now.

While we're on the subject of winter, I remember my first Christmas at the orphanage. I was about three-and-a-half years old. The boys and girls were all seated in the dining hall at a big table, the girls at one end, then the senior boys, then junior boys and then us infants at the other end. We had all been told that Father Christmas was coming to see us, so we were all quite excited. Then he came out of the kitchen and started walking down my side of the table giving every child an apple while saying, 'Ho ho ho!' When I saw him, such a big man with a big beard and red robe, it terrified me. So when it was my turn to receive an apple I dived under the table screaming, 'Go away!' I remember that. All the children who had seen Father Christmas before couldn't understand what was going on. The House Mother came over saying that he had an apple for me, but I just screamed that I didn't want it, that he was a horrible man. Eventually he worked his way through the room handing out apples and exited once he had finished.

So the people who ran the orphanage did make sure that Christmas was celebrated.
Oh yes, they put on a Christmas lunch, which was when Father Christmas came to visit, resulting in my reaction. Also, the house mothers told us to put a sock at the end of our beds. In the morning

everyone had a little mouse made out of sugar and a tangerine in their sock, all of us except for the oldest boy at the end of the dormitory, who was seven. He would often misbehave, so he received a bar of soap. He was so upset by it that he burst into tears. It was the only time I saw him cry.

What sort of things would be deserving of punishment in the orphanage?

One example was that at the end of each room there were chamber pots that we would use to urinate in overnight. We were only allowed to urinate in a chamber pot, nothing else. One morning, a number two was found in one of the pots. We were marched downstairs in our pyjamas. The Sisters then put us over their laps, took our trousers down and proceeded to examine our bottoms for evidence. It turned out to be the oldest boy, so he was dragged away for punishment. I never found out what punishment he received. This was the same boy who had a bar of soap put in his sock at Christmas.

Another example that sticks in my mind was when I was being taught how to put on boots for the first time, as opposed to the shoes I was used to. Boots, of course, require lacing up, which one of the Sisters was showing me how to do, but whenever I made a mistake she would whack me over the knuckles with a ruler.

These were just two examples.

What did you do at the orphanage on a day-to-day basis? What did they try to teach you?

The day began with us all getting up together at the same time, then downstairs to have a shower or strip wash, then back upstairs to get into our ordinary clothes. After breakfast we would go to school if it was a school day, and if not, then the day was spent playing games inside or out in the yard.

On one occasion, I was playing tag with another boy out in the yard. He tripped over, broke his leg and began howling. He was carried inside, and I was called in soon afterwards. I was told that I had been a wicked boy for breaking his leg, despite the fact that I was nowhere near him. But even so, I was still caned over the knuckles for being such a naughty boy.

You entered the orphanage when you were three-and-a-half years old and left at the age of seven?

I arrived when I was around three-and-half years old and was there for roughly three-and-a-half-to-four years, until I was seven.

It's always hard to get someone to analyse themselves and the effects that spending their first years in a place like that can have. But did being raised in such an environment and experiencing what you did have an effect on you as a person growing up?

Very much so, but not only in myself. I noticed a lack of confidence in anything I tried to do that was a bit out of the ordinary. It was a very unusual beginning to life, and I would notice that older boys, say twelve or thirteen, were partaking in activities, mainly sports, and I would say to myself, 'There is no way that I will ever be able to do that!' Even then, I had no confidence in my own ability.

It seems as though living in that orphanage resulted in you not being allowed to explore, to form your own personality, and as a result you were quite limited in self-esteem and a belief in what you could achieve.

Yes, exactly. Life was spent either in the orphanage, school or on the grounds of the orphanage. Aside from school, the only time we went off the grounds was across the road to church on Sundays, and even that was regimented; we had to march there. It wasn't a natural life like I saw other boys having with their own parents.

When you had the option in school to take part in a sport, to be part of a sports team, I assume that those things never came naturally to you.

What stood out in my mind was when teams were being assembled to play football, or something like that, I was never picked on any team, or if I was, I would be the last one, as the captains knew that I wasn't any good. In cricket, for example, there were two or three occasions when the batsman hit the ball straight at me and I turned around and ran away rather than try and catch it.

Eventually, you left the orphanage. What was it like to step into a slightly more normal environment, going from the orphanage to a foster family?

From the age of around seven right until I was called up by the RAF, I was brought up by foster parents. One day, the welfare officer of the orphanage collected Harold and myself. The three of us were taken by bus to Victoria bus station. From there we walked to Victoria railway station and were then taken by train to Orpington railway station. Once there, we were met by a couple who were to be our first foster parents. To my surprise, the man was wheeling a pram with a toddler inside. I tumbled over and was asked by my new foster father if I was tired, to which I replied that I was. So he took the toddler out of the pram and put me inside, and I fell asleep. Once at their house, we were bedded in a box bedroom, with myself in the bottom bunk and Harold in the top one.

Overall, despite monthly visits by the Welfare Officer to check up on us, living with them was a terrible experience. At first it was Harold and I, but after a few weeks he left. The reason I was given was that 'he was a bad example to you.' One occasion that comes to mind is when my foster father asked me to fetch a tool from the shed. I remembered that I had done it obediently on a previous occasion and that Harold had told me that I was a timid mouse, and that I should stand up for myself and next time tell him to get the bloody thing himself. So when my foster father asked me to get a tool from the shed, I said to him, 'Get the bloody thing yourself', in a raised voice. He was furious and asked me to repeat myself, so I did. He then downed his tools. I ran into the kitchen, but he caught up with me, bent me over his knee and gave me a really hard smacking. The foster father was a violent, nasty man, in my opinion. I have memories of him beating his wife and beating me.

One particular memory that shows how horrible a man he could be was when I witnessed him violently attacking his wife whilst he was drunk. He had her on her back on the sofa in the living room, and she was screaming and trying to fight him off. I tried to drag him off, but he simply picked me up with one arm and hurled me across the room. Luckily, I landed in an armchair, but he threw me with such force that if I had hit the wall it probably would have killed me. I was only eight years old when that happened. Fortunately, the postman, who lived next door, knew I was being mistreated and reported it to the council. He told me this later when I ran into him when I was twelve.

Was your first foster mother any different from your first foster father?

Yes, she was a nice person, but the trouble was that she couldn't go against her husband. One thing about my first foster mother is that she would sometimes bake cupcakes in the morning, and they would be cooling in the tray as I left for school. I would take one so I would have something to eat. I thought that she never noticed until I ran into her after the war, and she told me that she had known every time but had never mentioned it to her husband or he would have beaten me.

It was while I was living with the first foster parents that I saw the sea for the first time. I was eight years old. All the parents on our road organised a trip for the children to visit the sea. For this, we went to Margate. A girl of around twelve, who was in charge of our small group of children, said, 'Look, there's the sea.' On a road which ran next to the sea, there was a roundabout with a fountain in the middle, and I thought she was referring to the fountain, so I came out with something like, 'Is that it?' 'No,' she said, as she directed my eyes to the sea. Upon seeing it, I was absolutely transfixed: it was love at first sight. We went on the beach, and since the other children who had been to the beach before were taking off their shoes and socks, I followed their lead. While I was paddling my feet in the sea, the girl told me to dip my finger in the water and taste it. It was then that I learnt that the sea was salty. I remember that we then went for fish and chips. I have always remembered seeing the sea for the first time. I still love it, even now.

On one occasion my first foster parents went to the circus. I was left in the house on my own. The house was lit by gas lamps, and I was warned not to try and light them. They hid the matches anyway. This was during the winter as it got dark quite early. I was in a pitch-black house on my own and was scared, so I went and sat on the front step and started sobbing. Mr Davidson and his wife, who lived over the road, heard me. He came and comforted me and invited me into his house, where he poured me a glass of milk and gave me some cake, which cheered me up. Eventually my foster parents returned and me not being there, started calling my name, which caused Mr Davidson to go out and give my foster father a piece of his mind. This caused quite a row. Once it was over, my foster father ordered me to bed.

Not long after that event, my first foster father brought home a goldfish that he had won at a fairground. It inspired me to write a story for a contest at my school. I was still at infant school, but it was a new one that I had transferred to when I moved in with the first foster parents. I wrote a story about how goldfish could breathe without lungs and won first prize, which was a book about Robin Hood.

Later on when I was still in junior school, I believe that the headmaster also raised concerns with the council about my foster father. Basically, if you arrived after the school bell was sounded by the prefect, a mark was noted in their book. If you received three marks in one week you were caned. I usually went without any sort of breakfast, and I was made to wash all the dishes that were covered in cold grease before leaving for school. If I was lucky I received a strip of bacon or something else. Anyway, all of that caused me to be late more often than not, which resulted in weekly canings. One day I just broke down and started sobbing. The headmaster asked me what the problem was and I told him everything. A few weeks later I was sent to live with the second pair of foster parents at 33 Gladstone Road, Farnborough, and I transferred to another school there.

Were the second pair any better than the first?
When I arrived at their house for the first time, my new foster mother opened the door and said the following: 'Oh good, a darkie. Perhaps he will bring us some luck.' They were her exact words. I have never forgotten that. She was always quite a superstitious woman.

But yes, living with them was much better. I was given some freedom and a deal of responsibility that I didn't have in the orphanage or with the first foster parents. For example, we had a canary named Mickey, a cat named Peter and a dog named Max. I was allowed to take Max out for walks on my own, and I could go on shopping trips for my foster mother by myself. However, they are only two of the few examples where I can say that I had any freedom. I wasn't allowed out to play with other children, for example. But I will say that I wasn't alone there. I had been with my foster parents for about a year when I was joined by a boy named William, known as Billy, who was four years younger than me. Though he was younger, it still provided us both with a partnership, as we were both in the same situation. There was also a boy named Tom, he was three years older than me and was there before I arrived.

What were the second set of foster parents like?

My foster mother was very strict and was fifty-two when I went to live with them in 1934; I was nine. She was born in 1882, so as you can imagine, she practically embodied the Victorian era. She never showed any affection or love towards me or anyone, not even when I returned from overseas after the war. She viewed herself as of a higher class than she actually was. Once, when I was twelve, word had got around that one of the female members of the Royal Family had injured her leg and was walking with a limp, so my foster mother started to limp, too, even though she was fine. I brought it up at the time, why she was walking that way, and it made her really angry. In her mind, walking with a limp brought her closer to the level of the Royal Family. She also had two ways of speaking, one to the welfare officers, neighbours, people like that, to make her seem better educated than she actually was, and then her actual way of talking, which was littered with grammar and pronunciation mistakes. She hated it if you tried to correct her. These things made her feel special, as though she was of a higher class.

A good example of her strictness was when she gave me a block of jelly marked out in cubes, which she told me to break up and put in hot water. I complied. As I was breaking the cubes, I started to say a rhyme of, 'jelly belly, jelly belly' to myself. She yelled at me to stop and told me that she would not tolerate language like that in her house.

My second foster father was a lovely man, but he could only walk with great difficulty. He was disabled due to an accident involving his back, suffered before my time, that had left him bent over. He was quite an understanding man. I only ever saw him lose his temper once. I can say that we really were good friends. He taught me many mechanical things, like how to repair punctures on bicycles, look after the chain and reconnect the links if they came apart, and he offered practical advice in the house and out in the garden too. I would have liked him to have been my own true father; he was that kind of man. He was very good at woodwork, and he also enjoyed gardening. He used to grow his own vegetables and even used to cut the back lawn with hand shears.

Did you ever see Harold again?
Yes, but unfortunately it wasn't to last long. After he left the first foster family, he went to a village named St Mary Cray, which was a couple of miles away from Orpington and Farnborough. After that, I didn't see him for a few years until I was in secondary school. I must have been eleven, he was well into his teens by then. He waited for me outside the school gates and said that he wanted to talk to me, to have a proper conversation about the past. I had to be home straight after school, so I didn't stick around; otherwise I would be in trouble. I told my foster mother what Harold had told me, and she warned me that he was 'a very wicked boy' and that I was never to speak to him under any circumstances.

So when I ran into him for the second time at Farnborough bus terminal, I just ran away. I never saw him again. I later learnt that during the war he joined the Merchant Navy and was on the cargo ship, MV Nottingham, when it was torpedoed in the North Atlantic on the 7th of November 1941. There were no survivors. How I wish I had spoken to him. I would have learnt so much and filled in so many gaps regarding my background and what happened. His name is on the Merchant Navy Memorial in London.

Not long after joining the second pair of foster parents you broke your neck.
I must have been around nine when that happened. I was playing in the playground and tripped over and banged my head on the ground, on a very hard surface. The result was that vertebrae five and six in my neck were broken. I was taken home; I didn't go to hospital. I was placed in a position with pillows around my neck so I couldn't move. The family doctor was called. He was quite elderly, and he said that I had a sore throat and gave me something called Friars Balsam to treat it. It was disgusting, a very bitter taste, so my foster

mother used to pour it onto a sugar cube to mask the taste. It didn't really work, as I could still taste it. I can still taste it now.

Eventually, the two vertebrae fused together. I would not find out about it until 1956, when I was in Malta and suffered another neck injury, which resulted in a hospital visit.

When people look back on the 1920s or the pre-war period, many tend to think of a stricter society, where among other things, public behaviour and expectations were clearly set. Is this perception of what it was like true in your opinion?

I found that life changed considerably at the outbreak of war, which coincided with the time I left school at the age of fifteen and started work. The way it most noticeably changed for me was that the men I had been working with were called up and I suddenly had more responsibilities. I found that I thrived on those responsibilities, and not just at work, but after work at night school, where I went to study accountancy.

When the night school had to close because of the wartime blackouts, I joined the Air Defence Cadet Corps, later renamed the Air Training Corps, and I really expanded my abilities there. I passed exams and gained certificates and was finally able to tell myself that I was just as good as everyone else. For me, life changed in that way.

If we go back a bit, I recall you telling me once how your secondary school was quite modern in its design for the time, but that the style of education, shall we say, stuck to the older methods. What was the school itself like?

It was very large. There were around 500 boys in the boys' school and a similar number in the attached girls' school. I first went there in September 1935, just after I had turned eleven and had passed the equivalent of the eleven plus. The school was named Orpington Central School.

The headmaster was a very strict man, very strict indeed, and he would not only impose his strictness on us boys but also on the masters. In class, we weren't even allowed to whisper let alone make any other noise without the risk of punishment, as indeed I once discovered. All I did was whisper to the boy next to me, 'I can't find my pen,' and he replied, 'Well, look in your desk.' To that, I replied that it wasn't in there. The master heard this, so I had to go to him and was promptly caned across both hands, three times in total. He was the sort of man who really caned you. It wasn't a tap; he would raise his arm above his head and put everything into it, to cause maximum pain. Those canes were only thin bamboo canes so they really hurt. Caned three times just for saying that I couldn't find my pen; it was that sort of discipline.

On another occasion, I had received a fountain pen as a Christmas present from the sister of my second foster father. The problem with it was that it constantly leaked. Once, I was using it to complete some geography homework when it started to leak everywhere. I tried to clean it up with blotting paper, but it wouldn't soak it all up so there were still stains on the paper. When I was back at school I handed in this homework. The geography master was quite angry and gave me a big lecture on the standards he expected for the homework he gave out and that mine was the most disgusting he had ever seen. I was then told to put out my hand and was then caned twice, but I disliked that master so much that I refused to let him see me cry. So I took it, and then just left the empty classroom. He was a big fat man; I can picture him now.

Punishments did not always lead to canings though. On one occasion, I was eating an apple, trying my best not to get caught, when the boy sitting behind me put up his hand and told the master that I was eating. The master asked me if I was eating, I tried to hide the contents of my mouth under my tongue and attempted to give an answer. I was told to spit the contents into the bin and not to do it again. The boy who told on me was then called up to the front of the class, and the master asked him how it felt to be a sneak, which was quite an insult.

As he made his way back to his seat, I whispered to him that I was going to sort him out at playtime. The master heard this and said in a quiet voice that nothing will happen at playtime. However, I was so angry with the boy that I would have half-killed him if given the chance, but by the end of the class it was mostly forgotten about.

Looking back at your time in that school, do you feel as though the standard of education was good?

That school had a whole range of classes. It was on two levels, had around ten classrooms on each level, plus a full-size gym with a range of sports equipment, and every subject had its own master. The assistant headmaster taught maths. Then there were separate masters for science, woodwork, gardening, geography, history and English.

Judging by the story you told of being caned for whispering about your pen, it seems like you were taught in an environment of fear and strict discipline.

Again, I go back to the word discipline. It was very, very disciplined. For example, when we went from class to class we would have to walk in silence, in single file. The headmaster would patrol the corridors with his cane tapping against his heels, looking for anyone to step out of line. A prefect was appointed for each of the two levels of classrooms, and they were responsible for reporting any boy who was caught running down the corridor or breaking any other rules. The prefect would then have to report it to the headmaster, and if he didn't, then the prefect himself would be in trouble; it was that kind of discipline.

What sort of things could get you in trouble? What sort of things were the prefects expected to report?

I have just given two examples: anyone caught running through the corridor, or any boys caught speaking to each other; these were against the rules. We had to concentrate on going from wherever we had left to wherever we were supposed to be going.

But I do have one story to tell you that shows how extreme discipline in schools could be.

What happened?

As I have mentioned, the school had two wings, one for the boys and the other for the girls, who were completely separated from us boys, even on the playground. On the occasion of this episode, a boy from a very poor family, who didn't have a father, was caught red-handed stealing from boys' coats in the cloakroom. He must have been around thirteen at the time. He was immediately taken to the headmaster. The headmaster informed him that he would be caned in front of the school.

All of us boys were assembled in the hall. This boy was brought out onto the stage, stretched out facedown on a table by masters and then caned across the backside by another master until he was screaming for mercy. It went on for several minutes, during which the boy must have been caned around twelve times. The master caning him started with the cane above his head and really put a lot of force into it. It was such a cruel event that half of the boys in the hall were in tears at witnessing this cruel spectacle. The headmaster eventually called a halt to it, and the boy himself was expelled. It left such a strong impression.

That is a truly horrific story. Do you know what became of that boy?
Sometime later, after the war had started, I heard that he had gone into the army and had reached the rank of sergeant.

Was that discipline evident in society at large, or was it just limited to a few institutions like schools?
Oh, it was quite evident in day-to-day life. If a child was running around in the street making too much noise, then adults who knew the family, even if it was more as acquaintances, would often go and report it to the child's parents. That was quite common.

A classic example was scrumping for apples in an orchard, which we had in our rural village. Before the war that was definitely frowned upon and would land you in trouble with your parents. After the war, people didn't care so much.

Fortunately, things seemed to change after the war. Incidents like the one I spoke about, with the boy being caned for stealing, that sort of brutality wasn't allowed to happen.

So, when you were growing up, would you say that there was a certain way that men, women and children were supposed to behave, and that the people and society would enforce it?
Yes, certainly before the war, there was a very Victorian mindset, shall we say, the opinion that children should be seen but not heard

being an example. My foster parents were typical examples of people who had been brought up during the Victorian era. My foster mother, especially, had very strict rules and regulations over what could and couldn't be done.

You have spoken about how the girls in your school were educated in a different wing to the boys, but were boys and girls generally kept apart outside of school too?

Yes, they were, especially in my case. I remember once when I was about ten years old, a group of us boys were in the playground talking about girls we liked. When it was my turn to speak, I told everyone that I liked a girl named Joan. Everyone else thought that Joan was ugly because she wore a black eye patch, but to me she was beautiful. Anyway, one of my friends told me that if I liked Joan so much I should write her a note telling her, so that's exactly what I did. My friend gave it to her and in it, I wrote, 'Dear Joan, I love you very much, and one day I want to marry you. Love Denis.'

One day I came back from school, and my foster mother ordered me into the front room, which meant I was in trouble. Standing there was Joan's guardian. It transpired that Joan had put the note under her pillow, and it had been discovered by her guardian. So I was asked what that note was and if I had written it. When I confirmed that I had written it, I was chastised. Then my foster mother said the most unbelievable thing. She asked me if I loved the cat, and when I said yes, she said something like, 'See, that's love. What you wrote in that note isn't love.'

Joan's guardian did everything to keep us apart; she would even keep watch outside their front gate after school. However, as Joan and I got older, we did meet up a few times. I would pretend to my foster mother that I was going to the ATC, but I have no idea what Joan told her guardian. Once, we went to a play about Latin American dancing, another time we went to the circus. I was posted out to Malta a few years after the war had finished, and she asked me for an address to write to. I wrote to her three times without response, and when I arrived home on leave I noticed that their house had been boarded up. My foster mother told me that they had vanished in the middle of the night. To this day I believe that my letters were intercepted and that my foster mother knew where they went.

How did things change for you as you got older?

For the first few years I still lacked self-confidence and wouldn't stand up for myself, but that changed as I got older, especially when I started work at fifteen once I left school.

In the first three years that I was with the second set of foster parents, there was an older boy who lived there, named Tom, who I have already mentioned. I didn't really like him or get on with him too well. He was three years older than me and had quite a big build for his age. Because he was older and bigger than me I looked up to him in the beginning, but despite this he used to bully me and bend me to his will. But on the other hand, he would also act like a protector and ensure that no harm came to me. For example, he would force me to act as lookout for the police when he wanted to steal things like bicycles; anything that could be sold. I didn't want to but wished to avoid conflict, so I went along with it. Though as I said, he would often protect me. He also taught me how to ride a bicycle.

Once we went to visit a friend of his who had a sister who must have been around sixteen. I was around twelve. She was a natural bully and started slapping me for no reason. Tom quickly saw what was going on and put a stop to it.

Tom had to leave the house when he was fifteen over a disagreement regarding his pay packet when he started work. What happened is that once a foster child started work, the council would stop paying the allowance that they gave to the child's foster parents. Our foster mother expected him to hand over his pay packet for her to keep to make up for this financial loss, with him keeping the rest of it. But when she asked for his pay packet he absolutely lost it, and a blazing row took place, a screaming match between the two of them. In his eyes, he had done the work, so he deserved to keep every penny of it. In the end, he stormed upstairs, grabbed a suitcase, packed all of his belongings in it and stormed out.

Our foster father, in the only time that I saw him angry, had tried to whack him with his stick and had accidentally caught me. At that point, he lost all of his anger, and his immediate concern was for me. He kept asking me if I was alright. So Tom went to live with his friend, who had the sister who slapped me. But that didn't work out too well, as his friend's mother began demanding money as well, to cover his upkeep. In the end, he intercepted me walking home from school one day and asked me to tell my foster mother that he wanted to come back. When I told her about this conversation that Tom and I had, she asked me if I wanted him to come back. I informed her that I didn't, and her reply was that in that case, he wasn't coming back.

So, there was Tom, Billy, yourself and their fostered daughter Daisy who you mentioned earlier. Did they have any children of their own or look after any others?
They had a biological son of their own named Bert, who when I went to live with them, was already twenty-seven; he worked as a nurse at the hospital in Orpington. Daisy was fostered by them when she was two and was ten years older than me. Then there was Tom and myself, and then Billy joined us. I was eleven at the time, and he was four years younger. So, including my foster parents, seven of us lived in the house at one time.

1929 to the early 1930s are synonymous with the Great Depression. Though you were young, do you remember the effects it had on Britain and on your two foster families?
I remember realising at the time that life was becoming more austere. But we lived in a tiny rural village, where life generally seemed to carry on, and the horrific conditions that the industrial parts of Britain went through didn't seem to affect us to such an extent. Our milk was still delivered by horse and cart in glass bottles. Everyone would watch the horse to see if it would have a poo in the road, and if it did, it was quickly scooped up and put on allotments or on flower beds.

But I remember throughout the thirties, if we had toast, we would be allowed to have either butter or jam on it but not both. Despite both Bert and Daisy working and money coming in from the council, money was still very tight. There were also a lot of men, many First World War veterans, out on the streets begging or selling matches or some other items in an attempt to earn some money. Many of them had a limb or two missing, and all of them on the street suffered from a shortage of money. There was no welfare state back then.

Aside from school and being at home, what other activities did you partake in?

My main activity was being a member of the church choir. The first choir I joined was at All Saints Church, when I was with the first set of foster parents in Orpington. The second choir I was with was at St Giles Church, when I lived with the second set of foster parents in Farnborough. I was with that choir until January 1939. The commitment to the choir included mid-week practice as well as Sunday services.

I remember that I used to take my own Bible into church services so I would have something to read. One day, one of the other boys stole it, and I know that because I saw him holding it. When I asked him to give it back, he told me that he wasn't going to, which resulted in one of the older boys stating that there was going to be a fight for it at the back of the church. We all went there after choir practice, and the other boys formed a rough circle. I threw a punch that landed on the boy's nose, causing it to bleed, and he started crying. By this time the fight had been broken up, and I got my Bible back.

Another thing that really sticks out is when I was out with Max the dog. I heard the distant rumble of thunder and decided that it was best that I make my way home. Unfortunately, the storm moved faster than I did, and before long I was caught in torrential rain. To get home I had to cross a lane, which was bordered by thick hedging. I went through a gap in the hedge and pulled Max close to me, giving him more shelter than I was getting myself. But eventually the rain eased enough for us to make a run for it. Once we were inside, my foster mother told me, 'You're soaking wet, get everything off.' I was eleven years old.

CHAPTER TWO

THE EARLY WAR YEARS,
SEPTEMBER 1939 – OCTOBER 1942

*Entering the workforce, the Air Training Corps, Biggin Hill
and witnessing the Battle of Britain and the Blitz*

**On the 3rd of September 1939, Britain declared war on Germany.
Where were you at the time of the announcement?**
I was in church listening to the vicar's sermon when a warden
walked in and handed the vicar a piece of paper. It was read out, and
it informed us that Britain was now at war with Germany and that
we should all go home and listen to our radios. On the way home an
air raid siren suddenly went off, but it turned out to be a false alarm.
But at least everyone got to know what it sounded like, as no one
had heard one before.

When I arrived home, the atmosphere was one of apprehension.
One couldn't help but talk about anything else but the war. I asked
my foster father how long he thought the war would last, and he
looked at me and said, 'Oh, you'll never be involved.'

How did day-to-day life and society change?
Society quickly changed. Overnight, all the men who were fit and
of military age were called up and children were soon sent off into
the countryside, which affected almost all families. Rationing was
quickly introduced on the essentials like petrol, sugar and butter,
but it soon expanded to include things like meat, eggs, cheese
and children's sweets. Eventually, clothing became rationed too.
Britain's entire industrial output was soon geared towards the war,
so a factory that made cars was soon making tanks.

People were quickly encouraged to do more, so scouts were
instructed to find things like metal gates, which they were told would
be melted down and turned into tanks and Spitfires. Women were

encouraged to knit more, things like scarves and balaclavas, and they were soon encouraged to join the labour force, mainly being sent into factories to make up for the number of men being called up.

But despite the apprehension, many people didn't believe that the war would last too long. It was the view that, 'It will soon be over.' It wasn't until Dunkirk happened that people really realised the significance of the situation and that the outcome wasn't so secure.

You had left school in the summer of 1939. What were you doing during those first war years?
Immediately after I left school, I started working in a town named Hayes, as an assistant in an electrical showroom, which itself was part of a chain. But there was a problem, which resulted in my last name being changed. When I began working there, they required proof of age, so they contacted the authorities - I assume Kent County Council - to get a copy of my birth certificate. However, they were unable to find one. The result was that my birth certificate was found but that my name was 'Denis Elliott' and not 'Denis Kimber'.

Why did you have the last name of 'Kimber' for the first fifteen years of your life?
The reason I had been given the last name Kimber was because I went into the orphanage with my brother, whose last name was Kimber, so they just gave me his last name. I had it until the truth came out when my actual birth certificate was found.

What was it like working in the showroom?
Very quickly I was given a lot of responsibility, and before long I could quote the items that we stocked and could basically run the shop myself. The reason for that was that a lot of my superiors were called up to the armed forces, so I had the opportunity to advance quite quickly. I remember that the superintendent of the shop smoked so much that he was deemed medically unfit for army service, and another supervisor was called up to the RAF. Years later I would run into that supervisor on an island just off the Burma coast, by which time I was a pilot.

A lot of women were brought out of retirement to fill the posts that the men had left empty, which eventually resulted in me being the only male working in the shop until one week before I was called up. That is when I began to train another male to take over from me. During that time, the Luftwaffe was conducting air raids. I remember on one occasion hearing the high-pitched noise of a falling bomb. I was outside watching these planes fly over with the supervisor, who was only in her twenties. Recognising the sound of a falling bomb, we both ran inside, and I yelled at everyone to get down. The supervisor dived onto her hands and knees, and I did the same and landed not far behind her. The cashier, she had been brought out of retirement to do the cashier job, had not heard the bomb falling and didn't know what to make of the two of us on our hands and knees so close together. The bomb fell on Hayes railway station.

Despite most people's purse strings having to be tightened, we sold a surprising amount of goods, especially electrical. People were starting to buy electrical goods in much greater numbers. One way to purchase things was through something called 'Hire Purchase', which for many was the only way to buy goods like that at the time. With 'Hire Purchase', the customer would fill in a form where he or she would agree to pay back the cost of the item in instalments.

The popular items were electrical kettles, irons, fridges and cookers. Though basic, they were becoming very popular. However, the wiring was very basic; no earthing wires in those days. I remember having to connect lamps in the showrooms to the mains, which involved putting a positive and negative wire to the mains. If you mistimed it, you would receive a shock, like a kick.

The responsibility I was given increased to the point that I became 'Assistant Cashier' and was put in charge of the storeroom where things like cables and bulbs were kept, among many other things. Once, the supervisor instructed me to lock up the store. The other staff member had gone home and the supervisor was running late for her bus due to a late customer, so I was given the keys.

So I locked up, but I then began to worry about having the keys because if the place was hit by bombs, questions would be asked as to why I had been left with the keys. So I cycled after her bus. It was the no.119 bus, which ran from Sidcup to a place called Wallington, which was the name of a district on the other side of Croydon. I caught up with the bus. She was the last passenger, and once she got off, the look on her face was quite a sight when she saw me. I gave her the keys and she admitted that she had also been worried about me having them.

But in December 1939, I had to have my appendix removed. Before Christmas, the two male staff at the electric showroom where I worked had been called up, and in their place a retired lady had been brought in to become the cashier, and a much younger lady became the supervisor. I have already mentioned them.

I'm sure it was in early December. I had to clean the floors of the showrooms. I was sweeping the floor behind the counter where the cashier worked when I heard a customer say to the cashier, 'Is that boy alright?' In the next instant, I dropped the broom and fell to the floor with intense stomach pains. It was decided that I should go home, and the person in charge of the clerical office above the showrooms had a car and kindly took me home. At that point I was still in pain, so my foster mother decided that the best place for me would be my bed. Once I lay down, the pain eased off somewhat, and I went to sleep. During the afternoon, my foster mother brought up a bowl of porridge. She was a great believer in porridge being the cure of all ills, but on this occasion I couldn't touch it. I decided to go downstairs. I had hardly got downstairs when the intense pain returned, and I just collapsed to the floor moaning that I wanted a doctor.

My younger foster brother, Billy, was sent to the doctor's house to ask for him to make an emergency call, which he did. After examining me, the doctor told my foster mother that I had appendicitis and that he would immediately phone for an ambulance to take me to hospital.

At the hospital, they inserted an enema and put me to bed. Not long afterwards, I was put on a trolley and wheeled to the operating theatre. Unfortunately, the surgical team was not ready. The nurse who was with me kept on trying to reassure me that I had nothing to worry about and that everything would be fine, when in reality I was a bundle of nerves. Before long, I was wheeled in and my pyjamas were removed, at which point I noticed that there was an anaesthetist by my side holding a mask, which immediately caused me to remember that at the age of eight I had seen the same type of mask when having my tonsils removed. The memory of the awful smell came to mind when the mask was clamped to my face and the ether administered. I immediately jumped up and made a run for it, but I was grabbed and dragged back by the staff who clamped the mask on, and then the operation went ahead. What made it worse was that this was a theatre where students would sit and watch from above. It was after five in the afternoon when I came around and became aware that my foster mother was sitting by the side of my bed, along with a neighbour who I had no liking for. Fortunately, I made it home for Christmas.

After being discharged from hospital, not much changed for me until the late summer of 1940, when I volunteered with the firefighters. It was expected that able-bodied people, even those too old or too young to go into the armed forces, would volunteer to help the nation, so joining the firefighters was my way of doing that.

The team I was in covered a very small area, so fortunately during my time there we never had to tackle any fires. My time was mainly spent playing cards. They taught me some new games too.

But I was only there for a few weeks, as in October 1940 I joined the Air Defence Cadet Corps with a friend of mine named Cyril Goldsack, who lived on the same road as I did. In February 1941, the ADCC was renamed the Air Training Corps, and we were given new uniforms. Originally, I wanted to go into the Sea Cadets owing to my love of the sea, but my foster mother vetoed that. Her reasoning was that the ADCC was further away from London than the Sea Cadets. She felt I would be in more danger if I was closer to London. The capital was being bombed quite badly, especially in the area of the docks.

At first, I went once a week after work, but that quickly became five times a week, plus a social event on Saturday night. By the way, I was in 173 Squadron.

What sort of things did you do and study with the ATC?
The lectures in the ADCC and then the ATC covered a wide variety of aeronautical subjects: airmanship, meteorology, navigation, aircraft recognition and Morse Code, which, in turn, served to help us through the necessary exams to be passed when joining the RAF proper.

We also took the 'Air Training Corps Proficiency Exam', which covered English, maths and navigation. If you passed, which I did, it allowed you to skip a few exams during the pilots' ground course. I also passed a test for Morse Code; I reached twenty-five words a minute.

After work, I would cycle home, grab whatever I could to eat, usually something on toast, then cycle down into Orpington to attend the ATC lectures. These took place in two flats that had been rented for that purpose. Sometimes we even had lectures in the stairwell between the two flats.

First, it would be decided what the lecture would be, then it would take place in the main room, though there would sometimes be more than one subject lectured on per night. As this was going on, a different lecture would be going on in the other flat. If you were lucky, you got a chair, though most of the time you would end up sitting on the floor.

Lectures would generally finish around 9pm, and invariably we would head outside and hear all the noise, which was mainly from anti-aircraft guns. Shutters would block out most of the noise when we were inside. Most of us had to cycle around two or three miles to get home, in pitch darkness. There was no street lighting or anything like that. It was a full blackout at the time.

While cycling in that eerie darkness, I would often be accompanied by the sound of wave after wave of aircraft going overhead to or from London. You have to understand that in 1940 and 1941, air raids on London were a common occurrence. This rather gruelling existence, which went on for week after week, eventually became too much for me, to the extent that one night I arrived home exhausted, and refusing to go into the shelter, I went straight to bed. It was quite a rebellious act for the time. I nearly paid the price one night when a bomb caught our house in its blast, which buckled our front door and broke plaster off the ceiling. The falling plaster then covered my bedclothes, yet somehow, I slept through it and didn't hear a thing. My foster mother quickly came rushing in and ordered me down into the shelter, claiming that, 'Bombs are dropping all around!' Those were her exact words. Ironically, there was only one bomb. But I was so exhausted after dealing with this sort of thing for so long that I just grunted, rolled over and went back to sleep.

However, the ATC wasn't just lectures; there were many practical things as well. For example, we had to learn how to fire and take apart rifles, which could vary in sizes from .22 to .303 calibre. We had to do the same with Vickers machine guns. For a sixteen-year-old boy, it was good fun.

There were also days where flying was the main objective. These took place during the two occasions when our squadron was allowed to camp for two weeks at Biggin Hill airfield. On our first occasion, I was taken up in a Blenheim bomber, and ironically I hated every minute of it. The Blenheim had three seats in various positions for the crew. We all drew lots as to who would sit where, the most sought-after seat being that of the co-pilot. I drew the co-pilot seat but quickly traded it for the seat of the gunner after discovering that the previous person seated in the co-pilot's seat had vomited everywhere. What I hated about sitting in the gunner's seat was the view and G forces imposed on me when the pilot went into steep turns. It caused me to swear to myself that I would never go up in an aircraft again.

There was also a big emphasis on lectures while we were at Biggin Hill. I remember that we once went to the camp cinema to see a film about aircrew training. One scene showed a formation of aircraft and how disciplined the pilots were in maintaining that formation. All the while, gentle music was playing as a backing to the film, and it appealed to me, as the music was so pleasant; I wondered what it was called. I had seen the film with B flight, but when A flight went to see it, I tagged along, just so I could hear the music again. The surprising thing is that it took many years before I learnt the name of the song.

About ten years later, whilst sitting in my own room, while still in the RAF, that same song wafted through the air. I quickly found the source of it and asked the guy what it was called; it was 'Magic Fire', by the German composer, Wagner. That piece has always stirred something deep inside me. I can picture the film now, and the aircraft flying in formation to that track.

Biggin Hill is such an iconic airfield in Britain. It played a major role in the Battle of Britain and beyond and was very important for the RAF. What memories do you have of it?

Our first time at Biggin Hill was soon after the Battle of Britain ended. We were billeted in Nissen Huts and had our meals at the same time as the ground crew had theirs. On one occasion, a group of us were surrounding a Spitfire, and the pilot asked me if I would like to sit inside it, to which I gave an enthusiastic, 'Yes, please.' Once I was inside, he asked me if I would like to start the engine, and once again I happily said, 'Yes.' I followed his instructions and the engine roared into life. Then he said, 'push the throttle a little way forward,' but my push was more like a shove. The engine roared even louder, and the Spitfire nearly jumped the chocks that were preventing the wheels from moving forward. The pilot had to reach in and pull the throttle back to the closed position; otherwise who knows what would have happened.

What was the atmosphere and day-to-day life at Biggin Hill like?

The impression I got while I was there was the cheerfulness of the place; the aircrew and groundcrew all seemed to be a happy bunch. It also struck me as quite a large airfield.

Cyril and I used to cycle there when we were both in the ATC. We would bike up Cudham Road, which leads through a village named Downe. Eventually we would reach a hedge just outside of the perimeter of Biggin Hill.

On one occasion when we cycled there, again, both of us in the ATC at the time, we asked the sergeant in charge of air traffic control if we could have some training on the Link Trainer. This was a ground model of a machine that had the same controls as a plane. It would lift up on bellows, and one could 'fly' it like a regular plane. On entering air traffic control - I was in front of Cyril - we went through the door and saluted, then immediately apologised to the sergeant there, as I thought he was an officer. He replied, 'No son, you did the right thing. You salute the office of an officer, whether he is there or not.'

When we asked about the Link Trainer, he informed us that the instructor wasn't there, but he said that we looked sensible enough, so he asked us to promise that we wouldn't be too rough with it if he gave us the keys. There were two Link Trainers; I got in one and Cyril in the other. We switched them on, and then we had a pretend dogfight which meant manoeuvring them for about an hour in quite a violent fashion until we got bored. Once we had finished, we switched them both off and returned the keys to the sergeant.

He thanked us both and asked if we would like a real flight if it could be arranged, to which we agreed. He phoned around the different dispersal areas, which resulted in a Belgian pilot offering to fly us. Another dispersal had a Tiger Moth available, so we had to make our way over to that dispersal. Upon arrival, I won the toss to go up first and got into the cockpit.

Once we were in the air, the pilot asked me if I had flown before and at the same time pushed the stick forward into a steep dive, then pulled it back and did a loop. This thrilled me into hoping that he would do it again, but he didn't. After a bit more flying around, he landed. I got out, Cyril got in, and I watched him. I quickly reached a state of jealousy when the pilot did not one loop, but two. But I got compensation when Cyril got out, and I saw that he had been sick. He proceeded to swear that he would never fly again. Later on, we were reprimanded by the ATC adjutant for going up on a flight that he had not authorised. But it was much different from my first flight; I thoroughly enjoyed this one.

Living in Kent at the time, and being so close to London, what are your memories of the Battle of Britain and the Blitz?
During the Battle of Britain and the Blitz, the entire area was on tenterhooks. Life carried on as normal as possible, but if people were out and heard a plane overhead it was natural to duck into a doorway or somewhere to take cover. But overall, not a lot changed. The buses still ran, people went to work and milk was delivered when available. People seemed to socialise more. However, all windows had to be blacked out, and there were air raid wardens whose job it was to enforce the blackout order. The propaganda was also very strong. It was designed to keep morale up, you know; 'Dig for Victory' and all that. One cannot underestimate the influence that Winston Churchill had personally in keeping morale up. His speeches had quite an effect on people.

Once during the Battle of Britain, Billy and I were returning home from a church service when suddenly the air was filled with noise as Spitfires and Hurricanes engaged German Messerschmitts in the skies above us; there were probably half a dozen aircraft in total. We saw a parachute open, which we later learnt was a Hurricane pilot baling out of his plane. He landed in an allotment, and the Hurricane crashed in a field. We started running towards a woodland area when a man called out to us to come over into his shelter, which was a converted double garage. Once we reached the wall surrounding the man's house, Billy, who was crying due to the noise and the odd bullet casing hitting the ground, was hoisted over the wall, and I scrambled over it myself. The shelter was well stocked; it had a 'kitchen' at one end, and the rest of it was made up of beds, chairs and sofas.

On another occasion with Cyril, we decided to cycle to Biggin Hill. We reached the boundary fence at the end of the airfield and before long witnessed ten Spitfires take off in a loose formation. Due to our position, the left flank of these Spitfires flew right over our heads, but not long after taking off, the Spitfire at the head of the ten started to slowly drop out of the sky. It disappeared out of sight and crashed. Fortunately, the pilot was ok. To witness ten Spitfires taking off in such a fashion and to hear the noise coming from their engines was really impressive.

During the summer of 1940, it was quite common to see Spitfires, Hurricanes and Messerschmitts in the skies. Even when it wasn't possible to see them, one could hear them.

During the Blitz, any family who had an air raid shelter spent night after night in it, but even a shelter wasn't guaranteed to keep its occupants safe. At a house quite close to where I lived, about a quarter of a mile away, the Anderson shelter of a family there was directly hit by a bomb that was believed to have been jettisoned, killing everyone inside.

Another family I knew, who lived on the next road to me, took a taxi into London and were directly hit, killing everyone. There were quite a few casualties for such a small village.

There were several instances during that period where, after attending the ATC lectures, and while cycling about two miles to get home, I was caught out in a raid, such as the time that a bomb fell so close to me, falling on a field, that it blew me off of my bicycle. This resulted in a torn left trouser leg and an injured left knee. The most ironic thing of all is that my foster mother was more concerned about the trouser leg than she was about myself due to the cost it would be in clothing coupons to replace a pair of trousers.

An unbelievable story is that of the adjutant of my ATC unit. One night, he and his wife were at home during an air raid and were sheltering under the stairs; they didn't have an Anderson shelter. Their house was destroyed by a bomb, and by sheer luck they survived, as the staircase that they were underneath was left standing.

Looking back over those first war years, which occurred and affected me during an impressionable age, there were so many incidences that all crowd together in my memory. It was a period which served the average adolescent well, in that we respected authority, but at the same time we had free hands in other ways. This gave us more time to enjoy life rather than be under the restrictions of the authoritarian rules of the older people in charge. People themselves became more open and would crack jokes. For example, if it got to nine or ten at night and no German aircraft had appeared, people would start joking that they were late and not on time. When the Luftwaffe aircraft would approach, there was a psychological effect, in that many of them would purposefully not have their engines synchronised, resulting in a sound which had quite an effect on many people; it was done to instil fear.

Fortunately, there were occurrences during the war which, as fate would have it, I was to miss due to being overseas. The first ones were the V-1 flying bombs, which were commonly nicknamed 'Doodlebugs'. They were essentially engines with wings and explosives attached, and with a simple guidance system, the result being that they would fall out of the sky once their fuel ran out and explode on contact with the ground. The public had an advance warning of a V-1's impending crash, because its engine had quite a distinct sound, and once the engine cut out one knew it would be a matter of moments before it crashed. Over a period of time, however, RAF fighter pilots learnt the trick of flying alongside the Doodlebug and positioning the aircraft's wing just underneath the

V-1's wing. At this point, the pilot would bank left or right, thus tilting the Doodlebug off-balance and causing it to crash, ideally away from built-up areas.

The other major occurrences I missed were the V-2 rocket attacks. The V-2 was a straightforward rocket, packed with explosives, that was fired straight up into the sky and aimed mostly towards England and Belgium. There was no approaching sound to give the V-2 away.

But back to those first war years. When I was around fifteen, I was cycling home from work, trying to get home before a storm hit the area, and in desperation I sought shelter under a rather large oak tree. After a few moments, a man came along on his bike and stopped close by. He warned me that it was not unusual for large trees to be struck by lightning, which made them dangerous places under which to seek shelter. Taking his advice, I cycled off in the heavy rain to the first house, which fortunately wasn't too far away. A few days later, I learnt that the same tree had been struck by lightning, and a man sheltering under it had been killed. I knew it was the same tree, because I later saw that the trunk bore the marks of a lightning strike, but I don't know if the victim was the man who gave me the warning.

CHAPTER THREE

INITIAL EXPERIENCES IN THE RAF, OCTOBER 1942 – JANUARY 1943

Being called up, initial RAF training, sailing on a troopship to South Africa, crossing the equator, rail travel and a posting in Bulawayo, Southern Rhodesia

You were called up when you were eighteen-and-a-quarter, which according to my calculations must have been in the autumn of 1942. Do you remember that day?
Very much so. However, I went to the recruitment office in Catford six months prior to my call-up in order to volunteer as a wireless operator. Cyril came with me to do the same thing. We did it because if we didn't, then when our call-up dates arrived, we could, in theory, have been called up to the army or navy. We wanted to ensure that we went into the RAF. But when we told the chap in the recruitment office of our desire to become wireless operators, his reply was, 'We have enough of those already. I will put you both down as pilots.'

Anyway, my call-up papers arrived at the beginning of October 1942. I discovered that I had been called up when I arrived home one day and my foster mother said, 'Your call-up papers have arrived.' She had already opened the letter and gone through it. The letter itself detailed where I had to go, what I had to take and by what time I had to be there. I had to go to Lords Cricket Ground in London and report to entrance gate E at 08.00 hours on the 12th of October. The gate one went to was decided by one's surname, so a chap whose last name was 'Brown' would report to entrance gate B, and so on.

Once there, we were all assembled into a large room where we were kitted out with uniforms and RAF clothing, including footwear. When it was my turn, I was asked, 'What size?' for each item of clothing. I told him, and he went to the table behind him and grabbed the relevant piece.

We then went into a big hall for refreshments, which in my case was tea. People were spitting out the tea, saying how disgusting it was. I was later told that this was because they put Bromide in it to kill our sexual desires. Crazy, isn't it? From there, we were shown our quarters for the first few nights, which were dormitory-like, with many in one room.

My rank upon joining up was aircraftsman 2nd class, the lowest rank in the RAF.

On the second day, we had to parade at 8am, and from there we were marched to a place named Seymour Hall, which we entered through a rear fire escape. Once inside, we had to prepare for inoculations. Most men had three inoculations, though I only needed two. After that, we were all given permission to go to Regents Park and relax, though most of us were sick. In my mind, that had to be down to the inoculations. In my case, on getting back to the billets I went straight to bed and spent most of the night still feeling sick, crying with pain. In fact, one of the older people, who was in his mid-twenties, took care of me for the whole night.

On the third day, following breakfast, we had to go to another large hall and completely undress. In the hall were several tables used by doctors to carry out medical examinations. I was passing all the requirements until the doctor in charge of the other doctors took me to one side. He told me that he had almost decided to fail me on the hearing side because he noticed that I had suffered two punctured eardrums. He then said that he had decided to let me proceed on the principle that the changing pressures that I would be exposed to once I started flying would help to heal my eardrums. His theory was correct, in that at the end of my first year in the RAF, when I underwent another medical, my eardrums had fully healed. They had initially been injured by our family doctor when I underwent a medical for the ATC. He had cleared both ears of wax but had been rather rough in doing it, causing both eardrums to perforate.

As an eighteen-year-old, was there a big sense of impending adventure in those first few days?

Not at first. As I have said, those first few days were taken up with medical examinations and being supplied with clothing; things like that. But when I arrived home on that first weekend, I really looked forward to reporting back. There was such a sense of anticipation for what was to come. I felt as though I was on the cusp of a big adventure, but my first adventure was somewhat of an anti-climax.

On arrival back after the first weekend, we were formed into one big group, probably around 200 men, and put on a corridor-less train. It meant that those carriages lacked facilities, including toilets. A few of the chaps on the train actually wet themselves on the five-hour train journey. Our destination was a town named Ludlow, not far from the Welsh border.

Our three weeks in Ludlow consisted of manual labour: digging trenches and filling them up again, building walls and then knocking them down and other similar tasks. We slept in bell tents, eight to a tent, and discovered that the best way to keep warm was sleeping side by side, body to body. Remember, winter was approaching, so it was very cold and damp. We had one water tap for about fifty of us, and the best wash we could have was by going into a nearby river.

After about three weeks, we got the message that we were to be up at five in the morning the following day in order to catch a seven o'clock train back to London. Thankfully, that train had corridors and toilet facilities. As we approached the outskirts of London, we became enveloped in thick pea soup fog. The train had to stop short of our destination, somewhere on the outskirts of London, as all the signals were at red due to the fog. When we got off the train, we were divided into small parties of ten. The leader of each party had to navigate their party back to our residences in crocodile fashion, where you hang onto the person in front of you, like a chain. The group I was in took the underground into London. It took us a long time to reach to our billets.

Nothing of any importance happened over the next few days. We were given marching sessions in order to learn the various disciplines in marching. It reached the stage that the sergeant in charge decided to call us on parade, and then he shouted out, 'Atten!'; everyone thought he was going to shout, 'Attention!', but he actually said, 'A ten-shilling note had been found.' Then he shouted, 'About!', which we thought was going to be, 'About Turn!' This is when you turn 180 degrees - there is an art to it - you swing around on your heels. Anyway, he then shouted, 'At about ten this morning!' The point of all this was to learn to wait until the entire order had been given.

I had the opportunity to return home again too. At the conclusion of my visit, I told my foster parents, 'I am not sure when I'll see you again.' My foster father replied in such a casual manner, 'I'm sure you'll be back next weekend.' In actual fact, I never saw him again, as he died on the 8th of December 1943. His passing really upset me; he had been like a real father to me.

We took another train, this time to Blackpool. Upon arrival, we were divided into small units. I was one of three men billeted in a rather large house, with a middle-aged married couple who owned the house. They had a daughter of nineteen. We three boarders were in a rather large bedroom with a shared bathroom. Our meals were excellent.

We had to parade at eight in the morning, every day. After a few days of this procedure, the sergeant called out a list of names of men who had to step aside from the main group and wait. It turned out the group that had been called aside, of which I was one, was destined for overseas. We were told not to reveal the fact of an overseas posting to anyone, including our parents; it was to be kept secret. I don't know what happened to the other group.

During all of that, Ludlow, Blackpool, digging trenches and everything, what was the atmosphere like? Was there a feeling of camaraderie and friendship?
Yes, we established friendships and there was a feeling that we were all in it together. During that time, we all began to learn the differences between civilian life and forces life. Once, one of the guys misheard an order and said something like, 'I thought you said,' and the sergeant replied, 'In the RAF, you don't think; we think for you.'

Those of us who were in the group going overseas were looking forward to it; at least I was.

Eventually, you were all sent by train to Liverpool.

Yes, eventually the day came when we, the group who were going overseas, were all put on a train and sent off to Liverpool. Once there, we joined up with other units, including those from the army. I estimate that there were about 200 air force and 1,000 army personnel.

We were transported to the docks and told to make our way to the deck of our vessel. We were then taken below to begin getting acquainted with where we would be spending the next five weeks. We started learning about things like hoisting hammocks, which caused much amusement when it came to getting into them. Bodies were falling over the place, but luckily I got used to mine fairly quickly.

We set sail on the 16th of December 1942, only nine weeks after I had been called up. I remember going up to the open deck as we pulled away from the docks and witnessing crowds of people waving us off. Once the ship was clear of the docks, I went below again and met a lad called Mervin. He was a year older than me and had made friends with a chap named Laurie, who was in the army and was, coincidently, his neighbour back home. We became a little unit of three, two in the air force and one in the army, for the remainder of the journey.

For someone who had grown up in the countryside and had little experience at sea, sailing on the open ocean for the first time must have been quite an adventure.

The freshness of the open sea, I found it to be very exhilarating. I could see the other ships in the convoy all around, and I didn't suffer from seasickness. I took to the sea immediately, to the extent that the word 'love' came into it. I loved the fresh sea air and the sounds of the waves. There is a certain magic about the sea. I loved and still love everything about it, even if the weather is rough. I remember that once out into the open sea we were soon in rough weather, and I took great delight in hanging onto the rails at the bow of the ship, while watching and smelling the sea. It was like being on a giant seesaw. But one of the crew noticed me and ordered me below, saying that if I fell overboard nobody was going to stop and rescue me.

In the following days, we had to get used to eating off long, narrow tables that would seat eighteen at a time, and in the first fortnight I ate quite well because half of my table friends were seasick, whereas I was never affected. It meant that I ate their food, as well. But after about ten days, they had got over their seasickness and were eating normally again, so I had to go back to eating just my own meals.

What was day-to-day life like on board? The threat of German U-boats must have been there.
On finer days, we as a group used to be on the open deck, where we were given exercises to perform, similar to what one would do back in a school gymnasium. We also had lectures on various subjects given by selected personnel on the crew, all of which helped to pass the time away during each day.

Our ship was named the SS *Rangitiki*, and it was one of three troopships in the same convoy. Our convoy totalled about fifteen ships, including escorts, which were naval frigates. The SS *Rangitiki* was the slowest of the lot and could apparently only manage fourteen-and-a-half knots at maximum speed, whereas others had much faster maximum speeds. From its time of formation, the whole convoy had to do slow zig-zags from port to starboard as a defence against German U-boats. We were told by one of the crew that on two occasions we had been attacked by U-boats, and in return the U-boats had been attacked by our frigates. It was claimed that at least one U-boat had been sunk by depth charges.

Another danger that the escorts had to be aware of was high-flying reconnaissance German Condor aircraft, which shadowed the various convoys travelling to and from the UK and reported their positions to the waiting U-boats. The defence against the Condors was that one of the ships in a convoy carried a Hurricane fighter on board that would be launched into the air to shoot down the Condor. After attacking the enemy aircraft, the pilot would fly close to his own ship, then ditch his plane and be picked up.

After crossing the Bay of Biscay in very rough sea conditions, we asked one of the crew roughly where we were, and the answer he gave was, 'Approximately 1,000 miles due west of the French coast.' In other words, in the Atlantic.

Judging by the time frame you have given, you spent the Christmas of 1942 at sea. How was it celebrated?
The Christmas dinner was marvellous: roast turkey, vegetables and potatoes, followed by mince pies and Christmas pudding. It was in stark contrast to back home, where everyone had to get by on rations. It was quite a Christmas to remember, and I can still picture it now, in full detail.

As we continued, the seas gradually got quieter, and soon afterwards the convoy stopped at a West African port; I believe it was Freetown, in Sierra Leone. It being hot and humid, quite a few of us slept on the top deck, which caused me to hear mosquitoes buzzing around for the first time. It could have been on that occasion that I was bitten by one. It was definitely during that time, as not long after reaching Southern Rhodesia, I was taken ill with malaria, which was consistent with the period of incubation.

Once we were refuelled, we carried on, travelling to and around the Cape of Good Hope, eventually arriving in Durban on the 18th of January 1943. All of us air force personnel then disembarked, but we weren't allowed to look around the city. We were split into separate groups of four. Mervin and I were in the same squad, but Laurie had to stay on board, as the convoy was carrying on up the East African coast. I believe that the troops on board were to join the Eighth Army in North Africa. Laurie eventually became a tank commander. In total, we were on board for just under five weeks.

It's well-known that life at sea involves various traditions and initiations. Did you or any of the other passengers experience anything like that?
The one that really stands out was when we crossed the equator. A couple dozen of us had gathered on deck, not knowing why, but we just presumed that we were going to do some exercises; that was what we had been told to dress for. On this occasion, however, the 'Crossing the Line Ceremony' was the ulterior motive behind the gathering.

A sailor, dressed in a gown and representing King Neptune, was seated on a platform before us. On his head was a silly sort of crown, probably made out of something like cardboard. I was grabbed by two sailors and smeared with some sort of muck; I have no idea what it was. Everyone else thought it was hilarious until they were ordered into the well deck and were drenched with powerful sea hoses, which would knock a man over. I was up on the platform with 'King Neptune' and was also sprayed down. An officer soon appeared and stated that the captain had ordered all this to be stopped, as there were ladies on board, WRENS, as I recall. At the end of it all, I was given a certificate by 'King Neptune', saying that I had officially 'crossed the line'. The others down below didn't receive a certificate, as they had 'crossed the line' without King Neptune's permission.

Despite those amusing events, the risk of coming under attack must have been there. You have already mentioned being informed that U-boats had attacked your convoy on two occasions and that defences were in place. A sense of danger must have been an ever-present thought in the back of your mind.
Oh yes, it was, and remember that this was in late 1942, early 1943. By then, German U-boats had been operating in wolf packs for quite a while. One occasion that really brought it to the forefront was a time when we were all ordered below deck. Questions were asked, and it soon transpired that a convoy, which was around three days ahead of us, had been attacked, resulting in ships going down; I don't know how many. The reason that we were ordered below was that bodies had been seen floating in the sea, and the captain didn't want us to see them, as the sight might have lowered morale.

All of that happened in the South Atlantic, far from home, and closer to South Africa than to Britain.

Stepping off the ship onto a new continent on the other side of the world, what was going through your mind? Your first time out of Britain must have been quite an experience.
It was, indeed. I was looking forward to sightseeing around Durban. Before the war, it was such a well-known city to those in Britain; we had even learnt about Durban at school. But that feeling quickly turned to one of disappointment when we were told that we were not allowed to explore the city.

After disembarking, we were soon put aboard the Blue Train. Each compartment could take four people and had its own wash facilities, bunk beds and armchairs to use. The train carried all 200 of us. The views from the train as it climbed the mountains were magnificent.

Eventually, we stopped in the city of Johannesburg. The whole platform was lined with tables, which were stocked with chocolate, magazines and newspapers. We got plenty of phone numbers from women, but senior officers told us that they would be quite useless, as once we reached Southern Rhodesia, we would not be allowed back into South Africa. After Johannesburg, we stopped once more in South Africa, in Mafeking. Once again, the tables were lined with things to buy.

We carried on northwards for a total of two days and two nights until we reached the Southern Rhodesian city of Bulawayo, which was reputed to have the longest railway platform in the Southern Hemisphere, and it was indeed long.

When we reached Bulawayo, we were marched to an area called Hillside, which was a complete air force camp. To our surprise, our beds were located in small pens which had once housed pigs. We learnt that Hillside had in previous times been the site of a cattle market. Each pen now housed a single iron bed and hooks from which to hang clothes. We arrived at Hillside on the 20th of January 1943.

Fortunately, things were soon to change. The cadets on Course 26 completed their training and were posted to various flying schools. That allowed the cadets on Course 27 to take over the better huts that the previous cadets had occupied. This also meant that the cadets on Course 28 moved into the huts vacated by the cadets on Course 27, which were an improvement. But most importantly of all, the cadets on my course, Course 29, could vacate those horrible pig pens. I was meant to be on Course 28, but malaria put a stop to that.

CHAPTER FOUR

SOUTHERN RHODESIA, JANUARY – DECEMBER 1943

Malaria, learning to fly the Tiger Moth, Victoria Falls,
dicing with death, piloting the Oxford and two grisly murders

Hillside, in Southern Rhodesia, was where you undertook the pilot's course. Did the course begin straight away?
Nearly, in that within about ten days we learnt that the actual course would start on the following Monday and that we would be on Course 28. However, on the Friday before, whilst being put through army-type drills on the parade ground, I heard the flight sergeant in charge of us call out, 'Catch that man!' That man happened to be me, as I had fainted and dropped my rifle, and within seconds I was lying on the ground beside it. I was carried to my bed, and after the medical officer visited I was quickly sent to hospital. What I had was the onset of malaria and the beginning of a two-and-a-half-week road to recovery.

The care in hospital was great, especially in the first two weeks, where a team of nurses worked on getting my dangerously high temperature back down to normal. My main memories of my stay there are of me moaning in pain and pleading to go home. Eventually the profuse sweating eased, as did the pain. But by that stage, my feeling of homesickness had increased, which led me to write the following poem:

IF ONLY
If only I could tread the green of England's fields again,
and gaze upon her countless streams, her woods and rolling hills
and plains, and lay on new mown hay.

If only I could smell those flowers, which I have known from birth,
and walk with ease and comfort, on soft, enchanted earth,

and listen to those singing birds be near or far away,
and gaze with awe and wonder, at plumage bright and gay.
If only I could see her skies of ever changing mood,
and watch the raindrops falling, as darkened clouds do brood,
and see the lightning flashing, and hear the thunder roar,
while howling winds grow angry, and shake against my door.

If only I could welcome Spring with all its colours rare,
and when hot Summer bids adieu gaze on those trees, so bare,
and when the snow begins to fall, feel Winter's icy hand,
if only now that I could be in that romantic land.

It's a beautiful poem, so much depth and emotion flow from its words. However, though you felt homesick, you were in the armed forces, so you couldn't just leave and go home. What did you do?

Fortunately, it was a feeling that didn't last long. Once my appetite returned and I was back to full health, I was allowed to return to my unit, and my homesickness disappeared. But when I was released from hospital, I had missed the beginning of Course 28, and it was only a week or so before Course 29 began, so I was put on that course. On each course there were about 200 cadets. My friend Mervin, from the troopship, was still at Hillside, he was on Course 28, studying for the exams. Instructors would use the results of those exams to decide on which cadets to send to which flying schools, assuming they passed.

My poem got some of the other cadets suggesting that I should have it published, but course work was taking up too much time. Eventually it got tucked into an exercise book to disappear for many years. To this day, I am still surprised that I wrote that poem, as when I was growing up I never read or wrote poetry.

At the end of each course, which lasted about four months, exams covering a wide variety of aeronautical subjects were undertaken. At the end of the exams for Course 29, those of us who passed were posted to our first flying schools so we could learn how to fly the Tiger Moth.

Going back a bit, you once told me that you almost didn't even start the pilot's course, and that just before Course 29 began, you decided that you wanted to be a wireless operator.

I learnt from other cadets that most of us taking part would end up with a personal interview, either with an assistant from the school staff, or with the squadron leader in charge overall, and that those who were interviewed by the squadron leader were 'special cases'.

I was interviewed by the squadron leader, but due to a lack of confidence in my abilities, I told him that I wanted to be a wireless operator rather than a pilot. He became very angry, and almost shouting, he told me that if I studied hard, then I would do well and become a pilot. He lectured me to forget about becoming a wireless operator, as the RAF already had an abundance of them. So I decided, then, to go on the pilot's course, though the squadron leader had not really given me much choice.

How was the course structured? I imagine that there must have been a lot of theory to cover before you got behind the controls of any type of aircraft.

Yes, there wasn't even a single aircraft at Hillside. Our four months there were spent occupied with lectures, exams, parade drills, and map reading exercises with a radius of up to about fifteen miles from Hillside. Some of these map reading exercises were purely classroom-based, but on others, we were dropped off with a map and a compass, in a group of six, with a leader in charge, and told to report to a certain point.

There were tests on our English and maths skills, but because I had passed the ATC Proficiency Exam, I didn't have to do those tests. We also had to learn how to disassemble, reassemble, and fire a Vickers machine gun. On top of that, we had lecture after lecture on ten subjects without even seeing an aircraft. At the end of the four months came exams on the ten subjects. They were: airmanship, navigation, meteorology, aero engines, flight instruments, signals (which included Morse Code), bombing theory, gunnery theory, pyrotechnics and aircraft recognition. The results of those exams decided which flying school one went to. A student had to get at least fifty-five percent per subject and an average of sixty percent overall to pass. I only managed fifty-eight percent on my worst subject, which was aero engines, but I finished with an average of eighty-one-and-half percent overall, which put me eleventh from the top on the course.

Cadets who passed could select their choice of Elementary Flying Training School, though it wasn't guaranteed that they would go there. I had heard that Induna was reputed to have the best instructors, so that's where I chose to go. There were two other Tiger Moth schools: Guinea Fowl, located near Gwelo, and Belvedere, in Salisbury, the capital of Southern Rhodesia. A good friend on Course 29, Ron, rather overconfidently, was sure that he would score highly on his exams and be posted to Induna. On the day that the exam results were published, we both went to a big board which had everyone's results on it, to see how we had scored. He started at the top and I at the bottom, working our way down and up, respectively, and we found each other's name. Having finished eleventh in my class, I was able to go to Induna, but Ron had finished much lower; he had just passed, and he was posted to Guinea Fowl. Those exams took three days to complete.

During that four-month period of intense study, what was day-to-day life like?
Unsurprisingly, they were mostly filled with lectures. They would begin at around nine in the morning, then there would be a break for lunch, and then we would carry on until about four or so in the afternoon.

It must have been quite stressful studying for all of those exams. When the time became available, how did you all relax and take your minds off it all?
In the case of Ron and I, we would often go to the gym in our spare time. Once, when we came back from the gym and were making a racket, a group of older cadets studying for their exams told us to shut up or else. One of us, I can't remember who, replied with something like, 'Or what?' They quickly grabbed me, pulled down my shorts, and got a tin of 'blackie', which was black shoe polish. I had the sense to yell out that if they did anything to me, I would

stop teaching them Morse Code. They let me go, grabbed Ron and blackened the cheeks of his bottom. He ran outside once they let him go, and when I caught up with him, he asked me to help him wash off the polish. Unlike him, I saw the funny side of it all. Another way to relax was to go into Bulawayo to use the swimming baths, and yet another was to visit the NAAFI, which stood for 'Navy, Army and Air Force Institute'. The NAAFI was basically a glorified canteen. There was a piano there, and occasionally one of the cadets would play classical music on it; he was an excellent pianist.

On one occasion, I was stuffed into a laundry bag, which was tied up. I had said something cheeky. Luckily, I had quite sharp nails and managed to split the bag open and get out. I went and replaced the bag with one from another billet.

I remember you telling me that those who passed the exams had a five-day period during which they could go and travel anywhere within the country. Where did you spend your five days?

A group of eight of us had a joint interest in going to see the famous Victoria Falls. As the visit would count as a geographical exercise, we were issued a travel warrant to cover rail expenses; it was a distance of nearly 300 miles one way, so the travel warrant was a welcome help. We had to allow a full day to reach the Falls and another one for getting back, so that gave us three clear days at the Falls. The train was ordinary; there was nothing special about it. I was sure that the engine was log-fired, but I later learnt that it was coal-fired. Though a day spent on a train sounds like a long time, the varied landscapes we saw made the time go by rather quickly. Rhodesia sits at quite a high altitude, exceeding 4,000 feet in places, and I remember passing many hills. We also travelled through a few towns on the way, one of which caused us great amusement as it was named 'Wankie'; it was well known for its coal.

When we reached Victoria Falls station, which was close enough to the waterfall to hear its roar, a Dutchman approached us and said that if we were looking for accommodation, he could help. When he said that it would be of no cost, it made us all wonder what the catch was, but fortunately there wasn't one. It turned out that he had been doing this for years, in gratitude for allied forces defending his country. The Dutchman lived alone in a house with two large spare bedrooms, each having four single beds, and out back the place had its own swimming pool, hewn out of solid rock and speckled with flakes of gold. One of our group even took a nail file to it but was told by the Dutchman not to bother, as it wasn't worth anything. The water was changed once a week via a pump set-up, so the condition of the water was good. The Dutchman told us that we were free to use it at any time, but without swimming costumes, to allow for the water being static. That raised a few eyebrows in our party, and one commented to the rest that perhaps our host preferred to see naked young men.

The Dutchman also owned a small open-back van, which he said we could use. But only one of us could drive, so he offered lessons to the rest of us. When it came to my turn, I found it was great fun to zigzag between the bushes along the riverbank, but the short piece of land that we were driving on ended at a flimsy fence, and if you went through it, you would end up in the river. As we approached the fence, my friend told me to press on the brake pedal, but I accidentally pressed the accelerator, which caused us to shoot forward. Managing to kick my foot off the pedal, my friend grabbed the steering wheel, causing us to sharply swerve; we stopped about three feet short of the fence. I lost interest in driving after that.

What was Victoria Falls like?
It was a stunning sight. The sound was deafening, and the spray went high into the sky. There were small offshoot falls, too, adjacent to the main length of waterfall. Victoria Falls carried a large novelty value; none of us had ever seen anything like it before.

I remember you telling me that during your time in Southern Rhodesia, you spent a good amount of time in Bulawayo, a place that you have already mentioned. What was the city itself like? Obviously things were very different then than they are now in Zimbabwe, as the country is now known.
The place was quite lively. It had a good range of shops, cafes, and a lovely swimming pool, in which I taught myself to swim.

There was a nice church named St Johns, which I believe is now a cathedral. There were also two cinemas. To me, Bulawayo came across as perfectly safe and peaceful. You could go there on your own and be fine, though we were advised to stay out of the south side of the city, not for safety reasons, but because, apparently, there wasn't anything there of any interest. From what I understood, the white population mainly stuck to the north, and the black population stayed mainly in the south. However, if a white person was walking along the footpath and a black person was coming the other way, then the black person would have to get off the footpath. I never experienced this myself, but that is what I was told. To me, it was a lovely place. I went swimming there practically every weekend.

Having passed your exams with flying colours and having been on an interesting five-day break, what was there left to do at Hillside before your move to Induna?
The weekend after we got back to Hillside from Victoria Falls was spent packing our gear and loading it onto the coaches that were going to take us to our various flying schools. When those of us who were posted to Induna arrived there on the 4th of June 1943, at 27 Elementary Flying Training School, we were billeted into huts which were divided into rooms, with two cadets per room. A separate hut contained baths, showers and toilets. I was at Induna for around two-and-a-half months. Having passed my exams and been posted to a Tiger Moth school, I was promoted by one rank to leading aircraftman, which also meant an increase in pay.

Induna, about ten miles northeast of Bulawayo, had quite a good bus service into Bulawayo. Flying was from a rather large grass field which was kept in good condition. There were no actual runways.

My roommate was named Wally. He was a pleasant chap, one year older than me, of medium build and the same height as me. He was from Brighton, and he surprised me by confessing that he could not swim.

On our first day, we met our instructors. Mine was named Flying Officer Cond (FO/C), a very calm man, I would say in his early thirties, who described every part of the Tiger Moth and its purpose while standing next to it. Then he climbed into the front cockpit, and the descriptions continued, including details about the instruments. He went through the start-up procedure, but we didn't fire up on the first day. FO/C tried to make everything about a Tiger Moth, including the flying, very easy. The Tiger Moths used for training cadets had two sets of controls joined together. One set was in the front, the other in the back, so if the cadet moved his joystick, then the instructor's joystick would move in the same way. This was so that when the cadet was flying, the instructor could take over if anything went wrong.

The next day, I was shown how to start the engine, which is done by swinging hard on the propeller. A taxiing demonstration followed, and then I had a go at it myself, which was interesting, as a Tiger Moth has no brakes or rear wheel. Instead of a rear wheel, it has a skid, which digs into the ground and acts as a brake. The next step was to learn the way to operate the main controls, via a single joystick, as it was called. All of this happened over the course of a few days, and each exercise had its own number, which was useful for log book entries. After taxiing came take-offs and landings, with my instructor doing the landings. While taxiing to the take-off point, he told me that we had to turn thirty degrees to port and then swing back the other way so we could see ahead, as the engine blocked our view, and, additionally, my instructor also blocked my view forward. This swinging motion continued until the take-off point was reached.

My own first landing attempt was a bit bumpy, but all the exercises were practised day after day until we could do them all. On the tenth day, after take-off, my instructor told me to head for 'Satellite Number One', which was a small airfield used for first solos. Another instructor and his cadet were already there. My instructor was going to test his cadet, and that cadet's instructor was going to test me. What I didn't know was that FO/C had placed a bet with the other instructor that he, FO/C, would get me off solo within ten hours; the course average was thirteen-and-a-half. During my test, the other instructor kept asking me how many hours I had done until we reached ten. We communicated through the Gosport, which is a rubber tube that allows the student and instructor to speak to each other. He asked me to do one more circuit and to land, which I did. I was then joined by FO/C, who jokingly told me that I had lost him a pound.

Both of us cadets had passed our tests. As the other cadet had arrived first, he was allowed to attempt to go solo first. I watched him take off and then started my own run. I became airborne but was horrified to see that the other cadet was slightly veering to the right, which meant that when he turned left to keep on the circuit, at 800 feet, he would turn into me. To avoid a collision, I stopped my climb at 600 feet, while the other cadet continued climbing. Sure enough, he eventually turned and flew right over me; he later admitted that he had not even seen me. I then continued my climb to 800 feet and completed the circuit. I could see his landing approach, and I was astonished when he lifted away to have another go. This left the way clear for me, and I made a nice landing.

It must have been quite an experience to go solo for the first time, and exhilarating to be up in the air. You must have felt a great sense of achievement.
Oh definitely, no doubt about it. I remember singing to myself as loudly as I could. I did a few more hours with FO/C, but then to my horror he went on leave. I then had an older instructor, who I will call Flying Officer T (FO/T). He had been a pilot during the Battle of Britain. Each instructor normally worked with two cadets, but FO/T already had two, and I believe that having to take me on as a third really annoyed him.

After our first introduction, we both got into a Tiger Moth. He then told me to taxi down to the take-off point in the way I had been instructed. I had hardly started taxiing when FO/T called out very sharply, 'Stop!' After asking me what I thought I was doing, he told me that if I had been taught to angle thirty degrees to see ahead, it was now going to be sixty degrees with him. This lengthened the time to get to the take-off point. He then ordered me to take off, which I did, but he started telling me how it was the worst take-off he had ever seen. He was in the front, and we spoke via the Gosport. I carried on with the circuit, and soon we landed. When we rolled to a stop, he said, 'Your landing was the worst I have ever known.' Though in my mind, I had done quite well.

He yelled at me to take off again, so I did, and on the downwind leg he gave me an instruction, which I didn't quite understand. Instead of answering, I kept quiet, but he quickly asked me if I could hear him. Bearing in mind that I was still only eighteen and feeling the typical anger of a teenager, I replied, 'Yes, I bloody well heard you!' He then did the most remarkable manoeuvre that I had seen up to that point, and haven't seen since. Somehow, he dipped the plane down, swerved steeply to the left, pulled the joystick back sharply into my body and bang, we were on the ground. I have never known a landing like it; it was truly brilliant.

He then told me to get out of the Tiger Moth, which I did. He stopped the engine and got out himself, and then began the lecture. First, he asked me what I had said to him when I replied to his last question. I told him that I had responded with, 'Yes, I can hear you, Sir.' His response was, 'No, it wasn't. Try again. Do you realise that you swore at me, an officer of the Royal Air Force?' I thought he was going to scrub me, to take me off the course. He glared at me and said, 'One day, you might be awarded the Victoria Cross, or the Distinguished Flying Cross, or the Air Force Cross, and it will all be thanks to me.' He then said, 'Now get back in the aircraft, take off and go and kill yourself.' Those were his exact words. The awful thing was that I nearly did.

On my first landing attempt I bumped too hard on the ground and did what is known as the 'kangaroo hop'. In the nick of time I saw that I was heading towards the windsock, which is like an empty pillowcase attached to a pole. The windsock blows in the wind, thus giving the direction of the wind. I put the throttle on full power, increased my height and just cleared it.

On the second attempt, I came in too high and plunked onto the ground, just clearing the hedges at the end of the landing strip.

On the third attempt, I said to myself, 'Please, God, don't let it hurt'; those were my exact words. I turned onto the final approach, put the aircraft onto what I thought was a good landing height and crouched down into the cockpit with my arms covering my head, waiting for the crash. Instead, it was just a thump, and then another. I felt the tail hit the ground, sat up quickly and saw that the plane had landed itself. I taxied back to dispersal, hoping that I had given the impression that I had done the landing myself, forgetting that the instructors on duty would have seen everything.

A red light showing on the control tower indicated that I had to report to the Chief Flying Instructor. I did so and was informed by the adjutant that the CFI was at a meeting and to come back at two o'clock. So I decided to go to the mess and have lunch. There I met up with Wally, who was usually a very happy chap but now seemed to be rather glum. He should have gone solo by this stage but was nervous about doing so and had decided that he was not meant to be a pilot, so his instructor had taken him off the course. Other cadets were similarly affected and were choosing to be navigators or flight engineers. They were posted back to Hillside, and eventually to the UK.

After lunch, I went to lie down for a while and then went back to the adjutant at two o'clock sharp. Yet again, the CFI wasn't there. I was told by the adjutant that there had been a major crash that the CFI was attending to and to come back at four.

When I returned again at four, I entered the CFI's office, fully expecting to be scrubbed from the course then and there. Instead, he pointed to a single chair and told me to sit down. Then the questions started, as he told me to recount all of my experiences with FO/T. In the process, I decided to be honest about my swearing at an officer, which had caused FO/T to lose his temper and to send me off to fly, unprepared for his style of landing. The CFI was quiet in thought for a while and then said, 'Elliott, you are not yet nineteen. So from tomorrow, I'm going to place you with Flying Officer Wright. He is our most experienced instructor, so if he can't get you flying again, then nobody can.' Then he added, 'Off you go, and no more swearing at officers.' So I wasn't scrubbed at all.

I imagine that your new instructor was better than FO/T.
He was much better; he was a very easy man to get on with. When I first met Flying Officer Wright (FO/W), the first question he asked was, 'How old are you?' I replied, 'Nineteen next week sir.' He then told me that he had two grown-up sons both in their twenties. I think he was trying to imply that he was old enough to be my father.

On our first trip he taught me several things, but no landings. The next day ended up with him telling me to do the landing, but I was hopeless at it. The day after, I tried again, but still it was no good.

So we got to Friday and he told me that it would be my last chance, as the CFI had told him that if there was still no success that day, he would take me off the course.

After take-off, FO/W told me to head for satellite two, another small reserve airfield. He told me that it was only a long narrow strip, on which planes could land from either direction. He kept stressing to look ahead in case of other planes; I did and made a perfect landing. He jumped up in excitement saying that he knew that I could do it, and why had I been holding back on him.

He told me to take off again and give him 'Another landing, just like the last one.' I did it! Then he climbed out, saying, 'It's all yours, give me two landings, then it's back to base where you can land there, too.' I did so, and they were both good, so I had finally solved the problem.

What changed with your landings that allowed them to go from horrendous to successful?
The difference was that my first instructor and FO/W told me to look straight ahead and judge the height that way. But FO/T had told me to look down when I was landing; to judge my height by the shadow of the wheels approaching the ground. Going back to what my first instructor and FO/W had told me to do was the big difference that changed everything with my landings.

For the next month, with FO/W as my instructor, I continued flying the Tiger Moth, completing exercises that increased in complexity, until the instructors were satisfied that I had met the requirements to move on to either the fighter stream or the bomber stream. The same applied to everyone else on the course.

My final flight with 27 EFTS at Induna was on the 5th of August 1943.

Did you have to study for and pass anymore exams?
While we had ten exams on ten subjects at Hillside, we only had to take seven exams on seven subjects at Induna; the lectures were more light-hearted too. I think that a big factor in it was that from Induna onwards if you failed the exams, then you had another chance to take them. Gunnery theory, bombing theory and aircraft recognition

were the three that we didn't have to study for. The other seven subjects were the same subjects as before, just at a higher level.

Was the Tiger Moth a nice, enjoyable plane to fly?
Yes, it was an easy plane to fly. It was such a simple layout with two fixed wheels, a tail skid, rudder pedals and a joystick. However, not everyone enjoyed it. We had a chap transfer from the Middle East. He originally worked as an engine fitter but somehow ended up on the pilot's course. After a while, he became sick of flying Tiger Moths, or 'toys', as he called them. So one day, as a form of protest, he came in to land on the part of the airfield where the Tiger Moths were parked, in two rows facing each other wingtip-to-wingtip. He hit the ground just before the first one and carried on going. He wrote off seven in total, including his own. He survived and wasn't even injured. Everyone thought that he would face severe repercussions and be kicked off the course. But astonishingly, he was just given a stern talking to and was back on flying the next week. It was unbelievable, utterly unbelievable.

You would have bet everything on him being kicked off the course.
Yes, absolutely. Seven Tiger Moths written off in such a way; I wish I had seen it really.

Having passed the ground course and completed your Tiger Moth training, what came next?
Cadets who successfully completed the 'Elementary Flying Training School' then had to choose to go onto either the fighter or bomber stream for further training. Fighter schools were equipped with American-built Harvards, and the bomber schools were equipped with twin-engine Oxfords, built in the UK. These schools each had the title of 'Service Flying Training School'.

I told FO/W that I wanted to join the fighter stream, but he vetoed that and instead entered my name onto the bomber stream. When I asked him why he had done this, he said it was because I was too gentle on the controls, and added, 'If caught in a dogfight, by the time you had nursed your plane into a gentle turn, you would have been shot down several times.' So the next stage for me was bomber training. The school I was posted to was 21 Service Flying Training School (21 SFTS) at Kumalo. I was posted there on the 13th of August 1943. Kumalo was also on the outskirts of Bulawayo, only two-and-a-half miles northeast of the centre of town. That location was handy, plus I had a room to myself, which was also nice. I was at Kumalo for around four-and-a-half months.

Did you ever find out what had caused the crash that the CFI had to attend?
Yes, I visited the cadets involved at the hospital. I was told that FO/T was in a Tiger Moth with one of them, preparing to take off, and was warned by the cadet that the other cadet, in the air, was coming in to land, and that they would collide. The cadet was told by FO/T not to worry; that the cadet in the air had overshot the airstrip several times and would do the same again. Unfortunately, he didn't. As a result, he landed on top of the Tiger Moth on the ground. FO/T was sitting in the front and came out of it with only minor injuries, but both cadets suffered appalling injuries. Both had broken backs and other breakages. They were still in hospital when I eventually left Southern Rhodesia.

Did FO/T face any punishment for what had happened?
I don't know. He was taken off instructing and posted back to Britain, but I don't know what happened after that.

So it was decided: you were put on the bomber stream and posted to Kumalo. Was there much difference between Kumalo and Induna?
Very much so. Kumalo was completely different. While Induna was quite a small set-up without a proper runway, Kumalo had a main runway of concrete, and a grass field that could be used, owing to Rhodesia's lack of rain. There were two hangars on the southern end.

On the 17th of August 1943, I met my first Oxford instructor and was surprised, as he was only twenty-one years old. He went through the usual aircraft introductions, which were quite different from the Tiger Moth, a biplane. The Oxford, a monoplane, was a much larger aircraft, and able to carry six passengers, in addition to the crew. Instead of a tail skid, it had a conventional tailwheel. It also had flaps, hydraulic brakes and two engines, whereas the Tiger Moth only had one. Even taxiing was different in the Oxford. Quite a lot of the early instructions concerned the different characteristics of the Oxford versus the Tiger Moth.

The next stage of my introduction to the Oxford involved flight. I watched carefully as my instructor took off, circled and then landed. He then backtracked to the take-off point, and off we went again. I expected him to hand over the controls so I could have a go, but instead he repeated everything as before, including the landing. Both of these circuits were done in the morning.

By the 19th of August, I had been on several flights with my instructor but still had yet to take off and land on my own. That really bothered me and conjured up fears that I was on the path to repeat what had happened with the Tiger Moths, mainly the problems I went through with landing. I went to see the CFI and explained my issues. He then told me to come with him, and we went to a hangar where an Oxford was stationed. He told me to get in, taxi to the take-off point, take off, do a circuit and then land it, and that's what I did.

At Induna, a lot of time was taken up on lectures and the theoretical aspects of flying, which kept you on the ground. Was it the same at Kumalo or was more emphasis put on flying?
At Induna, the ratio of flying to lecturing was pretty much even, but at Kumalo, it was definitely skewed to the flying side. What made it much more difficult was that we had to do the same syllabus as those before us had completed, but in much less time, as the powers that be were desperate for aircrew due to the high casualty rate. While the course originally had to be completed in twenty weeks, for us, it had to be done in twelve. To put this into context, on the 27th of November 1943, I flew four times.

On quite a few occasions when I went up, another cadet, named Jack, and I would swap positions; one would pilot the aircraft and the other would navigate.

On one occasion, after a Saturday morning flight, I returned to my room and fell fast asleep, without even bothering to take my flying clothing off. I eventually woke up thinking it was seven in the evening and that I would need to get a move on to avoid missing the evening meal. I quickly changed and made a dash for the mess, but I soon discovered that the sun was in the wrong part of the sky and that it was actually Sunday morning. I had slept for sixteen hours! So I made my way back to my bed and slept for another two.

If that story is anything to go by, it sounds like the course itself was very demanding.
It was, especially as we had fewer weeks to complete everything. Cadets never used to fly on weekends, but there we were flying on Saturdays, trying to make up the hours. However, as we had already passed the various exams, the lectures we had were a lot more informal, if you will. They were more on the lines of tips and advice on the various aircraft and what was to come in our piloting careers.

Despite having our own rooms, we slept under canvas for the last two weeks of the course. The point of that was to get us used to the conditions that we would likely face during our travels and on our future postings. I remember that the rain tipped down on the second week, which was unusual for Southern Rhodesia. It was so heavy that we all took the opportunity to shower in it. Unknown to us, the camp photographer, as a joke, had photographed us naked in the rain, and to our horror it was an elderly lady who was tasked with developing them.

What sort of exercises did you have to do with the Oxford? With the Tiger Moth, it seemed like it was more about setting a foundation with basic flying and getting used to being in the air. While I imagine that exercises when flying the Oxford were designed to resemble the actual operations that you would soon be undertaking.
Yes, it resembled operational flying to such an extent that we would sometimes be ordered to pretend that we were on operations. We would take off, navigate to the site, drop our 'bombs', navigate back

and land. Before we took off for these 'operations', we would all assemble and have people tell us the various facts and figures about the 'operation'. It included where we were going, what targets we were going to strike and what the weather would be like on the way there and back. The intelligence people would have their say on the known state of any defences. It was a mock version of the briefings we would have before undertaking real operations. When we returned from our imitation operations, we even had mock debriefings. Each of these mock operations happened twice, with Jack and I swapping the roles of pilot and navigator.

There was one pretend operation when Jack was piloting, where we had to fly low, pretending that the enemy had radar. The main ravine we were over had little offshoots, and we worked out that if we chose the third ravine, it would take us close to the bombing area, where we would climb, drop the bombs and return home. Unfortunately, we picked the wrong ravine, and as soon as we turned we had cliffs in front of us, due to this ravine being much shorter in length. Jack had to put on full power, and we steeply climbed over them. I was acting as the navigator, and I was absolutely mesmerised by the sight of the cliffs coming ever closer. When we got back to base, we told our instructor about this experience, and he informed us that we were lucky on several accounts: one, it was a brand new plane; two, the engines gave us maximum power as they were new; and three, we were probably aided in our climb by an updraught.

On another occasion, I was flying into the sun; in other words, the sun was ahead of me, which affected my vision. Coming from the opposite direction was another Oxford at the same height as myself. Fortunately, it was being flown by an instructor. When we saw each other, I pulled back hard on the controls to increase height, and he dived down. It was one of those things that was over in seconds. It wasn't spoken about once I was back on the ground, and I never heard any more of it. Thinking about it, I must have been slightly higher than he was for me to have chosen to go up and for him to have chosen to go down.

During those navigation exercises, there seemed to be a risk, in that if you made a mistake and became lost, you could run out of fuel while trying to make it back, or face a similar potential tragedy. Was that ever a concern?
Yes, it was always in the back of my mind. Two cadets force-landed as they were running low on fuel while on a navigation exercise, and they were murdered while trying to find their way back.

That's tragic. What happened with the two cadets?
Well, during the Oxford course, say a couple of weeks after it began, it became known that an Oxford in the hands of two cadets on a cross country exercise had gone missing. A big search party was assembled, and all training flying ceased while the search was on. But after three to four days, flying continued and the search was called off, as it was believed that no one could last in the wilderness of Southern Rhodesia for that long. Eventually, around six weeks after they had gone missing, a story went around Kumalo that their Oxford was found after a native of Bechuanaland had walked into a police station to report that he had seen a big yellow bird on the ground; Oxford training planes were painted yellow.

According to the story, the authorities of Southern Rhodesia got permission from the Bechuanaland authorities to search the site. They found the abandoned Oxford, with the chocks in place and with the engine and cockpit covers on, but two things were missing: the navigator's maps and the compass. The two cadets had left a note which stated the direction they were going to take from the aircraft to reach a river they had seen from the air. However, when our people followed the track that the missing airmen had marked out, they didn't find anything at all.

Then the chief navigator of the unit had a brainwave regarding all of our compasses - big magnetic ones with the needle floating in alcohol. He remembered that every fifteen degrees, the compass had to be compared with another compass at least fifty yards away from the aircraft, to account for the magnetic pull of the aircraft. The search party discovered that the course the airmen had chosen did not take into account either the magnetic pull of the aircraft on the compass, the variation between magnetic north and true north or possibly both.

It was said that they ended up in a native village and that they had been murdered and their remains stuffed into termite mounds. When the authorities arrived, the village chief and the witch doctor were both found to be wearing RAF clothing. The two of them were taken to trial, confessed to the killings and were ultimately hanged in Bulawayo jail. The village was then destroyed; burnt to the ground, I believe.

However, it's only recently that I discovered what actually happened. After running out of fuel, the two cadets, Walter Adamson and Gerald Edwards, force-landed on a salt flat in Bechuanaland. The next morning, they left a note stating what direction they were going to head in and left the aircraft with their parachutes, a compass and a medical kit. Not long after they left, they were picked up by a hunting party of Bushmen and taken back to their temporary shelters. The two cadets were then fed and watered, and then they went to sleep. The three men in the hunting party then discussed the situation around the campfire and decided to kill the two cadets for their money and clothes, and because of their fear of being caught illegally hunting. The two cadets were then shot, but one of them was finished off with an axe. Bits of their bodies were cut up and boiled down into tubs to be used for medicine and magic.

One of the members of the hunting party went to a police post about four weeks later and reported his sighting of the missing Oxford to the police. An investigation was launched by the Bechuanaland Police, which resulted in the women from the hunting party implicating the three men, so the case then went to court.

During the trial, in September 1944, the judge found them all not guilty, despite fairly compelling evidence. The main reason was that the description of the two cadets given by the hunting party witnesses differed to that of the RAF officer who served as a witness for the prosecution; photos of the two cadets proved that the RAF officer's description had been wrong. Other reasons were the language barrier and the two cadet's bodies not being found. Though the three men in the hunting party were rearrested, charged and found guilty of illegal hunting.

What a horrific story.
It must have been a horrible ending for the lads. What I don't understand is that we were all instructed to stay with the aircraft if an event like that happened. But I guess that following a crash in the middle of nowhere without any communications, and with supplies running out, many would try and find their way back.

Before passing out of Kumalo, you had to complete the famous wings exams.
Yes, they were on the same seven subjects but at a more advanced level. The same rules applied as at Induna: if you failed any of the exams, you were allowed a second go. I passed the first time, but seven cadets failed on the first attempt. I believe that they all passed on the second attempt.

Having received my wings, I was promoted to sergeant, which once again meant an increase in pay, as every increase in rank did.

What do you remember about receiving your wings?
It took place on the 17th of December 1943. It was rather a quiet affair. We all lined up next to each other, and the air vice-marshal in charge of the Rhodesia Air Training Group, he had flown to our airfield in his own personal Harvard, then pinned them onto our chests. We sewed them on later. Once given our pilot's wings, we were told that unless we did something really dire, they could never be taken away.

The air vice-marshal then gave a speech in which he said that we were now pilots in His Majesty's Royal Air Force, and that we think we know it all and are now going to show off. He told us to go ahead and do it, to go to our girlfriends' or parents' houses and show off, but to only do it once. To do it a second time would be dangerous, and to do it a third time would lead to us killing ourselves. It was RAF superstition, like in the First World War, where the men in the trenches were told not to flick on a cigarette lighter three times, or a sniper would get you.

Speaking of Harvards, my friend Cyril, from the ATC, was a few months younger than me, so he followed me out to Southern Rhodesia on a later course. By the time he arrived at Hillside, I was at Induna, so we were unable to meet, except once in Bulawayo. He in turn went to the Tiger Moth school named Guinea Fowl, so we were unable to meet due to the distance. I went onto the bomber stream, and he went onto the fighter stream and flew Harvards. Unfortunately, he failed the pilots course. Like others in a similar situation, he was posted back to Britain and received compulsory orders to join what were known as 'Bevin Boys', young men sent to work in the mines in order to increase the rate of declining coal production. By the time I arrived back from overseas he was out of the mines, but unfortunately I never saw him again.

While we are on the topic of friends, I forgot to mention that while I was in Southern Rhodesia I used to meet up with Mervin from the troopship quite regularly on Sundays, as we went to church together. He was on the course ahead of me owing to me being struck down with malaria. He used to give me helpful advice and tips on what was to come.

What did you think of the Oxford at the time, and how do you look back on it?
It was quite an easy plane to fly. It had a particularity, at least in my opinion, in the sense that if you landed it badly it could bounce forward, resulting in its nose dropping and the propellers going into the ground, which generally resulted in engines catching fire. Once, I had been flying with an instructor and was told to do an exercise which involved taking off. As I waited at the take-off point, an Oxford came in to land, did the landing and tipped onto its nose. The propellers hit the runway, and the port engine caught fire. Then a second Oxford came in to land, and the same thing happened, except with the starboard engine. The fire engine that arrived to extinguish the fire on the first Oxford had its work cut out, as its workload quickly doubled. It was quite common, though. One of our cadets wrote off three Oxfords, two during the day and one at night. On the night flight, he overshot the airfield and went between two trees, causing the wings to be ripped off. The plane ended up sliding along on its fuselage.

I'm just glad that you managed to land them without any engines catching fire or ending up on your fuselage, and that you never had any incidents with them.

Well, I did have an incident. It's something I must confess to after seventy-five years. I was on a night exercise, with the objective of landing at Kumalo, but as I was coming back, I spotted the lights of the Hillside area; Hillside and Kumalo were not too far from each other. Being young, I couldn't avoid the temptation of going into a shallow dive and roaring over Hillside, breaking one of the basic rules of the air, which is to never do beat-ups. I knew that I would have been seen and tracked, that any plane would have been tracked - what direction it approached from and everything.

After my dive, I climbed back up to circuit height and returned to Kumalo from a different direction, to make it look as though I had returned from the exercise from that direction. Over the next few days there was a big investigation in both nearby Oxford camps, Kumalo and Heany. Everyone was questioned, and when my turn came I made up a story about how on my return I had seen a plane flying low down in that area. The Kumalo investigators thought that nobody who had studied at Hillside would beat-up his own pals. In the end, the belief was that it must have been someone from Heany, so they were all banned from leaving the camp for a while.

Another incident that comes to mind is when I landed at Kumalo on a very windy day and was rolling to a stop. There were two hangars at Kumalo that were quite close to each other. As a result, if the wind was strong and in the right direction, it would be sucked through the gap between the two and cross the runway, as was the case on this occasion. When I came to that section of the runway, the wind caught the tail fin and started to cause my Oxford to spin. I put on opposite rudder and increased the power to the starboard engine. I was soon out of the wind stream, which stabilised my Oxford, but the air traffic controller noted it down as a bad landing and notified the CFI. Later that day, I was called to see the CFI, and I explained what had happened. He asked me if I had learnt anything from the incident, and my reply was that, yes, I had learnt to take into account the dangers posed by crosswinds when landing. His reply was that it can happen to any pilot regardless of experience, and that the same thing had happened to him that morning.

CHAPTER FIVE

FROM SOUTHERN RHODESIA TO JERUSALEM, DECEMBER 1943 – FEBRUARY 1944

*Travelling through Africa to Cairo, memories of Egypt
and taking a train to Jerusalem*

**What happened after you received your wings? I assume that
you were posted to a new flying school that involved aircraft you
had not previously piloted.**
For a group of fifteen of us, three of whom were older chaps, the next
stage involved a lot of travelling. We were posted from Kumalo to
Jerusalem, which is obviously on another continent. We travelled by
three methods: train, open-back truck and flying boat. We left Southern
Rhodesia on the 30th of December 1943, arrived in Cairo on the
15th of January 1944 and were there until the 1st of February.

We were put on a train to Victoria Falls, the same rail line as I
had ridden before, but this time we only stayed at Victoria Falls
for a few hours. We then departed from Victoria Falls, carrying on
with our train journey, in order to reach our night's destination in
nearby Livingstone, Northern Rhodesia. First, however, we had to
endure an annoying incident not long after departing Victoria Falls
station when our train and one travelling in the other direction from
Northern Rhodesia met at a sweeping 180-degree bend, still on the
Southern Rhodesia-side of the falls.

It would normally have been possible to let the train approaching
from Northern Rhodesia pass through, but our rail crew found
that the last two carriages of our train, which were restaurant cars,
blocked the passage of the other train. Us RAF lads set out to solve
the problem. We went to the train crew to tell them our plan but
were told to mind our business. Their solution, in the end, was to
disconnect the two restaurant cars from our train and abandon them

on the main track. The southbound train then went forward, and its engines connected with the two restaurant carriages and pushed them the short distance, less than a mile, back to the Victoria Falls railway station. All of this took around three hours, and for the rest of the journey we had nothing to eat or drink.

From there, we skirted the falls and crossed over into Northern Rhodesia, now known as Zambia, and almost immediately arrived at Livingstone. The Victoria Falls and Livingstone rail stations were only about eight miles apart, by train, so this rail journey was short. We spent one night there, and what surprised us was how cheap everything was.

The next day, we were put aboard three trucks. During the journey, we were caught in the slipstream of the truck in front, so we were caked in dust. On top of that, the seats were rock solid, and as you can imagine, all of that led to an uncomfortable trip. Our journey, roughly 300 miles in length, ended at an army camp.

Once we arrived there, a load of us stripped down and made our way to the lake to go swimming and to wash all the muck off. Just as we were about to enter the lake, an army captain came rushing over, warning us not to go anywhere near the water. He shouted, 'Haven't you heard of Bilharzia?' We replied, 'He isn't with us.' The captain then told us that Bilharzia is a waterborne parasite, a worm that burrows into the skin and ends up in the urinary or intestinal tract. There was a group of natives swimming in the lake without a care in the world, but the captain's explanation put an end to our desire to swim. The captain then proceeded to tell us that as we were in an army camp, we fell under army orders.

We were billeted in two wooden huts, which could house twelve people each. The three older chaps decided that they would like to stick together in one hut, and the remaining twelve of us decided to stay in the other one. Apparently, the natives who worked in the camp were known to come in and steal things, so the army soldiers told us to look after our stuff, which we did. One man stood by the door keeping a lookout, and he would be replaced by a fresh lookout every hour. The three older ones in the other hut didn't do the same as us, and as a result they lost everything; literally everything. The rest of us had to give them what we could from our supplies; otherwise, they would have been completely naked.

After a few days there, we were all put on a train and eventually found ourselves in a second army camp, followed a few days later by another train journey, to Lake Tanganyika. After crossing that lake by boat, it took us two more days to reach Lake Victoria, where our train stopped. I remember that we had to sleep on the train. In charge of our party was a chap whose job it was to make sure we reached Cairo. He came up to me and asked if I wouldn't mind sleeping on the floor, as they were one bed short. I agreed. So, in my rail carriage, the chap in charge was on the top bunk, an army chap was on the bottom bunk and I was on the floor. In the early hours, I awoke to find the army chap trying to sexually interfere with me. But before he had any success, I was awake and swearing and shouting at him, and the racket woke up the chap in charge. He turned on the light and proceeded to call the army bloke in the lower bunk a bunch of explicit names, and that was the end of it.

From there, we crossed Lake Victoria by boat, taking twelve hours to do so. The boat had cabins, each of which had two individual beds inside. Most of the beds were taken, and anyone without a bed had to sleep on the deck. I was relieved to find a spare bed until I saw that the kitbag that was already there belonged to the army chap from the lower bunk on the train. I could tell by the name and handwriting on his kitbag that he was the man, so I chose to sleep on the deck.

We disembarked in Kisumu, but we were only there for a few hours, maybe not even that. We were told by a man that our billets were at the top of a hill, which we proceeded to climb. Within minutes of reaching these billets, we were informed that there had been a mistake and that we actually had to go back down and board a civilian Imperial Airways flying boat named *Caledonia*.

The first stop was a place named Juba, on the White Nile. We spent one night there. The next day was mainly spent flying, our destination being Khartoum. Because we were only there for one night and had to leave at five the following morning, we didn't get to see or do anything. When we left, there was a full moon in the sky; it wasn't light yet. That caused me to recall a song that we all knew. The part which came to mind was, 'We are leaving Khartoum by the light of the moon. We are sailing by night and by day!'

So, we departed and headed to Cairo. On our way there, as we flew over the desert, the plane suffered horrific turbulence, which the pilot counteracted by climbing.

By the way, sometime during the journey I had developed a cold that was giving me grief, especially in my ears. My discomfort eased once the pilot gained altitude, but the pain returned when he descended and then landed at Cairo. Luckily, however, I misjudged a step when I disembarked, and the jolt from hitting the ground after misjudging the step caused the pressure to be released from my ears. This left me in a much better state.

We asked the crew how much they were paid, and they told us that they received one farthing an air mile. After refuelling, they continued on to their next destination, as more time in the air meant more money for them.

After Southern Rhodesia, you didn't spend a lot of time in the African countries and cities that you passed through. Despite this, were you able to form any comparisons and opinions about them? After all, it's a giant and diverse continent.

Not really. After all, we were just passing through and didn't really have the time to speak to people and explore. It was a journey of highlights and was rather boring at times. At no time during the journey did I ever feel any antagonism or disdain from the local people, but again, interactions and time to explore were very limited.

You were in Cairo for two weeks before being posted to Palestine. What did you do while you were there?

In Cairo, we stayed in quite a nice hotel named 'The Heliopolis', we were five to a room. We didn't have duties during our two weeks there. The hotel was staffed by Italian prisoners of war, who struck me as being quite depressed; their sad demeanour was understandable.

As we had so much free time, we decided to do a lot of sightseeing. One of the first places we went to was the Museum of Hygiene; it was awful. They had detailed wax exhibitions of what all these dreadful diseases could do to the human body, and in quite graphic detail. Once we had finished downstairs, the museum curator asked us if we wanted to see what was upstairs. One of our party asked if it was as bad as what we had just seen. We were told that it was worse, which prompted us to decline his offer and leave.

We also visited the pyramids at Giza. There were two ways of getting to Giza back then, either by horse or by camel. My four chums had ridden horses in the past, but I had not. By the time I managed to mount my horse, the other four were already way ahead, which caused my horse to take off quite quickly after them. I was terrified, which is ironic considering that I had no fear of going up thousands of feet in a plane by myself.

Once we arrived at the pyramids, we discovered that we were able to go inside. As you can imagine, it was completely dark. The guides profited by selling strips of magnesium which could be set alight and used as candles, though they only lasted a few minutes, after which we would buy new strips, as needed.

What was it like to be standing in front of and then going inside one of the most significant and famous man-made structures in history?
What struck me about the pyramids was their size; they were huge. The tunnels we entered were narrow, but one could walk upright. We came to the edge of a chamber deep within one pyramid and had a look but didn't explore further. Just by being inside the pyramid I felt as though I was connecting with history. But at the same time, there was a certain uneasiness about it; I just wanted to get out.

The two cities that you spent the most time in on the African continent were Bulawayo and Cairo. How did Cairo compare to Bulawayo?
The people in Bulawayo were very friendly, and the city was clean and well laid out in regard to roads and avenues, while Cairo, by contrast, was anything but. Also, I don't recall Cairo having the entertainment facilities that Bulawayo had, like swimming baths and cinemas, though I'm sure that they were there.

Although we had free time, we still had to report to an RAF office every day to be updated on the latest situation regarding any future activity. There was also quite a big army presence in Cairo; this was not surprising considering that the North African campaign had only been won the previous May, around eight months earlier.

With so many British troops there at that time, and being aware of the historical relationship between Britain and Egypt, what was the general attitude towards the British from the Egyptian people?

I sensed quite a strong anti-British sentiment. We were told to never get into a confrontation with an Egyptian, because it would never be a fair argument or fight; it would quite quickly become you versus a group of Egyptians, and that was a fight that could never be won. The army lads always travelled in large groups, and the British and Egyptians seemed to stick to their own.

Did you see any other parts of Egypt while you were there?

Yes, we took a bus to Alexandria. Out of curiosity, one of my friends took his shoes and socks off and went for a paddle in the Mediterranean but soon came rushing out, saying that it was bloody freezing. There was a feeling of age about the place, as though you were many centuries in the past; I found Alexandria to be a very interesting place. I remember that we visited a small café and managed to find tea there. It doesn't sound like anything special, but it was the tea drunk in Britain, which stuck out to me. In my opinion, Alexandria differed from Cairo, in that I found the place quite friendly; there wasn't the antagonism I sensed in Cairo.

Travelling from Cairo to Jerusalem was by train, I assume.

Yes, it was a rather slow journey from what I remember. We didn't stop there, but we passed through a huge army camp where there were acres upon acres of tents. One story that sticks out in my mind is of children running alongside the train selling peanuts in paper cones. A chap, not in our group, wanted to buy a cone and leaned out the window with a banknote in his hand. The child took the banknote and made a run for it, with no intention of handing over the peanuts. The man grabbed the child by his shirt but ripped a huge section of it off. The child scampered away with both the peanuts and the banknote, leaving the man shouting explicit words. He then threw the ripped part of the shirt away. Amazingly, the child ran back, picked up the missing piece of his shirt, and ran off again.

What was also interesting was that the landscape kept on changing; one never tired of looking out the window. While there were areas that resembled a desert, especially in the beginning of our journey, as we continued on we would start to see small fields filled with orange trees and date palms, particularly near the coast. Small lakes were also noted.

We really looked forward to arriving in Jerusalem; it was a place that we had heard so much about.

CHAPTER SIX

PALESTINE, FEBRUARY – MAY 1944

Exploring Jerusalem, a tragic passing, forming a crew,
training on a Wellington bomber, taking a Wellington to
the breaking point and travelling to India

Jerusalem is a city steeped in history. It's significant to so many people around the world and has been occupied and fought over by so many armies and empires throughout history. Even now, the atmosphere one experiences there is hard to describe. What feelings and impressions did you get from being there?
Exactly that, the sense of being a witness to history. I was immediately reminded of things I had read about in the Bible when I observed that many of the Jews of Jerusalem wore their hair in ringlets and were touching the Western Wall. We were told that the reason their hair was worn in such ringlets was so when they died, they would be pulled up to heaven. The Western Wall, even then, had such a high turnover of people coming and going.

How long were you in Jerusalem? Was it a similar situation to Cairo, where you had few duties and plenty of time to explore?
Yes, I was in Jerusalem for six weeks, staying in what can only be described as an assigned building. We didn't have any duties during that time; we just had to report to the military officials. The rest of the time was spent sightseeing. It was quite similar to our time spent in Cairo in that sense. One thing that we did every day was to go swimming at the Young Men's Christian Association, also known as the YMCA. There was also a library there, on the top floor.

We explored the old town and walked around the outdoor market. I remember that we bought these delicious Jaffa oranges that the sellers would cut open and squeeze into a glass; the juice from these oranges had a very strong and delicious taste, but I must say that dates were my favourite. The market itself was always busy and full of life. It was great; we could have quite easily spent all day there. At one of the numerous clothing stalls, I took the opportunity to stock up on underwear, as the ones that the RAF supplied were quite poor.

We also took a one-day bus trip to Bethlehem, which was quite an experience. The atmosphere in the town was normal until we entered the Church of the Nativity, where Christ was said to have been born, and then it went dead quiet; the silence fit me like a coat, in some ways. Even my friend, who was never short of things to say, was completely silent while we were inside. There was a deep feeling of holiness when I was in there, a feeling of being blessed; it was a lovely feeling. I can't speak for anyone else, but that's how it felt for me.

The town itself was quite small. There was a steady stream of people, including locals and sightseers, but there weren't masses of them, or anything like that.

We also took a one-day trip to Tel Aviv. As it was an RAF vehicle that took us there, we had to return at a set time, unlike when we went to Bethlehem. It was not a problem, however, and we spent most of the day on the beach.

During those first weeks in Jerusalem, I received a batch of post that had finally caught up with me, around nine envelopes in total. In that batch was a letter from Bert, my foster parents' biological son. Bert informed me that my foster father had died on the 8th of December 1943. It was horrible. I was crushed, as I really liked my foster father. Later on, I received a letter from Mervin's mother. Mervin was my friend from the troopship and through much of my time in Southern Rhodesia. His mother's letter informed me that Mervin had been killed. He never completed the pilot's course in Southern Rhodesia, because he couldn't do two required manoeuvres at the same time. Instead, he became a navigator, and when returning from an operation over Europe, the aircraft he was in crashed due to heavy fog.

It must have been awful to receive Bert's letter.
Yes, and the five of us were just about to go out when our mail arrived. We decided to open our mail before departing, and the reason

I opened Bert's letter was because I recognised his handwriting. As I said, I was crushed, and I just started crying. The others went out, but I just stayed in with my thoughts.

The 1930s and 1940s saw an escalation in violence in Jerusalem for many reasons, the unpopularity of the British being one of them. To what extent did that situation impact you?
My little group always stuck together, not because of any threat, but because there was an atmosphere of tension, and various groups like the Stern Gang were getting a lot of publicity. We were on alert, but fortunately nothing happened to us. One could still go around sightseeing and also visit the market without any issue.

Eventually, you were posted to RAF Aqir, in Palestine.
Though fifteen of us arrived in Jerusalem, I was the last in the group to a receive a new posting. Why that came about was that the officials sorted everyone by age, and the older ones were posted first.

As far as I can remember, in Palestine, there were three fighter training units, two Spitfire and one Hurricane, or maybe the other way around, and two bomber training units. Each was a numbered 'Operational Training Unit', or OTU, and it was typically the last posting for a new airman prior to an actual operational flying assignment.

I was eventually put on a coach with about thirty others and posted to RAF Aqir, in order to convert onto twin-engine Wellington bombers at No 76 Operational Training Unit. Upon arrival, on the 18th of March 1944, we were taken to a big hangar where many other personnel were milling around. An officer told us to mingle and form crews. Basically, how it worked was that one man would walk up to a pilot such as myself and say something like, 'Do you need a wireless operator?' or whatever trade he held, and if the pilot didn't yet have a wireless operator for his crew and they all got on well together, then the wireless operator joined that pilot's crew. I formed my crew in this way.

At Aqir, it was a tradition for a newly-formed crew to have a drink together. That event was the first time in my life that I drank alcohol. At two in the morning I felt that I was going to be sick, but the nearest latrine was around 100 yards away. I made a quick dash under the full moonlight to the latrines; I made it there and was sick everywhere. It was then that I realised I was completely naked.

What happened once your crew was assembled?

After our crew formed, we started flying together, beginning the essential process of learning how to work as a team. We were in Aqir for a little over two months, during which time I only did around eighty-two hours of flying, which is nothing really, especially when you consider the fact that I totalled 157 hours in Oxfords.

During that time, I met an Australian pilot named Carl Fristrom, who preferred to be called 'Frizzy'. He would go on to become my best friend over the coming years.

How long did it take for your crew to gel? Was there instant rapport?

We all quickly got on well, and this transferred into flying, where we began to work as a well-oiled machine. Though I was the youngest, at nineteen, we were all within a few years of each other, except for my rear gunner, who was eleven years older than me.

There was one character though, my first navigator. He was quite a maverick, and a hard drinker. He was always making us laugh and pulling practical jokes. For example, once when we were in the Sergeants Mess, he got on the phone to the commanding officer and asked, 'Are you the CO?' Then once the reply came, he asked, 'Do you know who I am?' When the CO responded again, my navigator slammed the phone down and walked off, saying, 'Guess he's not in' while shrugging his shoulders.

Another time, we were coming back from a night exercise when some lights appeared off the coast, quite a cluster of them, obviously boats of some sort. My navigator saw this, leaned over and said, 'See those lights down there? They're Japanese trawlers. We should go after them!'

Eventually, he was posted back to Britain, which I'm sure was due to his actions, which often involved drunken brawls. Even before I arrived, he had a reputation for being a maverick, and he had been overseas for over four years.

I didn't get on with my next navigator at first, which is ironic, as we became good friends later. Our friendship developed quite quickly, though, once we discovered that we had worked for the same company, just in different counties, him in Essex and myself in Kent, before being called up. He was an excellent navigator; he could navigate you through the eye of a needle in the darkest of conditions. His name was Len Upjohn.

Seeing as you now had your wings and were a qualified pilot, did the procedure of learning to fly the Wellington differ from when you learnt to fly the Oxford?
Flying didn't start straightaway, as we had to do a period in the classroom being taught all the systems of the Wellington. We learnt how the plane worked and what to do in emergencies, along with the workings of the electronics, the hydraulics and pneumatics. We would start by going over a topic in the classroom and would then go to see it in person on the actual aircraft. This stage in our education was purely to prepare us for operations.

There was a system in the Wellington for transferring fuel from a tank on one side to the other, so if one tank was running out of fuel you could transfer the contents from the other one. It was intriguing to learn of this, and many other secrets of the Wellington, a more advanced aircraft than any of us had previously flown in training.

Another exercise was in learning the emergency procedure for baling out, and we learnt that on a non-flying Wellington in the hangar. Several mattresses were put in front of the hatch. We then had to put on our parachutes and pretend that we were baling out. In my case, there happened to be a loose screw on the side of the hatch which caught my uniform and almost ripped it off. I went back to try it a second time, knowing I had to master it, and the same thing happened again. The third time my trousers were torn. Frizzy thought it was hilarious.

An important exercise was in learning how high we could fly before passing out from lack of oxygen, measured as the crew sat side-by-side next to a doctor. We were in a decompression chamber, where the amount of oxygen was gradually lowered, corresponding to increases in elevation, as if we were airborne. In this manner, the doctor recorded the elevation when each crewman passed out. It was an important exercise for me, as otherwise I wouldn't have considered the possibility of passing out.

I did nearly pass out a few nights later while on a night exercise when my oxygen supply became disconnected. I started to believe that the plane was doing strange things, like flying upside down, as the stars appeared beneath me, but it was a false picture caused by hallucinating due to oxygen deprivation. I told my flight engineer to check my oxygen, and he managed to fix it.

Learning to fly a Wellington was the same as an Oxford in the sense that I went up with an instructor pilot who showed me, in precise detail, everything to do with taking off, flying and landing. Included in my training was guidance on specifics like when to lower the undercarriage and when to operate the flaps. My instructor was named Flight Sergeant P (FS/P), and I didn't like him. He used to try and make flying as difficult as possible, like when he would turn off one engine and force me to fly purely on the other one. On another occasion, when we were coming back over the Eastern Mediterranean, FS/P noticed searchlights in the night sky, probably to do with an exercise for another unit. He proceeded to fly into the lights, handed me the controls and told me to get us out of them, which I did by going into a sharp dive, then putting on hard left rudder to get us back on course. Looking back on it, his method of forcing me to fly under challenging conditions, while seemingly harsh, was great training for what I might face in combat.

At No 76 OTU, I first had to complete the exercises with FS/P that I have just mentioned. Then I had to be passed to fly a Wellington solo, without an instructor present. I practiced take-offs and landings at a different airfield, not at RAF Aqir. My practice, then the soloing test, lasted for three days, beginning on the 9th of April 1944. Once I passed, I soon started a programme of regular flying exercises, day and night, with my crew.

Going into the searchlights sounds like quite a baptism of fire, as far as exercises go. Were your exercises all so intense?
The exercises we had to do were mainly cross country, during which the navigator came into his own. A lot of those exercises were flown

over the eastern side of the Mediterranean. Having said that, my first night exercise involved an emergency when a red warning light came on. Now knowing the Wellington's systems, I concluded that it had something to do with the electronics. I radioed base and asked them what to do. In reply, they told me that it was probably an electrical fault but to divert to Haifa, an airfield that I had never been to before. The fault turned out to be an instrument failure.

Of course, all these exercises were designed to resemble actual operational flying. We had live bombs to drop at that stage, for bombing exercises, not for every exercise. Those bombs were only eleven pounders, whereas the bombs I dropped on operations were as heavy as 3,000 pounds each, which had to be dropped from a minimum height of 3,000 feet to be clear of the updraughts caused by the explosions.

Seeing as you and Frizzy were both pilots and such good friends, did you ever compete with each other on those exercises?
It wasn't planned as such, but if we were put on the same exercise, then we would compare results. It was a very friendly rivalry. But I remember that he boasted to me once that he had done what I 'could never do,' which was to go past the red line on the speedometer. This red line marked the maximum speed one could take a Wellington before it risked falling apart in the air.

Soon after Frizzy's boast, I was on a daylight exercise at a height of around 10,000 feet when my maverick navigator started to goad me into trying to go past the red line. I went into a dive and soon found myself unable to pull out, as I couldn't break the force I was experiencing.

My wireless operator became quite scared and started frantically telling me to, 'Pull out of it!' I luckily remembered the elevator trim tab, and by the time I operated this tab, our speed had far exceeded the red line. We couldn't have been much more than three to five hundred feet from the ground when I finally succeeded in pulling out of the dive. All of that took place just as I flew over the airfield. One of the engineers on the ground later told me that the diving Wellington was like 'a bat out of hell.'

That's crazy, though I guess that being nineteen, your concept of danger still wasn't fully developed.
Correct; it was anything but fully developed. It was all exciting at the time. I hadn't intended to travel at such a high speed or anywhere close to it; I just wanted to go one mile an hour faster than Frizzy had. But still, once I landed, the red light from the control tower came on, and I had to go and see the Chief Flying Instructor, who was not happy. He really gave me a talking to, but I think it helped that I looked so young.

On one exercise, we had to do night photography by flying over the target and dropping the photoflash so the camera would work. After Frizzy's Wellington and mine had returned to base, he started shouting at me, 'Bloody hell, Denis, you could have killed me! Your flash went off right in front of my cockpit!' He then started laughing. It was that sort of competition and that sort of humour.

I imagine that the day-to-day atmosphere was quite lively and that there was a sense of impending adventure, as once all of you had finished with the Wellington operational training unit, you would be posted to another corner of the globe and find yourself on the cusp of operational flying.
Yes, that's exactly right. Frizzy and I already knew that our next step was to be posted to a heavy conversion unit, which we knew was for four-engine Liberators. We also knew that we would be posted to India, which led to a lot of excitement and anticipation. Growing up, I had heard many stories about India, 'the jewel of the Empire'; it was a place etched in British history.

How did the Wellington compare to the Oxford? Was it a plane you liked?
I liked the Wellington. It was such a powerful machine, though not as powerful as a Lancaster. It was also a reasonably easy plane to fly. It was one of the planes that a pilot could land smoothly with relative ease, even though the cockpit was high off the ground. Ironically, the Warwick, the larger transport version of the Wellington, had different flying characteristics and was not a plane I liked. It wasn't as sleek, and it was a harder plane to land.

After you had passed out of the Wellington operational training unit, you were posted to India. From Palestine to India is quite a distance. How long did it take to reach India?
We left RAF Aqir and began our journey to India on the 27th of May 1944, and it must have taken about a week to get there. The first leg of our journey was by train back to Cairo, through the various fields of fruit and the desert. We were only in Cairo for a day, but while I was there I made a visit to the dentist, as my fillings were coming to the ends of their lives. I was at the dentist for just under an hour, during which time he removed the old fillings. There were about four teeth involved: two in the front and two molars. The RAF was particular about the front teeth for image reasons. We were partway through the procedure when my front gunner barged in and said that the flying boat was leaving in half an hour. In that time, I had to pack my kit in preparation to travel. We were like blue-arsed flies. The dentist wrote a note explaining what he had done and told me to find a dentist in India to complete the treatment.

Once we were packed up, we were all put on open-back lorries and taken to the awaiting flying boat. Ironically, there was a short wait to receive permission to go aboard. Unlike my last flying boat experience, this flying boat was an RAF Sunderland; it didn't belong to Imperial Airways. We were in the air for about two-and-a-half hours. We flew to Bahrain, our first destination, for what was meant to be a simple refuelling stop, but we actually ended up spending three days there, as a result of an important wedding that went on for the three entire days. The noise coming from the wedding was quite something. The music and sounds of people partying went on day and night, and as a result we got very little sleep. The engineers who were tasked with refuelling the plane were guests at the wedding, and with nobody else to refuel our plane, we were grounded. My fellow travellers and I, fifteen in total, were given accommodation in a Nissen hut-type of building.

How did you spend the three days?
We actually had a chance to go and explore. Even back then the waters around Bahrain were quite busy with oil tanker-type ships. Bahrain itself wasn't built up like it is now with its huge modern cities. In

fact, it was all quite undeveloped back then, at least compared to now. I remember hearing the call for prayer bellow out at various times. Another thing that stands out in my mind is the night sky. Due to the lack of light pollution, the night sky was so bright and vivid, it was amazing. Night skies like that are a navigator's best friend.

CHAPTER SEVEN

INDIA ADVENTURES BEGIN,
JUNE – OCTOBER 1944

*Arriving in India, jungle preservation training, pulling a gun
on a friend's crew, converting to the Liberator, W/Cdr
James Blackburn and RAF Liberator operations from India*

Once the wedding was over, did you quickly depart for India?
Yes. One morning, three days after we landed, we were put onto the
same Sunderland flying boat in the early hours, and then we began
our flight to Karachi, India. Despite the flight taking most of the day,
the nice thing about it was that we were all given a meal on board.
That was the highlight of the flight, and by the late afternoon we had
landed in Karachi. The fifteen of us were put on an open-back lorry
and taken to an army camp fifteen miles outside of Karachi.

Once we were in the camp, we had to queue up for blankets, and
then the most extraordinary thing happened. In the queue next to
me was a chap who was in the Air Training Corps with me back in
Britain. He was two years older than me, so he was called up when I
was sixteen. He recognised me first, and it was quite a sight once we
realised who the other was. We only had a few minutes to talk before
having to go our separate ways, but it was an amazing occurrence.

Within a few days, we realised that we were going to be there for
some time with nothing to do, so a few of us had the idea of going
into Karachi and renting some bicycles. This included Frizzy and
his crew, who had been on the same flying boat as me. Close to the
huts in which we were billeted was a flat patch of land, about the
size of a football pitch. We crushed up a tin can and devised a game
of polo using the bicycles. By the time we were finished with them,
the bikes were absolutely wrecked, and the chap who had rented
them to us was furious. He demanded money to cover the costs of
replacing them, and we agreed.

We were there at the camp outside of Karachi for about three weeks before we boarded a lorry to the Karachi train station. From there, our destination was Bombay, but we had to go via Lahore. On the way to Lahore, I saw the most unbelievable sight: a cow with five legs. The fifth leg was hanging from its chest, a few inches above the ground. It wasn't supporting the cow or anything like that. It was one of those things that caused me to do a double-take, as I just couldn't believe what I had seen. I spoke to a member of the train crew about it, and he told me that it wasn't as unusual as I thought, that he had seen and heard of such cows before and that it wouldn't be killed due to Hindu beliefs. Remember that before the Partition in 1947, when the creation of Pakistan caused Hindus and Muslims to migrate east and west, respectively, there was quite a large Hindu population in what is now Pakistan; we were then travelling within that part of India which became Pakistan a few years later.

It was dark by the time we reached Lahore. We took the opportunity to shower, but the heat and especially the humidity were so strong that even though we showered, we found ourselves unable to completely dry. We did the best we could and got back on the train. From there, we travelled to Bombay, which took two days. On that leg of the journey, I noticed that I had developed a sore on my left leg that I knew required medical attention. In our medical kits, we carried needles, thread, little bandages, iodine and the like, so I disinfected a needle with iodine, pricked the sore, dabbed it with iodine and repeated that for the duration of the journey. Once I arrived in Bombay, I went to see a medical officer and described by treatment. He told me that I had cured it myself and didn't need any further treatment.

I also took the opportunity to find a dentist to have the outstanding work on my fillings completed.

From what I remember you telling me, you were in Bombay for an extended period of time. Did you get a chance to look around? To many, Indian cities generally come across as quite chaotic.

Yes, but it was organised chaos. We found an air-conditioned cinema, which surprised us. Even back then the traffic was very heavy. It was a bustling city, and there was always the feeling that there was so much to do. For example, it had quite a big, lively market. We were in Bombay for about three weeks, though it wouldn't be my last time in Bombay; it was a city I really liked.

But having said all that, there was a really poor area of Bombay, which we visited out of curiosity. In that area, people lived in huts made out of basic materials, with roofs mainly constructed out of corrugated iron. Due to the lack of sewage facilities, there was an unsavoury smell in the air at all times. However, I never felt unsafe there.

After Bombay, you had to undergo a course known as Jungle Preservation Training.
Yes. On the 16th of July 1944, we were put in trucks and taken to 'The School for Jungle Preservation Training', just over 40 miles southwest of Poona. At the school, we spent exactly two weeks under canvas in a jungle-like environment, dealing with incredibly wet conditions and doing exercises under the command of retired army officers. The jungle area was named Mahabaleshwar, and in the fourteen days that we were there, we learnt how to recognise poisonous plants, which plants and shoots were edible, and how to make cooking pots out of bamboo. With maps of the area and compasses, we had to do daily exercises following trails that the instructors had laid out. These exercises involved wading through rivers and streams.

In some parts, the jungle was very dense and required the use of machetes to hack our way through. The instructors would attach certain objects to trees so we would know that we were on the right course. Though our boots were meant to be leech-proof, they were anything but. We concluded that the leeches entered through the lace holes; it was amazing, really. Leeches also got in under our clothes. Unfortunately, we were told that our boots were not snake-proof, and that if we ever came across a snake we had to kill it.

Once back at camp, we had to completely undress, dry ourselves off and put on clean clothing. Two charcoal fires provided the heat to dry our wet clothing. We all found leeches attached to our bodies by the end of the day. Luckily, one of our party smoked, so we were able to use his cigarettes and matches to burn them in to releasing; a leech couldn't be pulled off, because the head would still be attached.

How many leeches a man had on his body was pure luck of the draw. Sometimes only one or two would be found, and other times a man would find himself covered in them.

Though the leeches were bad, one terrifying event did occur. We had reached a point in the trail that we were on. To our right was a rather deep ravine, at the bottom of which ran a fast-flowing river. To descend the ravine to reach that river, one had to go down a small trail, which was rather muddy and slippery. As captain of the crew, I went down first and reached the bottom, but the person coming behind me, Lance, my co-pilot, weighed considerably more; I was around nine stone, and he was around fifteen or sixteen stone. When I heard a yelp, I turned around to see him sliding down the trail towards me while desperately trying to catch hold of anything to stop his fall. With nowhere to go, I grabbed onto a small tree and braced myself. Lance grabbed onto me, and fortunately the tree didn't break; if it had, I hate to think what would have happened. Luckily, that was the only dangerous incident that we experienced on the jungle preservation training course.

The jungle we were in was rated a three. I can't imagine what jungles rated a one or a two look like.

Another incident I remember from the jungle course was when I pulled my revolver on Frizzy's crew. Frizzy wasn't present, as he was in Australia on leave. What happened was that we were on a map-reading exercise through the jungle. My crew and Frizzy's crew were in separate locations when I heard gunfire in the distance. When my crew and I arrived to investigate the noise, we discovered that Frizzy's crew were standing around a pond and shooting at frogs. When I saw that, I immediately lost my temper because those innocent animals were being shot. I shouted to Frizzy's crew that they had better stop, or I would do the same to them. One of his crew proceeded to shoot another frog, so I pulled out my revolver and fired at the ground next to him, causing him to jump. He told me that it was all a bit of fun, to which I yelled that the frogs wouldn't see it that way.

Did any repercussions result from that incident?
No, no officers were present when it happened, and no one reported it. It was soon forgotten.

After you completed your jungle preservation training, did you go straight to a heavy conversion unit to learn to fly Liberators?
No, we were put aboard trucks and transported back to our quarters in Bombay. From there, we went to 3 Refresher Flying Unit in Poona, arriving on the 30th of July 1944. We were stationed there for just under two weeks, and while there, we were given refresher lectures on things we had already done and even a lecture on Bombay itself. We also received new clothing and took care of outstanding medical issues.

The next stage of our journey was by rail, then lorry. The train from Bombay took us to Bangalore, where we were then transported by road to 1673 Heavy Conversion Unit at RAF Kolar, arriving on the 14th of August 1944. It was unusual for the RAF to have situated an airfield so close to a huge hill, less than 5 miles away, rising nearly 1,300 feet above the elevation of the mostly flat surroundings. I can visualise that hill now, to the left of the western end of the single east-west runway. The hill interfered with the usual circuit taken by an aircraft in flight, so when a pilot took off to the west, he had to climb 1,500 feet in elevation to safely clear the hill, then he could descend back down 1,000 feet when clear, in order to complete the circuit. In good weather, it was not a problem, but one had to be mindful of the terrain if the weather was an issue. The peak of that hill was about 1,300 feet above the airfield.

As we entered the hangar at RAF Kolar, I saw a Liberator in front of me. It was such a majestic plane, and so much bigger than any other aircraft I had flown. Upon seeing it, I said to myself, 'Bloody hell, I'll never be able to fly that!' Frizzy, on the other hand, seemed excited, as though he couldn't wait to fly it. His attitude seemed to rub off on me over the next few hours and days, as I became more excited at the prospect of flying it myself.

The Liberator is an American-built aircraft, so were the cockpit and controls any different from its British counterparts, and if so, did you have to go back into the classroom and take lectures to learn how everything worked before being allowed to operate the controls in the cockpit?
Yes. The day after our arrival, my crew and I were taken to a Liberator at its dispersal site, and we slowly circled the plane while the instructor pointed out the various bits and pieces, what they did,

how they were positioned and things like that. It was all part of what every pilot knows as an 'outside check'. It was the duty of the engineer and the navigator to accompany the pilot or pilots on the outside check. We had to inspect the rudders and elevators to make sure that they were all moving correctly and to make sure that there was no elevator lock in place, or anything like that. If one failed to do those things, there could be serious consequences. For example, if the elevators were locked in place, the pilot wouldn't be able to control the rate of elevation.

If the aircraft was just about to be flown, a shield covering the pitot head had to be removed. A pitot head was a device protruding from the fuselage that measured the static air versus the speed of the slipstream air. The results were shown on the instrument panel inside the cockpit, indicating the speed that the aircraft was traveling. We would also have to check the tyres before any take-off, to see if there were any faults. On the inside of the tyres was a square of yellow paint. On the outside was a matching yellow square and then on the centre rim, another one. They had to match up within reason to make the tyre operationally safe. If they didn't match up, then it was obvious that the pressure on the tyres was unequally distributed.

There were other duties to perform too. For example, the engine covers and the cockpit cover had to be removed before a flight.

With the outside inspection completed, it was time to perform the inside walk-through, starting with the rear turret and progressing forward in the fuselage past the waist guns, one on each side. From there, the inspection made its way through the bomb bay area. If the plane had been armed, the bombs would be stacked in the racks on either side of the narrow catwalk traversing the bomb bay, or aerial mines would be hung so that each could be toggled, that is, released, as planned.

Carrying on, the examination centred on positions and equipment in support of the piloting, positioning and communication functions of the Liberator, in relation to the pilot, second pilot, flight engineer, navigator and wireless operator. On the Mark VI Liberator, the only model I flew aboard, the navigator's station was in the forward fuselage, ahead of the cockpit, but in earlier models the navigator was positioned behind the cockpit, back-to-back with the wireless operator. The navigator also filled the role of bomb aimer. The cockpit, of course, was an essential focus of pre-flight scrutiny. On our introductory first visit to a Liberator cockpit, the instructor showed us what each instrument and dial represented. Further instruction was transferred to the classroom. Lastly, an interior walk-through finished with a check of the nose wheel in the forward fuselage and also the front turret.

Were there many lectures?
There were around eight to ten lectures, about an hour apiece, but they were relaxed, and nothing compared to the lectures in Southern Rhodesia. We had no formal interviews or exams at 1673 HCU, but we did have one-on-one discussions with the instructors about various instruments.

One thing I did at Kolar, unlike other trainees, was to study within an actual Liberator every day, in order to see in person, what the instructors were talking about. Walking to where the Liberators were and later back to where the lectures were held was a four-mile round trip. The first time I went out to examine a Liberator on my own, the plane I found unlocked was unsuitable for all of my needs because the rudder pedals were missing. On probably my third visit to this particular Liberator, a voice asked me what I wanted. It was the flight sergeant in charge, and when I replied, he suggested that I come with him. He explained that the aircraft I was looking at was inadequate, because it was only used to provide spare parts, so bits were missing from it. Instead, he unlocked another Liberator. The controls on the one he opened were perfect.

We struck up a friendship, and when I told him that I was walking back, he offered me a lift on his bicycle; I sat on the handlebars. I met up with him the next day and quickly realised that he knew as much about the Liberator as any pilot. He suggested that I sit in the pilot's seat and operate the controls, so I could see what they do. The Liberator was stationary, obviously, though once he did let me taxi it. There was no danger, as he sat next to me the entire time.

My visits there went on for several days, and each time when I returned to where the lectures were held, I met up with everyone else. Most of the others chose to spend their free hours on the recreation ground, but one time, Frizzy asked me why I chose to make that four-mile trip every day. I told him that I wanted to know how the Liberator operated, so, by the end, Frizzy had caught on to what I was doing and accompanied me.

What came next?
After we had finished with all the lectures and theoretically knew how to fly a Liberator, we then went on to practical flying. Initially, we each went up with an instructor, who showed us everything, such as how to navigate the hill and complete a circuit. After he was satisfied, it was my turn. I completed my circuit, but my co-pilot was told that he would never be able to fly a Liberator after he had swerved off the runway twice.

At the end of our time at 1673 HCU, which was just under two months in total, we found ourselves at the noticeboard, looking to see where we had been posted. Frizzy and I were posted to 159 Squadron, which was based at an airfield named Digri, in West Bengal, 65 miles west of Calcutta. Once we arrived there, on the 15th of October 1944, we had to see the CO. Frizzy went in first. After he was done, I knocked on the door and entered. The CO looked up and said to me, 'Good Lord, I didn't know they were sending schoolboys.' He saw that I had gone bright red with anger and followed it up with, 'All I care about is that you can do the job.'

Both Frizzy and I were told that we would have to go with an experienced captain for our first few operations before being allowed to captain aircraft ourselves. In total, I went on five operations with an experienced pilot, and only after the first four was I given command of my own Liberator. On the fifth operation, flown on the night of the 7th-8th of November 1944, we had to jettison our bombs due to an American miscalculation. They thought that they had seen a group of Japanese naval and supply ships heading north, but what they had actually seen was a very small group of islands being hit by northerly winds, creating what appeared to be a wake. The Americans were observing them from an altitude of over 20,000 feet, so I can see how the mistake occurred. Still, we had to turn back.

Before we get on to your operational flying, I would like to briefly talk about your first commanding officer on 159 Squadron, Wing Commander James Blackburn. He was no ordinary CO. He had been held in Morocco as a prisoner of war, having survived the sinking of the troopship *Laconia* off the West African coast on the 12th of September 1942; he and the other prisoners were rescued by the Americans. He was awarded the Distinguished Flying Cross and a Bar to it. Additionally, he was awarded the Distinguished Service Order and a Bar to that, and the Americans honoured him with the bestowal of their US Distinguished Flying Cross, too. He seems like an exceptional man. What was he like in person?

Firstly, a bar is added to the medal's ribbon if the recipient, having already received the medal in question, is awarded it again. Anyway, as a person, I sensed that W/Cdr Blackburn had an air of authority about him, a sternness. He didn't take kindly to fools. Here's an example. On one raid, my Liberator was hit with a single bullet, in the nose, but it didn't affect the plane or hurt anyone. We didn't even know about it until the ground crew informed us following their post-sortie inspection. W/Cdr Blackburn was told about it in the debriefing, and a chap who was a squadron leader and a flight commander came out with something like, 'One bullet. Is that it?' He made fun of it. W/Cdr Blackburn turned to him and in front of all of us, intelligence people included, said, 'That proves that Denis got much closer to the enemy than you ever did.' The look on the face of the squadron leader was quite something.

As you will find out later, that was quite a prophetic statement. At the same time, however, W/Cdr Blackburn was quite friendly, too, to those who deserved it, that is. He had earned the right to act in this way, though; this was his fifth tour of operations! He finished the war with 200 combat operations to his credit – extraordinary!

W/Cdr Blackburn seemed like the type of man to inspire complete faith and trust, a true leader.

Yes, he inspired complete trust and confidence in his men. If he was taking part in an operation, I felt safe; that if nothing happened to him, then nothing would happen to me. He was a rare type of chap.

He was only interested in operational flying, as there was a sense of danger in such flying that he found appealing. Regular flying did not interest him at all, as he found it boring. He really led from the front.

On Christmas Eve 1944, Frizzy and I grabbed all the chairs and tables from the Sergeants' Mess and set up a celebration with bottles of drink. Joining Frizzy and I were some of our non-commissioned officer friends. W/Cdr Blackburn walked in, took a look around and said, 'This is where I belong.' He stayed and celebrated with us, not with his fellow commissioned officers. Imagine a table with fifteen or sixteen of us, talking about flying, life at home and what have you. It was nice.

Then W/Cdr Blackburn asked us all what we were going to do once the war finished. One or two had ideas, but not me. He told us that before the war, he enjoyed sailing. I think he had been with his father, and that on one occasion they were 'pooped', which is when a wave breaks over and swamps the entire vessel. He then went on to say that when the war was over, he was going to buy a yacht and sail it around the world and asked if any of us would join him. Everyone remained silent except myself. My hand shot up in the air, and I said that I would. He said that he would write to me with instructions once the war had concluded and I was out of the RAF.

Finally, before we get on to operational flying, what was the main role of the RAF Liberators in India, and what was 159 Squadron's role?
The primary role of the Liberator squadrons, based mainly in north-eastern India, was to attack Japanese-held targets across the Bay of Bengal, the Indian Ocean, and eventually beyond, mostly on land and rarely at sea. Targets included such sites as storage depots, port facilities and jetties, airfields, railway stations and bridges. Mostly the Liberators filled an important strategic bombing requirement, but on occasion, especially late in the war, they were call upon to directly support Allied ground forces, in a tactical role, by bombing such targets as enemy troop concentrations close to the front lines. In addition, Liberators, mainly from two dedicated RAF squadrons, were tasked with Special Duties operations, where agents and supplies were parachuted behind enemy lines. A couple of RAF Liberator squadrons flew exclusively on reconnaissance operations and maritime patrols,

never carrying bombs or mines. One RAF Liberator squadron flew only air-sea rescue missions, sometimes supplemented by aircraft, including Liberators, from other squadrons.

In 1942, when 159 Squadron began operations as the first heavy bomber unit in the theatre, the targets were all in Burma, and the operations, only flown at night, were almost all traditional bombing sorties. As the war progressed and Allied forces expanded, other RAF Liberator squadrons were established, as were American B-24 squadrons. Due to the progress of the war, the target locations became farther afield from the RAF bases and no longer just in Burma. Thailand was a more frequent destination, and ultimately Malaya and even French Indo-China, Cambodia and Northern Sumatra were the focus of Liberator attention. As the threat from Japanese fighter opposition decreased, eventually daylight operations were the norm.

During my tenure on the squadron, we still mostly attacked at night; in fact, only four of my operations were planned daylight strikes. Under W/Cdr Blackburn's leadership, 159 Squadron specialised in the aerial mining of Japanese waters, designed to severely curtail shipping and, thus, the resupply of Japanese fighting forces. Twelve of my twenty-three operations were mining sorties, while the others were bombing missions.

I should add that through my time on 159 Squadron, an airman's 'tour of operations' consisted of roughly 300 hours of operational flying or thirty operations flown, whichever came first. Because the distances we had to fly were ever-growing, the length of a typical operation increased. An average length of an operation during my tour, flown between the 20th of October 1944 and the 28th of January 1945, was thirteen hours and thirty-nine minutes. Thus, men like myself, unlike earlier airmen flying shorter operations, were reaching the 300-hour mark long before approaching thirty operations. My twenty-three operations were flown in 314 hours and 10 minutes, and in just over three months, in the dry season. Earlier, such as in 1943, it could take an airman one full year to finish a tour of operations, which meant that he would have had to endure a long monsoon season, when flying was often severely impacted by the weather.

I must admit that I lucked out. A directive to increase an airman's tour to 400 hours or one year, whichever came first, was announced in March or April 1945, soon after I had reached the 300-hour mark and had finished my 159 Squadron tour of operations. Some men were on the cusp of reaching 300 hours when the new rules went into effect, and naturally, morale took a tumble. Incidentally, the first crew from 159 Squadron to finish its tour by reaching the 400-hour mark came in June 1945.

159 Squadron was split into three sections. A Flight and B Flight, with separate flight commanders as their senior leaders, put up eight Liberators each on most operational bombing/mining sorties; these Liberators constituted the main offensive force of the squadron. I was in B Flight.

In addition, 159 Squadron had a third section, the ultra-secretive C Flight, which was commonly known as the 'Special Flight'. Originally attached to 160 Squadron in Ceylon, its role transferred to 159 Squadron at Digri in June 1944 when it was designated C Flight. Its members were kept apart from the rest of 159 Squadron, presumably because of the secret nature of their work. With sometimes only a single specially-configured Liberator, and other times with only two, C Flight's mission was primarily to identify and analyse Japanese radar signals. In November and December 1944, C Flight also performed reconnaissance and weather reporting in cooperation with bombing or minelaying Liberators from A Flight and B Flight, and C Flight even reported post-strike A Flight and B Flight bombing results. On one of my operations, from the night of the 15th-16th of November 1944, a Special Flight Liberator, slightly ahead of us, dropped flares to illuminate the jetties in Mergui, Burma, which were A Flight and B Flight's bombing target. In May 1945, the solitary remaining C Flight Liberator was transferred from 159 Squadron to 1341 Flight, and 159 Squadron again had only an A Flight and B Flight.

Finally, let me add that in April 1945, after I had departed, 159 Squadron changed its role and became the Pathfinder squadron in the Far East. The Pathfinder technique had proven to be an effective means of identifying and precisely bombing targets in Europe, so 159 Squadron became the elite specialty unit out of India. The best pilots, navigators and their crews, from other bomber squadrons, were transferred to 159 Squadron to create a super unit, and the scheme achieved a very high standard in bombing and navigation.

CHAPTER EIGHT

OPERATIONAL FLYING ON 159 SQUADRON, OCTOBER 1944 – JANUARY 1945

*Bombing and mining raids including three Penang
operations over eighteen hours, losing a friend, the brilliance
of W/Cdr James Blackburn, dropping napalm, escaping death
and the cowardice of a high-ranking officer*

You have already touched upon the fact that you had to act as co-pilot for an experienced pilot on five of your first six operational flights. What do you remember about your first operational flight?
It took place on the 20th of October 1944. My Liberator, one of the fifteen Liberators from the squadron sent out on this daytime raid, was serial number EV900, letter code 'H'. The pilot I was paired with, F/Lt Gordon Pendleton, taught me a lot. He explained how different types of operations were supposed to be flown in theory, in order to maximise the chances of success. For example, he explained that when laying mines in a river, which we were doing on this operation, it was important to keep the aircraft as close to the centre line of the river as possible. It was done to maximise the aircraft's distance from any gun batteries placed on either side of the river. He also taught me how to porpoise, which was a gentle moving of the controls forwards and backwards, causing the plane to move up and down. This was done in order to put enemy gunners on either side of the river off focus.

What I remember is that we laid mines in a section of the Pak Chan River's wide estuary, close to Victoria Point, at the southernmost tip of Burma. This estuary is more than two miles wide. We were warned by intelligence that there were gun emplacements on the banks of the river.

Victoria Point is a small town at the mouth of the Pak Chan River, which serves as the border between Burma and Thailand.

It was a pretty straightforward operation. From the south, we arrived at the mouth of the river and flew up the estuary, to the north. Fortunately, the anti-aircraft fire we came under wasn't too heavy, though the real concern for us was that we were in the range of Japanese fighter planes, so the crew had to be on a constant lookout for those. We carried eight mines to drop in pre-determined locations. Once the mines were released, we continued flying northward for a short distance, and then turned west, heading back to sea, before changing course to the northwest to return to base.

According to my log book, the flight took fourteen hours and thirty minutes.

Was your second operation as straightforward as your first?
The second operation took place on the 23rd of October 1944. The objective of our six Liberators was to bomb Japanese supply dumps in a town named Taungup, Burma, located near the eastern coast of Burma northwest of Rangoon and not far from Ramree Island. The dumps contained weapons, ammunition, food supplies and the like. Unlike the first operation, which was over 1,100 miles away, Taungup was only about 520 miles from Digri. This operation took seven-and-a-half-hour and took place during the day. One interesting thing was that not a single shot was fired; we flew there, dropped our bombs and came back, with no opposition. Our attacking force consisted of only six Liberators because earlier in the day 159 Squadron had sent out a separate force of eight bombers to mine the waters near Mergui in southern Burma.

On the way back from Taungup, I said something to myself like, 'Boy, this is a piece of cake. I hope they are all like this.' That was something you shouldn't really say.

Your third operation was a very important one. It was a legendary sortie to mine Penang Harbour far to the south and all the way in Malaya. Would you mind talking about everything that went into it and explain why it was such an important operation?
It took place on the 27th-28th of October 1944 and was the first

of the three operations by 159 Squadron to mine Penang. As this was only my third operation on 159 Squadron, I was yet to fly as captain of my own aircraft. Instead, I was screened by a seasoned pilot, WO L.A. Hendy, aboard his aircraft and with his crew. A narrow channel separated Penang Island from the eastern mainland coast of Malaya, but it wasn't the harbour itself that we focused upon; instead, it was the approaches to the harbour that we mined. There were two approaches, from the north and south. My Liberator, KH159 G, one of fifteen Liberators on the operation, was assigned to drop mines in the southern approach. Due to the incredible distance we had to travel, a 3,000-mile round-trip, each aircraft was only able to carry four mines, as opposed to the usual eight; each mine weighed 1,000 pounds.

What made Penang Harbour so important was that it was not only a vital location in the Japanese supply and fuel transport system feeding the Burma front, but it also served as the primary base for both German and Japanese U-boats operating in the adjacent Indian Ocean. Submarines were repaired, refuelled and resupplied here. Furthermore, it was a valuable transshipment point for materials being carried between Germany and Japan.

Our objective was to deny the Japanese use of this essential depot.

It was a very complicated operation to carry out. Our own 2,000-yard-long runway at Digri was too short to try and take off from. This was because of the extra weight involved in carrying overload fuel tanks; these were extra fuel tanks positioned in each aircraft's bomb bay to provide the petrol needed for the record-distance operational flight. As a result, we had to take off from an American B-29 Superfortress airfield, Kharagpur, that had a longer runway.

On Thursday, the 26th of October, the day before taking off on the actual raid, each of our fifteen participating Liberators was loaded at Digri with four mines, and the overload fuel tanks were filled, while the main tanks were only partially filled. We then took the Liberators to Kharagpur, which was about thirty-two miles to the south. Kharagpur had a runway of 2,500 yards, which was 500 yards longer than ours; this added distance was essential if we were to get airborne fully-loaded.

Upon landing at Kharagpur, we lined up our Liberators wingtip-to-wingtip along the perimeter track. The main petrol tanks were then topped up by American ground crews, who tried to get in every drop of fuel they could. By the time they were done, some Liberators were resting on their tail skids, front wheels off the ground and in the air. However, once an engine was then started, the slipstream from the turning propeller was enough for the Liberator to tip back forward onto its front wheel.

Each Liberator would carry 3,000 gallons of fuel, including 660 gallons in the extra bomb bay tanks. The petrol from these extra tanks was to be used first, and once empty, en route to Penang, they would be ditched by the flight engineer through the open bomb bay to lighten the load on the aircraft in order to achieve maximum efficiency with the remaining fuel in the regular tanks. It was all worked out by W/Cdr Blackburn.

The men of 159 Squadron were returned to Digri by Dakota aircraft, in order to spend Thursday night in our own quarters. The next morning, on Friday the 27th, after the same Dakotas took us back to Kharagpur, each aircrew lined up next to its respective Liberator.

The Americans came around to offer us sweets and snacks. They didn't believe that our operation could be done, doubting that the Liberator had the range to make it to Penang and back, even with the extra fuel tanks. A fifty percent casualty rate, minimum, was generally expected.

Because of the concerns that some of our bomber force might not be able to make the full round-trip distance, Royal Navy destroyers were put on alert. In addition, two British submarines were positioned to offer assistance, if needed, the first one a third of the way to Penang and the second two-thirds. Our navigators were given the coordinates of these destroyers and submarines with the idea that if anything went wrong and an attempt to ditch was necessary, the Liberator would do so as close to a destroyer or submarine's location as possible. It took a mind like W/Cdr Blackburn's to plan for assistance, and not just think of having help available, should anything go wrong.

The 3,000-mile round trip was the equivalent of a flight from London to Moscow and back, with no stopping halfway. The range of a Liberator without extra fuel was around 2,400 miles, but W/Cdr Blackburn's calculations showed that the distance could definitely be made with the addition of the extra bomb bay tanks – if the overloaded Liberators could even get airborne, and if no battle damage was incurred; opposition was expected. The doubts of the Americans and many in the British hierarchy were understandable.

Having worked hard to improve the Liberator's performance, W/Cdr Blackburn had ordered that each Liberator's guns and turrets be removed, except for the rear guns. He also ordered the removal of the armour plating behind the captain's seat in order to save weight, and the crew size to be reduced to only six men: captain, co-pilot, navigator, flight engineer, wireless operator and rear gunner; an American bomber crew typically numbered ten men at this time. Even with all of W/Cdr Blackburn's changes, no one knew for sure if we would actually be able to take off; the operation would be risky from the start.

W/Cdr Blackburn gathered all the captains around him for a final discussion. A Liberator that had already been to Penang to get the latest weather report returned, and W/Cdr Blackburn was informed that the weather report was good. He then told his captains that he was going to take off first, and that if he didn't succeed in getting airborne, each aircraft's captain could decide for himself whether to attempt the take-off. That's the sort of man he was, leading by example.

Also, before I forget, it was Blackburn who planned the Penang operation, without the support of the Americans and the higher echelons of the RAF, most of whom doubted that success could ever be achieved. Of course, his own staff supported him and implemented his plan; his leadership was extraordinary and inspirational.

So, W/Cdr Blackburn taxied to the runway and did what was known as a precautionary take-off. He applied brake pressure with both feet, as hard as he could, and opened up the throttles to maximum power, including the turbo boosters.

Then, when he released the brakes, his Liberator shot forward. It enabled him to reach take-off speed quicker, using less of the runway. We noticed that he took about 2,200 yards to get airborne, and his climb was painfully laboured. After that, each of the remaining fourteen Liberators took its turn taking off. We all made it into the sky – that, in itself, was a great achievement – though never with much runway to spare. In the case of my aircraft, we used the same length of runway to take off as did W/Cdr Blackburn. With all fifteen Liberators, the initial climb into the sky was challenging and not unexpected.

Your log book records a nineteen-hour round trip. What was the atmosphere like among your crew on the way there? Did the scale of what you were attempting to undertake reflect the atmosphere inside your Liberator?
Very much so. With so many hours sitting there doing little or nothing, the realisation of what we were attempting to do really hit us, and the tension rose further and further as we got closer to Penang. The last half hour or so, in the fading light of the early evening, was very tense; everyone was on edge. We had no idea what defences Penang had. We didn't know if fighters would have been alerted by radar or noise detection, or if any gun emplacements were primed to fire at us. I can almost feel the nervous anticipation now. Adding to the stress, the navigator had to be sure that we were over the exact release point for the first aerial mine, as plotting the drop locations, starting with that first mine, was essential. When all the mines had finally been released, you could feel the tension just disappear, as if someone had stuck a pin into a balloon.

We completely surprised the Japanese, to our immense relief. Not a shot was fired at our Liberator, to the best of my knowledge. None of the other aircraft met opposition, either, although one Liberator's crew spotted a single bright flash from mainland Malaya, which may have been an anti-aircraft muzzle flash, but if so, the aircrew did not see or hear the explosion. They also witnessed several flashes which may have been small arms fire, but they suffered no damage. Our squadron scored a magnificent victory that night.

When you reached Penang Harbour, did you have specific sites to target within the harbour complex?
There were two deep water channels feeding Penang Harbour. Eight aircraft were assigned to mine specific stretches of the northern

route, while seven Liberators focused on the southern approach. Sixty mines, in total, were deployed, as planned. We approached at probably no more than 200 feet, in case the Japanese radar was operational, but before dropping our loads we climbed to 400 feet, the ideal height for releasing mines.

There was huge tension as our aircraft's navigator counted off as each mine was dropped. Once the fourth and last one was released, there was a huge sigh of relief among my crew. We turned sharply to port and began the nine-and-a-half-hour journey back to India.

I imagine that the atmosphere inside the aircraft on the way back was a lot more joyful than on the way there.
We were totally relaxed. Though I was only co-pilot on the first Penang trip, I'm sure I flew the Liberator on the way back while the captain, WO L.A. Hendy, had a nap, up until we reached base. It was tradition for the captain of the aircraft to land.

Out of interest, how did Kharagpur, the American airfield, and its standards compare to Digri, the RAF airfield where you were stationed?
My impression was that the atmosphere at Kharagpur was a lot more relaxed. For example, at Digri, if two airmen met, depending on their ranks, one would salute the other; there was that formality in place. The Americans didn't seem to care about that at all, and they were really laid back. Also, they seemed to enjoy a higher standard of living than us. They had more money and more consumer products, a wider variety of food and, in general, much more was imported for them. There also seemed to be a higher level of activity at Kharagpur compared to Digri, with a greater number of men around and increased hustle and bustle.

The RAF appeared to only have the bare minimum amount of men on its airfields, while the Americans seemed to have a surplus. The British authorities were careful with what they imported. Even the estimated fuel consumption of our Liberators was calculated for every trip, and this figure determined how much fuel each Liberator would receive. The Americans didn't appear to face those restrictions. They were very kind to us, offering us sweets and the like. Nice chaps.

What was the aftermath of the first Penang operation?
The desired results were achieved, although 159 Squadron returned twice again to Penang to drop mines; I was on all three raids. Each of the three operations averaged, per Liberator, a little over eighteen hours in the air, making them the longest RAF bombing or mining operations ever at the time. The second Penang mining raid, on the 26th-27th of November 1944, was not a success due to the weather we encountered, but the third, on the 23rd-24th of January 1945, was another success. No major ships were sunk by our mines, but because the Japanese lacked the means to clear the mines we had dropped, the harbour's use was disrupted, as we had hoped. Furthermore, we had achieved a supreme victory by forcing the German U-boats to evacuate Penang for Batavia, thus eliminating the U-boat threat in the Indian Ocean.

Do you have anything else to add about this Penang raid?
Yes. Because we took off at twelve minutes after ten in the morning, we arrived at Penang just as the sun was setting and reached Digri just as the sun was beginning to rise the next morning, on Saturday the 28th of October. The timing of it all was planned so we would arrive just as the Japanese were winding down for the day, when they would least be prepared for an attack.

Two Liberators chose to land at Chittagong, on the eastern side of the Bay of Bengal, rather than risk fuel starvation and crashes en route home. They received more fuel at Chittagong and made their way safely back to Digri. All thirteen other Liberators had landed at Digri after having taken off from Kharagpur the previous morning.

One thing I find amazing about this operation was that we were so overloaded with weight, yet not one of the Liberators suffered an engine failure or anything like that.

Your fourth operation, a bombing raid on Bangkok, was quite eventful, wasn't it?
Yes. It was a nighttime bombing raid on the 2nd-3rd of November. Sgt Ron Clift was my screen pilot aboard KH211 'A', one of fifteen Liberators attacking the Makasan Railway Workshops in Bangkok from low altitude. Some of my regular crew were aboard for this one.

Approaching the target from the west, all was going well, with excellent visibility over Bangkok in a night sky illuminated by a nearly-full moon. In a shallow dive, we released all of our bombs in one run from 400 feet on the workshops, already aflame from the attack of previous 159 Squadron aircraft. Sgt Clift's plan was then to fly out to the south over the Gulf of Thailand, turn west, climb to 10,000 feet and cross Thailand and Southern Burma. From there we would continue on our way home.

What actually happened was that we were still quite low when we reached the Gulf of Thailand. Silhouetted by the bright moon, we were met with a horrific sight: four Japanese naval ships that were anchored next to each other and two more ships of note nearby. All hell broke loose when at least some of the six ships proceeded to open fire on us. Shells exploded all around; it was like being in the middle of a fireworks display. Sgt Clift's reaction was to take violent evasive action, which resulted in the plane being thrown around. Honestly, it really scared me. I was quite nervous on other occasions, but this was one time when I was truly frightened. After all, even at twenty years old, I appreciated the fact that it only took one shell to bring us down.

Did the plane suffer any damage?
Although we weren't hit directly, the aircraft sustained very minor damage when a shell fragment struck a blade of the propeller on number two engine. It gave us some vibrating trouble on the way home but didn't impede us or anything like that. After a flight time of fourteen hours, we were safely on the ground again back at Digri.

Incidentally, the fires we started at Makasan Railway Workshops were visible for 70 miles. The operation was considered most successful, causing severe damage to 75% of the buildings in the workshop area.

What a frightening experience it must have been.
Yes. Although it only lasted for about three minutes, it was terrifying, especially at my age. I was scared stiff.

You didn't complete your fifth and sixth operational flights. What happened?
Yes. But first, here are some facts. Before my fifth operation, I became captain, or 'skipper', after being screened by a seasoned pilot on each of my first four operations. On the night of the 4th-5th of November 1944, my fifth operation, I was given command of my own Liberator for the first time, but then on the next operation of the 7th-8th of November, I was screened one last time. From then on, however, I was skipper of my Liberator crew. In the latter part of December 1944, I was promoted from sergeant to warrant officer by W/Cdr Blackburn, skipping the rank of flight sergeant completely. Warrant officer was the highest non-commissioned rank that one could hold in the RAF. I was most grateful for this promotion.

Anyway, on my fifth operation, on the night of the 4th-5th of November, which was also my first operational flight as captain, aboard EW110 'B', the flight engineer reported that we had a fuel leak. We were at 5,000 feet and over Burma, one of eight Liberators on the way to lay mines in the Bangkok River, while seven other 159 Squadron Liberators were headed to bomb Bansue Railway Workshops, also in Bangkok. My flight engineer was supported in his claim by the smell of fuel in the plane. But what had actually happened, as I later learnt, was that my navigator, Sgt Len Upjohn, had accidentally kicked over a small tank holding fuel for the Auxiliary Power Unit, which gave a necessary boost to the electrical supply when starting the engines.

What did you decide to do?
Can you imagine the situation, at 5,000 feet above the Burmese jungle? I faced my first major command decision: either carry on to the target believing that we might run out of fuel and crash, or turn around, jettison the mines and return to base. I asked the flight engineer to use the Aldis lamp to light up the outside of the aircraft to see if we could find the source of the leak. No leak was found, but the instruments showed that there was a drop in the fuel supply, which pointed to a leak. Combined with the smell of fuel, it led me to decide to turn around, jettison the mines and return to base.

Ironically, as we approached Digri, the instruments showed that everything was normal, and not long after landing we were told that an airlock in the pipes connecting the fuel tanks to the engines must have led to the faulty fuel gauge readings.

Even though we did not make it to the target, we were still airborne for thirteen hours and twenty-five minutes.

I am sure that you had to explain yourself to the senior officers. What was their reaction to it all?
My report had to be given to the flight commander, who was the squadron leader that I have already mentioned. His reaction was one of fury. He told me that I was a disgrace to the Royal Air Force and that I could be court-martialled. He also accused me of cowardice in the face of the enemy. Remember that I was only twenty, and going through all these new experiences, so all of the flight commander's harsh language had quite an affect on me.

Anyway, his words infuriated me, so I went straight to W/Cdr Blackburn and explained what had happened. He assured me that given the circumstances, he would have done exactly the same as I did. He told me that he would much rather have a full crew and aircraft back than have a target hit but lose the crew and aircraft. He also told me not to worry about the flight commander, and that I would discover things about him in time.

Did that claim ever come to fruition?
Yes. I said earlier that W/Cdr Blackburn's statement following the 8th of December 1944 bullet-in-the-Liberator's nose incident, a month after the fuel leak confusion, was prophetic; I'll explain how it was. There were rumours going around that the flight commander would jettison his bombs just before reaching the target, and that on some operations he purposely stayed far away from the target. The rumours came about because he was often the first one back when he flew operations; the official 159 Squadron records verify this as true. He claimed that it was because he had a faster plane than anyone else, which is utter nonsense.

For his charade to have persisted for as long as it did, over several months, at least some of his core crew must have been in on it, too.

However, as flight commander, he sometimes flew with another pilot's crew, not his own, and these other crews were likely unaware of his motives. Also, no crew makeup was exactly the same from operation to operation, so he flew operations with many airmen who likely kept their mouths shut, for various reasons, even if anyone was aware of and disgusted with his methods. As he was a squadron leader, and a flight commander, fear of backlash from such a powerful figure may have stifled an airman or two. For many reasons, then, the secret was maintained for a long time. One certainty was that several men on 159 Squadron were very wary of the flight commander, and suspicious of at least some form of complacency among aircrew with whom he flew operations.

Incidentally, I learned that on the night my flight commander chastised me for my 'cowardice' in failing to reach the target by returning early to Digri, despite W/Cdr Blackburn calling it a legitimate reason, this same flight commander had been the first to return to Digri – a mere twelve hours and twenty minutes before my Liberator touched down! He was only airborne for one hour and twelve minutes. Still, he found it appropriate to talk to me in that manner.

Not long after the operation of the 8th of December, when the flight commander mocked me for being hit with the single bullet in the nose of the plane, a member of his crew told W/Cdr Blackburn that the flight commander was not taking them anywhere near the target, and that their loads of mines were being jettisoned. This was all confirmed, and the flight commander, without a court-martial we all felt he justly deserved, disappeared from the squadron.

A year or so later, I ran into him outside of the air traffic control office at Baigachi airfield, 25 miles northeast of Calcutta. Dressed in a white uniform, he had become a private pilot for a high-ranking air official. I quite deliberately tried to make eye contact, but he wouldn't look me in the eye and quickly scurried off somewhere. He must have had connections in high places to have landed that assignment. What he demonstrated on 159 Squadron, cowardice in the face of the enemy, was a court-martial offence, yet he became a personal pilot.

But to have had the gall to speak to you so harshly back at 159 Squadron is unbelievable.

Quite agree. During the war there was a process of automatic promotion. I'm sure that's how he got to the rank of squadron leader; I can't imagine him passing all of the exams that one had to take in order to be promoted in peacetime.

Do you think he was projecting himself in such a way in order to make one think that he would never be capable of such an act himself?

Yes, I think he was trying to put himself in a higher place than he could really attain and to create a false image of how brave he was.

Did his crew face any sort of punishment?

No, I don't remember anyone else facing any sort of punishment. W/Cdr Blackburn put it all on the flight commander's head. This man was a true coward. I would have loved to have been there when W/Cdr Blackburn was dismissing him, though I am disappointed that the flight commander wasn't brought up on charges.

W/Cdr Blackburn was a nice man, but if you got his rag up, then he was a force to be reckoned with. As an example, a sergeant on the squadron was once a warrant officer, but due to a drunken brawl he was in one night he was stripped of rank by W/Cdr Blackburn. To put it into context, when I first joined the squadron, I was a sergeant.

We have just covered why you turned back short of the target on your fifth operation, but why did your sixth operation have to be abandoned? From what you have already mentioned, several islands were mistaken for a group of Japanese ships.

American reconnaissance from high altitude was thought to have detected Japanese merchant vessels heading north. What had actually been seen was a group of small islands which were being hit by strong northerly winds, creating what appeared to be ships' wakes. As a result, on the 7th of November, fourteen of our Liberators were sent to attack that apparent convoy near Tavoy, in southern Burma. Flying aboard EW110 'B', I was screened for this operation by FO J. Goody because the target was a convoy, and I had never attacked shipping before.

When we reached the target area, we discovered that what the Americans had reported as ships were, in fact, islands. The Americans had observed these islands from over 20,000 feet above, so I could understand how the misidentification occurred. Nevertheless, a broad stretch of water was searched, but nothing was spotted except small craft, such as fishing boats. We were always briefed with a secondary target, usually in case cloud cover or ground haze obscured the primary target, and for this operation the secondary was the Ye, Burma railway station and facilities. The thirteen other Liberators dropped their bomb loads on Ye rail targets, where meagre opposition was encountered. However, my aircraft's prolonged search for the apparent convoy over more than 100 miles of ocean had compromised our fuel supply, so it was determined that bombing Ye would possibly leave us short of fuel for the long trip home. Therefore, the decision was made to jettison our bombs over open water, as it was considered too dangerous to land with bombs onboard.

My Liberator's flight time amounted to thirteen hours and thirty-five minutes.

The squadron took not finding a convoy in quite good humour, and we were relieved at not locating shipping, as well. Imagine having to attack a convoy of ships with bomber aircraft, in the middle of the sea. It was one thing to strike with nimble fighter aircraft, but imagine doing it with lumbering bombers.

If memory serves me correctly, we had a party that night to celebrate the fact that we found islands and not ships.

I assume that your seventh operation was a success and that the target actually existed.

Yes. On the 11th of November the crews of twelve Liberators, including the aircraft I captained, EW110 'B', were tasked with minelaying at the port of Moulmein, Burma, southeast of Rangoon. Three others were directed to lay mines near the Sittang River bridge over 80 miles to the north.

Before we all got into our aircraft, I saw my good friend, Johnny Hall, who was a navigator, get into his aircraft. I waved at him and said, 'Have a good trip, Johnny.' He waved back.

For my crew and I, the raid was a success, as, despite only fair visibility on a moonless night, we released our mines near Moulmein, but one terrible thing happened that I must mention. As I began to climb and bank away, I saw a Liberator in the distance begin to descend in order to lay its mines and then to suddenly explode and fall in flames to earth. Because defensive tracer fire was observed immediately before the explosion, we assumed that the bomber had suffered a direct hit, most likely in the bomb bay. At the time, I didn't know Johnny was in that Liberator, but this was confirmed when we were back at Digri. Canadian skipper Johnny Johnson and his crew in aircraft KH159 'G', seven men in all, failed to return. All were presumed killed, including my friend, Johnny Hall.

My Liberator's time in the air was eleven hours and fifteen minutes.

How did you deal with something like that, losing a close friend and actually witnessing the destruction of what turns out to be his aircraft?
My crew and I went to the Mess for an after-flight meal, where we found out about the missing plane and who was on it. After the meal, Frizzy's crew and my crew went back to our billets. We were in the same basha huts. All I can really say is that I kept my feelings to myself. After a while, I hardened myself to the losses of friends.

Did the loss of a friend like Johnny affect personal relationships with comrades and the friendships you made?
It did, but there was such a depth of feeling that is hard to describe. One way that losing Johnny Hall affected me, and still does, is that to this day, I have never said 'Have a good trip,' to anyone taking a journey.

Were these little superstitions common in the RAF?
Yes. I think a lot of it went back to the First World War, where there were superstitions about things, like not lighting a cigarette three times or a sniper would notice and get you on the third light. Although I believe that superstitions were quite common on 159 Squadron, they were not advertised or really spoken about. After all, they were quite personal.

What location did you target for your eighth operation?

For my eighth operation, which took place on the 15th-16th of November 1944, fourteen Liberators bombed jetties and waterfront buildings at Mergui, in Burma, on the Burmese coast nearly 340 miles southeast of Rangoon. The squadron took off at around eleven in the morning with a load of nine 500-pound bombs in each aircraft. For me, the assignment was soon to change, quite simply because one of the engines in my Liberator, EW110 'B', would not start up. It had to be completely replaced.

Although W/Cdr Blackburn had already taken off, by radio he notified me of a change of orders. Not only would my Liberator bomb the target, but, because I would be arriving over Mergui after it had already been hit by thirteen Liberators from 159 Squadron, I was commanded to provide photographic evidence of the success of the squadron's attack. To accomplish this added photo assignment, a vertical camera with an eight-inch focal length was installed while the bad engine was being replaced. W/Cdr Blackburn stated that if I had not taken off by two in the afternoon, then I was to remain at base. I really wanted to go, so I kept on pestering the ground staff, and eventually, with seven minutes to spare, and after a complete engine refit, I took off.

Arriving over Mergui about two-and-a-half hours after 159 Squadron's main force had struck, we witnessed a large area of active fire along the waterfront, estimated at 1,000 yards long and 200 yards wide. We noted two intense red fire centres, at the northern end and southwestern end of the target zone, plus fires spreading into the town. (This fire was seen 140 miles away by the main bomber force, returning to Digri.) My new orders were to first make two photographic runs over the port, followed by a bombing run. The first photo run was to be in a west-to-east direction, and the second would be north-to-south. Unfortunately, because of photoflash failure, we only attempted one photo, and one photo run: from west-to-east.

After we had finished the photographic run, we decided that we would make our bombing run over the port flying from north-to-south. The level of destruction from the earlier raid was most impressive to see, but the side effect of the fires was the obscuring smoke and unstable air, including updrafts. Consequently, we had to bomb from 10,000 feet, a higher altitude that planned, but we were still able to add our nine bombs across the length of the blaze.

Regarding opposition, there was none during our photo run, but during our bombing run we were subjected to considerable anti-aircraft fire, none of which caused damage. However, once the last bomb had dropped, I went into a starboard dive, so we were soon out of range of the guns and heading for home.

When I met W/Cdr Blackburn in Malta after the war, while I was with 38 Squadron, he told me that the Mergui operation I have just told you about was the only time he had been worried about me, simply because had things gone wrong he would have been asked to explain why he had sent a twenty-year-old to carry out such a dangerous mission.

For my ninth operation, on the 18th of November 1944, fifteen Liberators returned to Moulmein for a dusk attack, carrying bombs, not mines, destined for the Martaban jetties and railway sidings area. I was captain again of EW110 'B'. The raid was considered highly successful. The squadron took a different approach to the target this time, and it worked. The incoming force of aircraft, in a cloudless sky with good visibility, split into two groups, one of five aircraft and the other of ten. The two groups focused upon separate initial aiming points on their run-ups to the final aiming point. The results were the same: we hammered the target, which was well-covered by our bombs. My aircraft, actually, had to make two bomb runs due to faulty bomb release gear, but we did so without issue.

The opposition from ground defences was very meagre and inaccurate, and we saw no enemy aircraft; we greatly appreciated this lack of opposition.

My crew and I were airborne for twelve hours and five minutes.

I must digress to explain just a little bit more about 159 Squadron's operations at this point in the war; the mix of bombing and mining operations did not all involve maximum efforts on one target, as was the case on the Moulmein bombing mission on the 18th of November and the Penang mining raid on the 27th-28th of October. Most of the time, one day's operational assignment involved 100% of the scheduled Liberators going to one target – sometimes for mining, sometimes for bombing. Not always, however. On occasion, lesser numbers of Liberators were sent to one target, while other aircraft from the squadron focused upon a completely different target on the same day.

For example, on the 4th-5th of November, eight Liberators were sent on a mining operation to the Bangkok River, while eight aircraft bombed Bansue Railway Workshops in Bangkok. The two bomber forces were geographically close, but the nature of each's mission differed fundamentally. Another example was on the 11th-12th of November, when twelve aircraft were tasked with mining Moulmein and three aircraft mined the waters of the Sittang River, near the Sittang River Bridge. One final example from November 1944 was on the 21st into the 22nd. In daytime on the 21st, four bombers were sent out to search for and bomb merchant shipping in the waters between Mergui and Tavoy, Burma (though they bombed Tavoy, the secondary target). Then, that night, three Liberators mined Moulmein waters while three other aircraft mined the Tavoy River, over 160 miles from Moulmein.

The Japanese used numerous ports, as opposed to concentrating their incoming supplies at the major port of Rangoon alone. The idea, in part, was that supplying their forces via scattered ports would make it more difficult for us to effectively target a single primary source, thus giving them a greater chance of resupplying.

Some operations, from the moment we first heard the destinations and details at the briefings prior to the operations, were pre-judged as likely to be fairly simple. Yes, things could go wrong, very wrong, and we never knew the outcome in advance or whether an anti-aircraft shell might ruin our day. However, sometimes we all but knew that things would go our way, and on such flights the atmosphere onboard was cool and calm. Although it wasn't really talked about for superstitious reasons, these types of raids were known as 'piece of cake operations' because different factors would appear to be favourable, including light or absent ground defences, a low probability of meeting fighter opposition, the element of surprise and ease in locating the target.

When Frizzy and I would compare the targets we had been to, some of them were quite different, because we were not always on the same operations.

Your tenth operation was to mine an area of the main river that flows through Bangkok.
Yes. It took place on the 23rd-24th of November 1944. Four Liberators were sent out to mine the Bangkok River, while at the same time another four were assigned mining duties in Goi Sichang Harbour in the Gulf of Thailand not far away – approximately 30 miles southeast of the mouth of the Bangkok River. I captained KH211 'A'. Fortunately, the long journey to Thailand went without incident. As I dropped down to 400 feet in the brightly moonlit, cloudless sky, I prepared to turn to port in order to reach the starting point for dropping the mines. Suddenly our Liberator was picked up by searchlights.

Considering that being caught in searchlights spelt the end for many aircraft, were you scared?
Honestly, no. I was so focused on the operation at hand that I didn't really think about our predicament as much as one would think. There was a degree of apprehension, though, being that we were so close to the enemy under those circumstances.

I immediately told Blondie Whittle, my front gunner, to take out those lights; it was possible at our low altitude. He didn't need asking twice. He started firing at them, and the lights went out. I then lined up for the mining run, and the mines were successfully released and their locations plotted. Once done, we turned west, climbed to 10,000 feet and began our journey back to base. In the debriefing, the intelligence people told us that the men manning the lights had probably fled for cover. I'm not surprised, really, as 50-calibre bullets spraying the surroundings from such a low height, even if none hit the searchlights, would not have been a pleasant experience.

On the journey back, the rear gunner told me through the intercom that he could see an aircraft on the starboard quarter. I then turned to look in that direction, and, sure enough, there was an aircraft there; it looked like a Japanese fighter to me. When it banked towards us, I immediately took refuge in a nearby cloud, and when I emerged a few minutes later the presumably-enemy aircraft was gone.

I must add that the crew listing for my Liberator in the post-flight Sortie Report for this mining operation, found in the official 159

Squadron records, did not list a nose gunner. This was an error in the records, as Blondie certainly was aboard with me on that operation.

Your eleventh operation was a return to Penang, but this time it didn't go so well.
What an understatement that is. The second Penang operation, flown on the 26th-27th of November 1944, was the first time I was involved in a really vicious storm. That, combined with my inexperience, led to a situation which could have killed my crew and myself. It has been said that the weather in the Far East was as big an enemy, or bigger, than the Japanese, and on that operation I can vouch for the frightening reality of an encounter between a Liberator and a thunderstorm.

A return to Penang had been planned to repeat the minelaying success of late October. The assumption was that it would take a month for the Japanese to sweep the sixty mines we had previously dropped and to open up the harbour and sea lanes to maritime traffic. We didn't know at the time that the Japanese had insufficient minesweeping capabilities at Penang, and that our first raid had severely impacted shipping, including submarine repair and provisioning, for much longer than we imagined. One month after our first Penang mission, then, we again set out from West Bengal, India on another 3,000-mile round-trip mining operation. This time, the Americans and senior RAF leaders knew the flight was possible, based on the results of the 27th-28th of October assignment.

Aboard EW110 'B', my crew and I took off from Kalaikunda, a different American B-29 airfield than Kharagpur, from where we had begun our outward flight on the first Penang raid. These two American bases were only about 7.5 miles apart. Kalaikunda, like Kharagpur, had an extended runway, not found on Liberator bases, which was essential if our heavily-laden aircraft were to get airborne. Our bomb bay held four of the same type of mines as deployed at Penang a month earlier, and once again we carried extra fuel tanks. The primary difference from my October Penang operation was that I was captaining the aircraft this time instead of acting as co-pilot.

Fifteen other Liberators from 159 Squadron joined EW110 'B' on the operation. In the changeable environment of an RAF bomber squadron, personnel had come and gone in considerable numbers over the past month, as men finished their tours of operations and other men's tours were in their early stages. Furthermore, others who were simply not scheduled to fly last time were now called upon to participate. The bottom line was that just under half of the participants on this second raid down to Malaya and back had not been on the first Penang operation.

Like last time, a 159 Squadron C Flight ('Special Flight') Liberator was sent to the Penang area to report on weather conditions, but the aircraft suffered engine trouble 70 miles north of Penang and had to return to Digri. Consequently, we were unaware of the nature of the storm we would soon run into.

Taking off and travelling to Penang in the late morning of the 26th of November proceeded without incident, but in the final few miles on the inward flight everything changed. As we approached Penang in a darkening sky illuminated by moonlight, I noticed the storm ahead and had to choose a course of action. I decided to try and penetrate it in order to reach the target, but once into the storm, we were tossed around quite violently, to the point where I lacked the strength to hold the Liberator in level flight. I forcefully told Lance Williamson, my co-pilot, to help me fight to maintain control of the aircraft, but he made the potentially fatal error of trying to bank to the left. This could have ended in disaster, as the wings, not being level, would have put us at risk of being rolled over, with loss of control and almost certain death. I shouted at Lance to keep it level. Also, lightning flashed and thunder boomed all around us, and heavy rain battered the fuselage. Each flash of lightning illuminated the cockpit for a split second. Without warning, like a leaf in the wind, our Liberator was caught in an updraught at an altitude of 1,000 feet and thrown out at 3,000 feet.

Miraculously, we had survived our attempt to penetrate the worst of the storm, but visibility was still terrible upon breaking free of the most violent part of the storm. To reach our assigned drop zone, if it was even possible, Len Upjohn, my navigator, would have needed to work out where we were and to set a new course, but the conditions were such that we were blind to our surroundings, all the way to sea level. I decided to jettison the mines, given the dangers that the storm posed and the improbability of ever reaching our target.

We began the flight home, avoiding the storm, but we had to reach deep, open water before we could release the four mines. Before they were jettisoned, the parachutes were removed from the mines; mines were always dropped via parachute. Later on, we went into Digri and had the silk parachutes made into shirts.

What was going through your mind on the flight back to base?
Not a lot, as I was down on the rest bed having a nap. But I was quite nervous that everyone else had reached the target successfully, and that I was the only one to have jettisoned my mines. I was worried that I would be ridiculed, as a result.

What happened to everyone else?
As on the first Penang raid, all participating Liberators made it home safely, although, just like in October, two bombers first landed at Chittagong due to fuel concerns. After landing at Digri following a flight of over eighteen hours, I went with many other returning airmen to the debriefing meeting overseen by S/Ldr R. F. Cox, the Senior Intelligence Officer. W/Cdr Blackburn, piloting the last Liberator to land, made an appearance just as I was explaining my encounter with the storm to the authorities. I was a bit nervous, because I thought that there was a good chance that no one would believe that we were caught in an updraft, thrown off course and, unable to locate our drop zone, had to jettison our mines. When I told everyone that I had been thrown out at 3,000 feet, W/Cdr Blackburn looked at me and said, 'I beat you, Denis. I came out at 5,000 feet.' At that point, a big sigh of relief came over me, as I knew that W/Cdr Blackburn's account would squash any doubt that may have existed about mine.

Arriving in the Penang area at different times, and with each aircraft's pinpoint drop zone unique from any other's assigned target, the sixteen Liberators faced differing storm conditions. Despite varying weather challenges, each aircraft searched as best it could for its target area. Success in laying mines, however, was limited, and twelve other bombers, not just my Liberator, jettisoned their mines on the return to Digri.

Only W/Cdr Blackburn and I chose to fly into the storm, though, unlike me, upon emerging from it he was able to visually find his drop zone and release his mines. Two other Liberators, having avoided the full fury of the storm, recognised their specific drop zones through small breaks in the clouds and deployed mines as planned.

Looking back on it, the fact that W/Cdr Blackburn and I were the only two to enter the storm and attempt to get through it leads me to believe that other captains, having sized up the storm, decided that they didn't want any part of that game of marbles. You can't blame them, though. I only attempted it out of ignorance and because at that point I didn't have a fully developed appreciation of danger. W/Cdr Blackburn was different, it was just pure bravery on his part.

For a while, there was a lingering sense of disappointment around the aircrews that took part due to the fact that most had been unable to successfully complete our objective.

Few people know that the RAF did drop napalm during the Second World War, one such occasion being on the 2nd-3rd of December 1944, during your twelfth operational flight, to Bangkok.

Yes, and the reason we used napalm bombs was that because the target structures were of mostly wooden construction, napalm was determined to be an ideal incendiary agent. The size of the target was small and in a compact urban area, so conventional bombing from regular height could have caused blast damage to the surrounding buildings. Instead, on this operation the participating Liberators were used in an unconventional way: as dive-bombers! The load carried by each plane was still largely comprised of the usual high explosive bombs, but then one napalm bomb per load ensured that fire was an essential destructive component, more so than the small number of standard incendiaries that were also dropped.

The 159 Squadron records state that the target was the Rama VI Bridge, a railway structure across the Chao Phraya River in Bangkok, while my log book simply records the target as a 'bridge at Bangkok'. Though the Rama VI rail bridge was a legitimate strategic target, our actual plan was not to bomb the bridge, but to strike a pinpoint complex of huts and other buildings close to the bridge's southwestern end. The buildings housed an arsenal of weaponry plus supplies, all awaiting delivery to Japanese forces in Burma and the rest of the region. The destruction of the target, then, was a worthy objective.

The landmark bridge, easily identified in the good nighttime visibility and bright moonlight conditions of the 2nd-3rd of December, became the focal point of the entire raid; as a guide to where we released our bombs, it made the precision dive-bombing of the buildings housing the weapons and supplies fairly simple.

In preparation for this unique attack, 159 Squadron's pilots had undergone appropriate training in the use of the Liberator in dive-bombing. The technique, however, was quite different than the nose-down vertical drops performed by dedicated single-engine dive-bombing aircraft like the German Ju 87 Stuka.

As a pilot taking part in the raid, I can describe in detail how we trained for it. A line of empty oil drums, representing the bridge, was spread across our airfield. Each pilot then practised a shallow dive towards the 'bridge' diagonal to the line of drums, and with an imaginary Chao Phraya River to the left. It was like making an approach to land the aircraft, except that the pilot maintained a speed of 120 miles per hour. Each of our Liberators had been modified to add a bomb-release button to the control column.

The practice dive continued until the exact moment when the nose of the Liberator was directly above the end of the line of oil drums, and at an altitude of 800 feet, the pilot pulled back the control column and at the same time pressed the button to release the practice bombs. The goal was to 'throw' the bombs beyond the 'bridge' and into what had been marked out as the target area. Then, an observer on the ground told the pilot via radio whether the bombs landed short of the 'bridge', atop the oil drums, directly upon the target, or too far beyond. We trained like that for several days with eleven-pound practice dummy bombs until W/Cdr Blackburn was satisfied.

Did W/Cdr Blackburn organise that raid like he had done with Penang?
Yes, he organised it himself, although I think he had more cooperation from the higher-ups than when trying to organise the first Penang

operation. The target area in Bangkok was so small that a highly accurate mode of bombing was required to ensure that damage to surrounding buildings was minimised. This ruled out high altitude bombing. As the higher-ups were familiar with W/Cdr Blackburn's successes, I imagine that they were more open to his ideas for the 2nd-3rd December operation.

Was the raid a success?
The raid was a complete success, with the whole target area being virtually wiped out. Post-operation photo reconnaissance revealed no visible damage to the bridge, and there was a bonus: the bridge, not our target, was temporarily closed to all rail traffic.

To avoid any danger of collisions, each plane was given a time to attack. Just like in our training, we approached slightly diagonal to the Rama VI Bridge, out of the west and with the river on the left, so each attacking Liberator flew from northwest to southeast. The target, then, was just beyond the bridge, and southeast of it. We had been forewarned that the bridge itself would be heavily defended by a nest of machine guns, and that there were further guns sited in the surrounding buildings. Sure enough, gunners on the bridge and elsewhere opened up on us. A few of our Liberators fired back, and for once W/Cdr Blackburn had to break radio silence to shout, 'Stop firing or you'll shoot yourselves down!' Aircraft, not mine, were hit, but the damage was minimal and nobody suffered physical injury.

After our fifteen Liberators had dropped their bombs, we all then climbed to 10,000 feet to begin the journey back to base. The amazing thing was that from 50 miles away we could still see the firestorm that the raid had started. All bombers taking part returned safely to base.

What was going through your mind during it all? What you were expected to do required such precision.
Due to our extensive dive-bombing practice back at Digri, I felt quite confident about performing the technique with accuracy on the actual target. Intelligence had told us about the machine gun nest on the bridge, as well as suspected gunsites close to the target, so, course, there was tension on the way to the target due to the potential of coming under heavy enemy fire and the consequences that can

result from that. Once we arrived in Bangkok, though, everyone just completely focused on the job at hand. However, unlike on our return journey from Penang, the tension didn't exactly dissipate on the way back from Bangkok, because we had to be on the lookout for Japanese fighters. Luckily, none appeared.

This was my seventh operation aboard Liberator EW110 'B'. My crew and I were airborne for fourteen hours and fifteen minutes to and from Bangkok.

Talk me through your next operation.
Number thirteen took place on the 5th-6th of December 1944. In Liberator EW110 'B', I returned to Mergui, in Burma, to lay mines, joining six other aircraft. Five 159 Squadron Liberators were directed to mine the Ye River in Burma, 195 miles further north. I was airborne on this routine nighttime raid for thirteen hours and thirty-five minutes. We didn't meet any enemy opposition, and all aircraft safely returned to Digri.

Your next operation, number fourteen, presented a bonus target, right?
Yes, you are correct. On the 8th of December 1944, I returned with my crew to Victoria Point, at the southern limit of Burma, to lay mines in the Pakchan River; my very first operation was to the same stretch of water. While my Liberator, EW110 'B', and five other aircraft took care of the minelaying, nine Liberators simultaneously bombed the newly-established port facilities at nearby Khao Huagang, Thailand. One other bomber, having a fuel problem, opted to instead bomb and strafe Great Coco Island, north of the Andaman and Nicobar Islands in the Bay of Bengal.

The minelaying at Victoria Point and the low-level attack on Khao Huagang went smoothly, but then things became interesting. In the briefing before we set off, we were told about an island close to our route back, where Japanese seaplanes were based, attached to a little wooden jetty. A few of the Liberators on this operation were detailed to attack the seaplanes on the return leg.

While making our way back to Digri, I remembered the island and decided that I couldn't miss out on the opportunity to attack the seaplanes. It shows the type of person I was back then; it was all good fun to me, one big adventure. So, once we reached the island, I noticed that two out of the three seaplanes were already on fire, no doubt from Liberators that arrived before us. I descended to no more than twenty feet and told Blondie Whittle in the nose turret to let rip. Blondie began firing his twin .50-calibre guns and set the last seaplane alight. What we didn't notice was a machine gun nest that had begun firing on us, but it was quickly put out of action. Aside from hitting the seaplane, Blondie also hit the jetty, causing pieces of wood to be thrown into the air. As all of this was happening, I turned to Lance Williamson, my co-pilot, and said something like, 'We're going to be the first plane shot down by pieces of wood.' We had a good laugh about it. All of that took place while travelling at 150 miles an hour or so.

The island was quite narrow, so we quickly approached the other side. I came around for a second run and noticed a supply boat, which I told Blondie to open fire on. He did, and the two or three men onboard dove into the water, but before jumping, one man let off a rifle shot, which ended up embedded in our nose. It was the same bullet in our nose which I mentioned earlier, when the flight commander mocked me for only taking one bullet, followed by W/Cdr Blackburn mocking him.

Anyway, I came back for a third time. A parade ground in the middle of the island with a Japanese flag blowing in the wind presented an enticing target, so I told Blondie to hit the parade ground and the few huts surrounding it, which he did.

After that, we departed for home, leaving most of the huts and all of the seaplanes on fire. Interestingly enough, during all of our action at the island, where there were numerous opportunities to let loose on the guns, my only other gunner, Sammy, in the rear turret, didn't fire a single shot, claiming that his twin guns had jammed.

This operation was another lengthy one for me, at fourteen hours and fifty minutes.

Was your fifteenth raid as exciting and exhilarating?
No. It was really a standard bombing raid, but on a unique site. On the 17th of December 1944, the entire squadron force of sixteen

Liberators took part in an attack upon a recently-pinpointed mobile radar station. Our target was on the northwest tip of Great Coco Island, located in the Indian Ocean between the Andaman and Nicobar Islands and the Burmese mainland. The reason we targeted this specific island was because the Japanese radar station, which had been discovered by a Liberator from 159 Squadron's Special Flight, had the potential to signal advance warning of any incoming Allied air attacks or movement of Allied naval ships.

From our Liberators, we could not see the camouflaged mobile radar site, which had been previously photographed, so in good daylight weather from an average height of only 3,000 feet, our aircraft bombed where the radar equipment was known to have been located. It was an uncomplicated raid, and all sixteen Liberators came home, without any damage. Captaining EW110 'B' once again, I logged ten hours and twenty-five minutes of operational flight time.

There can't have been much of the radar installation left.
Yes, no doubt. The site was absolutely pulverised. We were told in subsequent weeks that there had been no transmission signals from the Great Coco Island radar since our bombing attack on the 17th of December. It could not be established from photographic evidence that we had destroyed the radar, but this was the logical conclusion.

Was your sixteenth operation as straightforward and without incident?
Yes, it was. Sixteen Liberators from 159 Squadron, including my EW110 'B', targeted the Martaban dockland area at dusk on the 21st of December 1944. Martaban was a small port to the east of Rangoon and across the wide Salween River from Moulmein. Anti-aircraft opposition was meagre, I was happy to learn, and our bombs, dropped in good weather conditions, destroyed two jetties and a rice mill and damaged rail facilities essential for the transfer of goods from the south onward to the Japanese battlefronts.

The operation was eleven hours and fifty minutes in duration.

However, my seventeenth operation, mining the Irrawaddy river near Rangoon, the capital of Burma, that was quite an experience.

What happened?

It took place on the 29th-30th of December 1944, and it was a tragic night for 159 Squadron. W/Cdr Blackburn had devised a plan to mine three separate bodies of water. Five Liberators successfully deployed mines in the Bangkok River, while another five Liberators successfully dropped mines in the nearby Goh Sichang anchorage in the Gulf of Thailand. Piloting EW110 'B', I was joined by five other Liberators on a mission to mine the Rangoon River estuary between the river's mouth at Elephant Point and the city of Rangoon 24 miles northward. As Rangoon was the most important port for resupplying the Japanese army in Burma, cutting this vital supply line would have a major strategic impact.

My experience on eight previous minelaying operations, six as captain, held me in good stead as we headed for our target zones up the Rangoon River. Each of our small force of aircraft was detailed to drop a record eight mines, as were the other ten Liberators headed to Thailand.

Laying mines was an art in itself, as the pilot had to be completely steady and dead on the course set out by the navigator. On top of this, precise timing of the release of each mine was essential in order to ensure it landed where it was supposed to, and that it could be plotted for reference.

The plan that W/Cdr Blackburn had devised involved fooling Japanese radar in the Rangoon area. He presumed that our sixteen incoming aircraft would eventually be picked up on radar while flying in loose formation in the bright moonlight. Therefore, once our force of bombers arrived south of Rangoon, the idea was that the six Liberators tasked with mining the Rangoon River estuary would rapidly drop out of the formation, one after the other, all the way down to 400 feet, our prescribed mining height. The hope was that the Japanese radar operators would only see the main 'blip' of the formation still heading eastwards and not be aware of six aircraft leaving the main group for our separate Rangoon River minelaying assignment.

But it did not go according to plan and nine airmen died. Once we reached Elephant Point at the mouth of the river, having descended to 400 feet, the first two Liberators came under intense, damaging anti-aircraft fire, though they still managed to lay their mines and fly on; no airmen were injured.

The third Liberator, however, was shot down. Before my eyes, I watched KH276 'X', piloted by WO Arthur Stewart, suddenly explode into a ball of fire and crash into the river. What had probably happened was that a shell had gone through the bomb bay doors and hit a mine. That's the only explanation I can think of that explains how that Liberator suddenly exploded like that.

Having seen all of that, I was struck with a brainwave. I knew that with the anti-aircraft guns primed to attack us as we flew past Elephant Point and up the Rangoon River in the bright moonlight, and with eight mines aboard, I would be a prime target, as I couldn't take violent evasive action for risk of a mine detaching and exploding. Instead, I took my Liberator off-course and out of range and asked Len Upjohn, my navigator, to rework the calculations so I could come around from the opposite direction. We could then release the mines in reverse order. The mines would still be dropped in the same designated places as planned, but the first mine released would be plotted as number eight, the second mine released would be plotted as seven, and so on. In doing so, by the time the eight and last mine had been dropped, the bomb bay would be empty, and I would be able to take evasive action and manoeuvre my Liberator out of the range of the fixed-position anti-aircraft guns, which faced southward towards the mouth of the river, the direction from which I was supposed to make my approach.

Once Len had worked out the calculations, I came around into range and dropped the mines successfully. However, we came very close to being hit by enemy fire. As the mines were being laid, I saw the flashes of Japanese guns, not the ones at the mouth of the river, and I said to Lance Williamson, my co-pilot, 'Those bods couldn't hit a barn door from ten feet.' In that instant, from our left we heard a low hum turn rapidly into a loud roar before fading to our right. A shell had only just missed us. I reached the end of my drop zone, went into a dive to the right, down to 100 feet and then levelled out to begin the journey back to base. From then on, I gave more respect to the accuracy of the enemy gunners.

Except for WO Stewart's Liberator, all fifteen other aircraft, including the ten sent to Thailand, returned safely to Digri, with no injuries to report. I added another ten hours and ten minutes of operational flying on this mission.

To say something like you did about the enemy gunners, while being fired upon, is incredible.
The thing is, nothing up until that point on that operation had really frightened me, not even seeing WO Stewart's Liberator being shot down. At that point, I was well on the way to reaching the end of my tour of operational flying on 159 Squadron, and I guess you could say that I was becoming a bit blasé about the whole thing.

What was the aftermath of the operation?
Despite the tragic loss of one Liberator, before its mines had been laid, the 159 Squadron intelligence people still rated our Rangoon River part of the operation a success because the goal of covering the waterway with mines had been accomplished. We laid forty mines into our designated drop zones, putting that section of the Rangoon River out of action for quite a while; no ship could reach the port of Rangoon from the Gulf of Martaban for the time being. To top it all off, during debriefing, when we were giving our accounts of the operation, I explained my brainwave to everyone and how it was successfully implemented. W/Cdr Blackburn congratulated me and told me that he would never have thought of it.

By the way, the pilot of one of the other Liberators to participate in the Rangoon River mining told me that, like the first three attacking bombers, he had also been hit by anti-aircraft fire but had managed to lay his mines and make it back. The fifth returnee from our subset of squadron minelaying Liberators had also suffered minor battle damage.

Your eighteenth operation was absolutely incredible but for other reasons. It's quite a story.
Blimey, yes. It took place on the 1st-2nd of January 1945, and we must have had a guardian angel overlooking us that night. I captained EW110 'B' again, one of fifteen Liberators from 159 Squadron to be

part of the attack; one Liberator had turned back before reaching the target. Our operational orders were simple enough: bomb the railway bridge which crossed the Nakhon Chaisi River, located 8 miles due east of Nakhon Pathom and 20 miles west of Bangkok. Because of unexpected headwinds, the fifteen Liberators were delayed in reaching the target, but bombing was well-concentrated. Subsequent photo reconnaissance images determined that we had completely destroyed the bridge, which carried the only rail line westward out of Bangkok. Ultimately, this vital rail line split southward down the Malay Peninsula, while the other branch continued westward as the notorious Death Railway to Burma.

Because of unexpected headwinds and weather, the fifteen Liberators were delayed in reaching the target, but bombing proceeded, nevertheless, in generally good conditions on a night with a three-quarters moon. To add to the moon's illumination, a couple of planes to the north of the bridge kept the area lit up with flares.

For my aircraft, it was when we reached the bridge that everything started to unravel. Upon approach, I heard, 'Bomb doors open,' in preparation to drop our bombs. At that moment, I glanced up to see another Liberator almost sitting on top of us, also with its bomb doors open. This time I was scared, as I didn't want to be on the receiving end of 8,000 pounds of high explosives. I had no choice but to slide out of the way using only the port rudder pedal, so as to keep the wings level. We were so close to the other Liberator that had I tried to use the control column to steer, the right wing would have risen and struck the other Liberator. Though everyone was late in starting the attack, my bomber was on time in the specific attack sequence; it was the other Liberator that was either too early or too late.

Although we were no longer at risk of collision or of being hit by the bombs of the other Liberator, we had yet to drop our own bombload. In the pre-operation briefing we had been told that should any Liberator miss its attack time, it was to circle until all the others had cleared the area before finally taking its turn at bombing, like going to the back of the queue.

After the incident I have just mentioned, then, we had to wait our turn, and eventually the way was clear for us to make our run.

We successfully dropped our bombs on the bridge and headed for home. However, at one point a huge storm chain loomed ahead. I looked for a way through at different heights, but that was no good, so I warned the crew that we faced a bumpy ride and ploughed into the storm.

Hailstones battered us and lightning bolts hit the sea, but fortunately not our aircraft. Eventually, we made it to clear skies, although we were far off track, which Len's navigational calculations confirmed. It meant that we no longer had enough fuel to reach Digri. I decided to head for Cox's Bazar, an airfield on the northeast coast of the Bay of Bengal, on Indian soil. However, when we were about thirty miles away, we came into the range of a British naval fleet involved in military action to retake Akyab. They mistook us for a Japanese aircraft and opened fire on us. As anti-aircraft shells began to explode around us, I immediately started flashing the navigation lights to signal that we were a friendly aircraft. The firing stopped.

When we finally made it to Cox's Bazar, it was still dark, and I realised that we had enough fuel to make it to Chittagong, located another 150 miles up the coast. The journey there was without incident, until we approached Chittagong. Suddenly, a huge shape seemed to glide past our port side, then one on our starboard, then another on our port side, then another on the starboard, and so on. In foggy coastal conditions, we had flown straight through a balloon barrage hoisted to protect ships moored below us.

I realised that the airfield was enveloped in the same fog that hid the ships from our sight, though I could just make out the runway lights. Being able to see these runway boundary lights, despite the fog, made it possible for me to land. In basic training in Southern Rhodesia, we had learnt how to get down in fog by means of timed runs on a stopwatch. I used this technique to safely land. How it worked was that the navigator, using a stopwatch, noted the time it took to fly level along the length of the runway. Once at the far end of the runway, the pilot made a rate one turn, also timed, which repositioned the aircraft at the end of the runway but facing in the opposite direction, and still level with the runway. The pilot again flew along the length of the runway. After the precise time it had taken to fly down the runway on the first pass elapsed, the pilot again made a rate one turn that was a duplicate of his first turn, only at the other end of the runway. Then, after the precise time recorded for the first rate one turn had passed, the aircraft was again known to be at the beginning of the runway, and a safe landing could be visually attempted despite foggy conditions.

Once the manoeuvre had been implemented you must have been relieved beyond belief, especially upon safely touching down.
Not entirely. Intelligence had told us that if we had to land at another airfield we should turn on our landing lights in order to identify to the people there that we were a friendly aircraft. So once we had lined up with the runway and were descending, I turned on the landing lights, and to my horror there was a steamroller sitting at the beginning of the runway. I pulled back hard on the control column, which guided the plane over the steamroller.

The problem I then faced is that I had lost about 200 yards of runway in which to come to a stop. When the wheels touched the runway, I had to slam on the brakes as hard as I could, which caused the brake shoes to catch fire. In response, I had to release the pressure on the brake shoes, but only for a few seconds, until the flames went out. Then it was back to engaging the brakes as hard as they would go, but not for as long as before, because we had significantly slowed down by then. With only two or three yards of runway left, I swerved onto the perimeter track, and finally we came to a stop. From there, we followed the airport jeep to the control tower.

To summarise, during that operation you faced a Liberator with its bomb doors open directly above you at the target, you had to navigate through a storm front, you came under friendly fire, miraculously flew through a balloon barrage, landed in fog and barely managed to avoid a steamroller sitting on the runway. You must have been in quite a state once you were out of your Liberator.
I breathed a huge sigh of relief, to say the least. We had landed at four in the morning, and by the time we taxied to the control tower it was just beginning to get light. In the distance, we could make out the balloon barrage through which we had flown, and, boy, did they

look clustered, and impossible to avoid. Lance commented that he wouldn't like to fly a Tiger Moth through there, let alone a Liberator, and he was not wrong.

We later discovered that we had only twenty gallons of fuel left in the tanks, which for a Liberator teetered on the brink of fuel starvation.

Some people would say that once I saw the steamroller, I should have aborted that landing, done another circuit, and then landed, taking the steamroller into account from the start. However, with only twenty gallons of fuel left, it's doubtful that another circuit and landing attempt would have been possible. Besides, in a situation like that, instincts come into play; there is no time to think through the options.

What I forgot to mention is that during that arduous flight we were hit in the bomb bay by a low-calibre shell, which damaged the structures that held the bombs and mines in place. The damage was so significant that my Liberator was downgraded to a training plane, and I received a new one, KH211 'A', already named 'Britannia V', which I flew on all five of my remaining operations on 159 Squadron.

The good news in all of this was that not long after the raid we were told that we had successfully wiped out our section of the bridge.

Did you ever discover why there was a steamroller sitting on the runway? Was it there due to negligence, or was it purposefully placed there?

An officer at Chittagong told me that the steamroller was put there to stop Japanese aircraft from landing. Even at that stage of the war, Japanese aircraft were still in range of Cox's Bazar and Chittagong. What surprised me was that we were not told about the steamroller in advance; we had been in radio communication with Chittagong prior to landing, and it was the sort of thing we should have been informed of. Come to think of it, warning about the balloon barrage close to Chittagong also should have been given to us.

I assume you were only there for a day at the most before you returned to Digri.

We were only in Chittagong for a few hours before flying the two hours back to Digri the same day. Remember, the senior staff on 159

Squadron had to wait for all of the planes to return before they could start preparing for the next operation.

Once back, we had to go through the regular debriefing and explain what happened on the operation.

Wasn't it around this time that W/Cdr Blackburn left 159 Squadron?

Yes. He was posted to Alipore, in Calcutta. On the morning of the 9th of January 1945, while I was asleep, he walked in with a group of officers, ripped off the covers and told me that I was flying him the short distance to Alipore airfield in Calcutta, and that I should bring along my entire crew.

We soon took off, with me as pilot and W/Cdr Blackburn sitting next to me in the co-pilot's seat. He didn't interfere or anything, but from his position in the co-pilot's seat he did teach me how to 'fly on the step'. What he said I had to do was to reduce the actual power of the engines, which of course slowed down the aircraft and caused the nose to dip. The plane went into a very shallow dive, increasing the Liberator's speed. The next step was to pull back on the controls and to adjust the trim tabs, which brought the speed back to what it was before the dive, but with the nose slightly up. W/Cdr Blackburn claimed that the aircraft's fuel consumption was more economical when flown in this manner.

Upon landing, he told me that he wanted to taxi the Liberator to air traffic control, and, blimey, did he taxi at some speed!

He also invited us all to lunch at Firpo's, the high-class luxury restaurant well-known to servicemen desiring a good meal in Calcutta. During the meal, he noticed that I was eating the bread rolls dry, and he suggested that I put butter on the rolls. He was surprised when I told him that I didn't like butter and, therefore, never ate butter on bread. I still don't like butter, all these years later.

After we had finished our meal, W/Cdr Blackburn told us to go shopping and to meet him at Firpo's once we had finished. This, we did, and from Firpo's we all went for tea to Christie's, an upper-tier hotel. He paid for it all - the lunch at Firpo's and the tea at Christie's.

Afterwards, he phoned up airfield transport and organised a taxi to take us back to Alipore.

Once we had been driven there, we went to the Mess to eat and drink before returning to the aircraft to fly back to Digri, but we didn't make the return flight that day, after all, because number one engine wouldn't start. As a result, we had a whole extra day and part of the next to spend in Calcutta. We didn't return to Digri until the 11th of January. Ironically, W/Cdr Blackburn later told me that he had phoned Alipore on the 11th to make sure that we had returned safely, only to discover that we were still there. That annoyed him, as he told me that he would not have let us sleep in a Nissen hut, as we all had. He said he would have put us up in a hotel if he had known that we were going to be stranded there.

How much of Calcutta did you get to see?
Quite a lot. With almost two days and nothing else to do, we explored the large, sprawling and quite an interesting city. It really was a city of hustle and bustle - very noisy and very busy. To give an example, the buses were always heavily crowded; even the double-decker buses had people sitting on the roofs.

We spent most of the daytime looking around the shops, and there were plenty of places where one could find a cup of tea. There was one main street that was particularly packed with people, though I always found it to be a safe city and the people to be quite friendly. Calcutta was a city I liked, and one I would return to more than once in the following year. It's hard to believe that two years later, India would erupt into violence.

One interesting fact is that we were not allowed to drink milk on its own anywhere in India as the milk was not pasteurised. If the RAF police caught us drinking milk, we would face punishment for it.

When you returned by Liberator to Digri on the 11th of January, 159 Squadron had a new Commanding Officer, W/Cdr Byron F. Burbridge. What was he like?
I didn't see much of him. He was nice enough but didn't have a charismatic force of personality like W/Cdr Blackburn. He was

Canadian, and 159 Squadron had more and more Canadians in its ranks, which changed the makeup of the unit. There was somewhat of a divide between the Canadians and non-Canadians, though it went unspoken. The RCAF men came across as more arrogant; they were loud and seemed to look down on the non-Canadians. I screened two of their pilots myself, and I got the impression that, in general, their training was not as rigorous as it was in the RAF. One chap I screened had poor instrument flying abilities, which I discovered when we were flying in cloudy conditions. That could potentially be very detrimental, because if the pilot was even a little bit off course, his lack of adequate instrument flying skills impeded the navigator. Even more vitally, the ability to fly on instruments was essential in keeping an aircraft safely airborne; the pilot's brain often sensed its environment wrongly, causing the pilot to react tragically, when faith in the instruments would have prevented incorrect decision-making.

Did the Canadian-versus-non-Canadian divide affect morale in any way?
It did, in the sense that to many of us, the Canadians wanted to be in charge, to be the top dogs and not work with us as equals. Then again, I was only on 159 Squadron for a few more weeks, as by that stage my tour was coming to an end, so I don't know the long-term impact upon the squadron.

Your crew didn't change in the last few weeks though?
Crew makeup on 159 Squadron evolved as W/Cdr Blackburn experimented with fuel consumption characteristics and the bomb or mine-carrying capabilities of the Liberator. Different operations, at varying distances from Digri, and at different times in W/Cdr Blackburn's tenure on the squadron, called for differing numbers of crewmen aboard any one Liberator. For example, for the 8th of December 1944's mining operation to Victoria Point, in Burma, my crew was comprised of eight men, but on my final operation on the 27th-28th of January 1945, again to mine the Pakchan River near Victoria Point, the crew count was down to six, including me. On the 1st-2nd of January 1945, I commanded a

Liberator with only seven men aboard. On the Penang operations, there were only six crewmen per aircraft. Consequently, then, not every operation called for the same core crewmen, and let's not forget that some crew positions, like the nose turret, were eliminated altogether on some operations. As an example of this, Blondie Whittle, my nose turret gunner, didn't fly with me again after the 29th of December 1944.

Furthermore, different mission requirements dictated who flew on any one of my final five operations. Lance Williamson, my usual co-pilot, flew with me on only one of my next four operations, when I screened one or the other of two Canadian pilots, and then on the final operation of my tour. Jock Balnaves, my wireless operator, was on four of my final five operations, but he was replaced by another wireless operator on one operation, for reasons I can't remember. Len Upjohn, on the other hand, was my navigator on all five of my remaining operations.

Despite the differing requirements dictating the number of crewmen per aircraft, four of my crewmates were with me to the end of my tour: Lance, my co-pilot; Len, my navigator; Jock, my wireless operator and Sammy in the rear turret.

I was on course to reach the required number of operational flying hours before any of these men. To complete a tour, one had to generally – but not always – fly thirty operations or 300 hours of operational flying, whichever came first. A factor in why I had more hours than any of these four was because I was screened on my earliest operational flights by a seasoned captain nearing the end of his tour. On two of these screen operations, I was with the crew of whoever was captaining the aircraft, not my own crew.

So you flew an extra operation so you could all finish together.
Yes. After twenty-two operations, I was twenty-five minutes short of reaching the 300-hour mark, but I had been told that my tour of operations was considered completed. However, not only did I want to cross the 300-hour threshold, but I also wished to join Lance, Len, Jock and Sammy one last time on what would also be the final operational flight for each of their 159 Squadron tour

of operations. So, I flew one extra operation. It meant once again returning to the site of my very first operation, Victoria Point, to lay mines.

After leaving 159 Squadron, I completed a one-off operational flight a few months later while I was based at Cox's Bazar. I will enlarge on that later on.

But before we talk about your final operation with 159 Squadron, you had another four to complete.
My nineteenth operational flight, on the 14th-15th of January 1945, was my first in twelve days, since my return from Chittagong on the 2nd of January. The squadron sent sixteen Liberators to bomb the road and rail bridge across the Mae Klong River at Rajburi, in Thailand, about 48 miles southwest of Bangkok. The operation itself was fairly routine with cloudless skies, slight haze at the target and meagre defensive fire. Two of our sixteen aircraft aided us in our bombing role by illuminating the bridge with flares.

The operation, aboard Liberator KH211 'A', was also the first time I screened someone; I was supervising and advising Canadian FO Gerald Schroeder, a pilot new to 159 Squadron, who officially flew as my co-pilot. The screening process was identical to what I experienced when I first joined the squadron, where a seasoned captain imparted his knowledge about our type of warfare to a newcomer.

We carried out our run dead on time, hit the target, turned around and headed for base. I was in the air for fourteen hours.

Only two Liberators carried bomb strike cameras. The photos, illuminated by photoflash pyrotechnics dropped from the aircraft and timed to explode when the bombs were detonating, revealed that bombs had scored a direct hit on the support structure of the northern end of the bridge.

Were cameras a common fixture on your operations?
Their use varied from operation to operation. For mining raids, because we were just deploying mines in water, there was no need for the extra weight of the cameras. A photo of a mine deployment would not have had helped to gauge accuracy, as would a strike

photo taken over a bombed target. On bombing operations, however, there was value in having visual evidence of our accuracy, although post-operation air photo reconnaissance led to a more accurate analysis of results, clear of sometimes-obscuring smoke from fires and explosions. On some bombing operations, where bomb strike cameras seemingly would have been useful, no Liberators carried them, while on other similar raids, such as on the 14th-15th of January 1945, only one or two aircraft were issued such cameras. Yet, on other operations, every bomber had a camera to record bomb strike images, and on some flights only oblique cameras, not downward-facing bomb strike cameras, were issued.

An example of the use of oblique cameras involved the same pilot who I screened on the 14th-15th of January, FO Schroeder. On the 9th of February, less than a month later, in a daylight attack upon port facilities at Khao Huagang, Thailand, near Victoria Point, his Liberator, KH255, took an anti-aircraft hit directly into the bomb bay, setting the overload fuel tanks, presumably, alight. It just so happened that men on other Liberators, carrying oblique cameras, directed their hand-held cameras in the direction of his Liberator and photographed a sequence of images of its ordeal, which ended in a crash and explosion which killed the entire crew.

The only reason I knew about the cameras on the 14th-15th of January was because the intelligence people told us about the direct hit seen in a bomb strike photo. My Liberator was not one of the two carrying a camera.

I know that the Americans used cameras a lot. For example, the Americans would attach cameras to their P-51 Mustangs and would show the films in their camp cinemas.

Operation number twenty was an 18th of January 1945 attack on the Martaban railway station and sidings.
The operation to Martaban, in Burma, went well. I captained KH211 'A' with a crew of seven. Joined by fourteen other 159 Squadron Liberators, and met by only meagre Japanese resistance, we came in, dropped our bombs in good weather with no clouds and came home. We were back on the ground at Digri after twelve hours and thirty minutes.

On the 20th of January 1945, for your twenty-first operation, you returned to Victoria Point, the site of your first and fourteenth operations.

Yes. As captain of KH211 'A', I screened FO Roy Borthwick, a Canadian pilot from British Columbia, and Len screened the Borthwick crew's navigator, PO Kennedy. This mission to mine the Pakchan River near Victoria Point was different than any previous mining operation in the sense that only two 159 Squadron Liberators were sent to mine this river, while fourteen other aircraft from the squadron were sent solely or in groups of two to mine eight other targets in Burma and Thailand.

Everything was going well until we approached the first mine's intended release point. The problem was that this was close to an island that was situated in the middle of the Pakchan River. We had received wrong information somewhere along the line, having been told that the maximum height of the island was around 300 feet, but in reality it was closer to 350. It meant that we had to alter our flight path, as we were supposed to descend to 400 feet, fly over the island and then drop our mines into a specific area of nearby deep water. Yes, we should still have been able to clear the island's highest point, but under potentially difficult circumstances, such as if atmospheric conditions were to negatively affect our visual sharpness or the aircraft's lift, it was wiser to increase the buffer zone for flying over the island to avoid the worst-case scenario of crashing into the hilltop. To do this, I circled around the area, added fifty feet to our flying altitude upon approach to the island, safely cleared the highest point and then dropped the Liberator to the mine-release height of 400 feet. We laid our eight mines on a timed run, where each individual release occurred after the same elapsed time interval.

During that operation near Victoria Point, I gave FO Borthwick the same advice I was given over the same stretch of the Pakchan River, and what I did whenever I was mining any river. That was to stay in the centre of the river, so that the aircraft would be equally distant from any guns positioned on either side of the river. I also explained and demonstrated how to porpoise, to make it more difficult for any enemy gunner to accurately aim at the Liberator.

This mining operation took us fourteen hours and fifteen minutes.

Your twenty-second operation was the third trip to Penang.
It took place on the 23rd-24th of January 1945 in generally good visibility, with diffused moonlight and no low cloud; the contrast in weather conditions compared with our second Penang operation was dramatic. I captained Liberator KH211 'A', one of sixteen Liberators participating in the third raid. For the second and final time, I acted as screen pilot to FO Roy Borthwick, the Canadian pilot who had flown with my crew on our most recent operation to Victoria Point three days earlier.

On the first Penang mining raid, on the 27th-28th of October 1944, the Japanese were completely taken by surprise, so there was no anti-aircraft fire other than possible inconsequential rifle shots. The second time, on the 26th-27th of November, only three aircraft dropped their mines because of terrible weather, but anti-aircraft fire was non-existent. The third time, however, on the 23rd-24th of January 1945, the squadron did face anti-aircraft fire. Luckily, the target zone that our Liberator was given for releasing our four mines was on the northern end of the northern section, so we faced very little defensive fire. It certainly didn't interfere with our minelaying duties. Two of our Liberators were hit, but not seriously. They laid their mines and made it back, as did every other aircraft involved. One Liberator suffered a mechanical malfunction on the approach to dropping its first mine, losing all four mines at once, but fifteen Liberators dropped sixty mines.

Even though W/Cdr Blackburn was no longer with us, we followed his routine from the first two trips. We flew to an American airfield – I cannot recall which one – the day before with the extra fuel tanks fitted. On the day of departure for Penang, the tanks were filled and the mines, four to a Liberator, were loaded. We then took off and completed the long operation. There isn't really much else to say about the third Penang trip, as it was essentially an exact copy of the first one.

I am proud to say that out of nearly two hundred individual airmen, total, who flew on the Penang raids, I was one of only six men to have participated on all three of the raids. Four were pilots and two were flight engineers.

We arrived back at Digri after eighteen hours and forty minutes in the air.

Now, as you have already mentioned, your last operational flight with 159 Squadron was one that you did not actually have to do.
Right. I did it so that I could join four members of my crew as they reached the 300-hour mark, and in order that we would all finish our tours together.

On the 27th of January 1945, the squadron once again sent small groups of Liberators, fourteen in total, to five different minelaying destinations. The aircraft I was captaining, KH211 'A', was one of four assigned to the Pakchan River, near Victoria Point. This would be my fourth, and final, visit to these waters.

In bright moonlight with good visibility and no clouds, we came under fire, but no damage was incurred. One thing I noticed was that the Japanese appeared to have more powerful guns than I had witnessed before, as their shells seemed to reach further. Our Liberator's minelaying and that of twelve Liberators in total were deemed a success (there were equipment malfunctions on the other two Liberators), and all fourteen aircraft returned safely to Digri. A final fourteen hours and thirty-five minutes were added to the operational tallies of Lance Williamson, Len Upjohn, Jock Balnaves, Sammy and myself, closing out our individual tours of operations on 159 Squadron.

The five of you must have been elated once you landed back at Digri and the reality that your operational flying was over fully sank in.
Yes, indeed. We had each exceeded the 300 hours required and were very happy for it. However, we didn't party or do anything memorable to celebrate. We were all wondering was where we were going to be posted next. Even though we had finished our operational flying, the war was still raging, and none of us knew what tomorrow would bring.

As it turned out, Frizzy and I were posted to Baigachi; we had finished our operational tours at the same time.

Do you know where the four tour-expired members of your crew were posted?
I'm not certain, but I believe that they were all posted back to Britain. I know that Len and Jock were, as I kept in touch with them.

CHAPTER NINE

REFLECTIONS ON OPERATIONAL FLYING AND 159 SQUADRON

Civilian casualties, flying fears, crew camaraderie, further thoughts on the Penang raids, W/Cdr Blackburn gets the US DFC, Frizzy and Denis are robbed of the British DFC, the Liberator as an aircraft and final figures of Denis's tour of operations

When you look back on your operational flying, what do you think about? After all, you were only twenty years old, in the Far East, and captaining a Liberator against a ruthless enemy. The things you did and witnessed are quite incredible in many ways.

What I have probably mentioned to you many times is that I had finished a full tour of operations by the time I was twenty-and-a-half. It's amazing to me that in such a short amount of time, I had gone from being a clerk in an electrical store to having completed a full tour as captain of a large bomber aircraft. It's amazing really. One must realise that at that stage the average age of a Liberator pilot on 159 Squadron was twenty-four-and-a-half. I think that the fact that I was so young helped me in the sense that I didn't have a fully developed sense of danger. To me, many of the operations were exciting, like with operation number fourteen; I did not have to attack those seaplanes, but to me it was all one big adventure. But trust me, I did appreciate the Japanese as a formidable enemy; I was under no illusions there.

The rest of the flying I did in the Far East seemed tame by comparison, as I wasn't actively facing the possibility of being shot down every time I took to the air.

When you were dropping bombs on places like docks, and targets within urban areas like Bangkok, there were inevitably going to be civilian casualties. Did you ever feel any guilt for what you were doing?

I find it best not to dwell on that subject, because what's done is done, and I was only doing my job. The hope was always that any loss of life would be the enemy and not civilians. I never felt guilt, but when we bombed targets in urban areas or dropped high explosive bombs, it was always in my mind that there would inevitably be civilians caught up in it all, whether killed or wounded directly from bomb blasts or during activities like manning hoses and fighting fires caused by incendiary bombs. Don't forget, being so close to London during the Blitz, I knew what it was like to be on the other side. After all, I had been blown off my bike by the blast of a bomb. Dropping napalm shocked me, due to its tremendous power and because I witnessed the target go up in flames, as a result. However, I looked upon it all as a job that had to be done; I had to comply with orders. Also, it has to be remembered that we were fighting a ferocious and fanatical enemy that was trying to kill us and many others.

You have mentioned that you lacked a fully developed sense of danger, but did you ever contemplate the possibility that you could be shot down and taken prisoner, or killed?

Yes, once or twice it happened at the beginning, before take-off, when I wondered what we were heading for. But once we were in the air, however, any doubts disappeared. One thing that I would occasionally contemplate was engine failure, a mechanical occurrence which was not common, but at the same time, wasn't unheard of. Not long after the flight commander I told you about had left 159 Squadron, another flight commander, S/Ldr John Gauntlett, was appointed in his place. S/Ldr Gauntlett had flown a tour on 159 Squadron in 1943 into 1944, serving with distinction, and had then been an instructor pilot at 1673 HCU at Kolar (where my first flight ever in a Liberator was with him) before returning to 159 Squadron to begin a second tour of operations. This friendly, but no-nonsense, senior pilot told all of us junior pilots that a Liberator could fly just as well on three engines as it could on four, and that losing one engine was no reason to abort an operation.

Ironically, on the operation following that lecture, I noticed that I was catching up with the Liberator in front of me. Their number four engine had failed – the outer engine on the starboard wing. I contacted them via radio and asked if I could be of any assistance. I received an abrupt reply from the captain, S/Ldr Gauntlett, telling me to maintain radio silence and to carry on my way independently, so that's what I did. S/Ldr Gauntlett and his crew completed their objective and made it back alright.

Honestly, at my age at the time, I almost never comprehended the possibilities of danger. I was nervous, but not fearfully so, more often than not. However, operation number four, on the night of the 2nd-3rd of November 1944, when I was screened by Sgt Ron Clift, on an operation to Bangkok, Thailand, really did scare me.

To put the possibility of losing a Liberator into context, soon after arriving at 159 Squadron in mid-October 1944, Frizzy and I asked W/Cdr Blackburn how many Liberators from 159 Squadron had been lost in the past four to five months, the average length of a tour at the time. The answer was five, all in just over the last month and a half: three downed due to the enemy and two which pranged on take-off or soon thereafter. (Going back to the beginning of 1944, two had been shot down on the 29th of February, and on the 2nd of April two crash landed after suffering battle damage).

Frizzy and I agreed that we had a decent chance of surviving, and luckily both of us did survive, but flying a Liberator against the Japanese was inherently dangerous business. Also, monsoon season weather was a formidable adversary, and then the odds of survival were poor should we have gone down over the jungle or in the vast bodies of water we flew over. Perhaps worst of all, we would have faced terrible hardship should we have been captured by the Japanese.

I have known pilots who became scared before their last-scheduled operations. For them, a superstition led to worry that, though they had survived all of their operations so far, the last-scheduled one might turn out to be when they wouldn't make it back. It did happen that men on the squadron failed to return from their final-planned operation.

Amazingly, Frizzy's Liberator wasn't hit by even a single bullet or shell, while another pilot on the squadron returned from an operation with around twenty-five bullet holes in his aircraft. In my case, I was only hit twice, a single bullet in the nose and in the bomb bay by a shell, and another time a shell fragment hit a propeller blade while I was being screened, and we came under fire from Japanese naval ships.

I was injured once, though I can't remember on which operation it was. On the journey back following a night operation, I had gone to lie down for a nap, handing over the controls to my co-pilot. I landed the aircraft, and we were transported to debriefing. My crew and I walked in, and W/Cdr Blackburn looked at me and said, 'Bloody hell, Denis, what has happened to you?' Unbeknownst to me, there was dried blood down the side of my face. While I had been sleeping, something had fallen down onto me, cutting me just above my left ear. I was brought to the Station Sick Quarters to be checked over and was taken off flying for a week. Fortunately, that's the only injury I or my crew suffered.

What did you and your crew do when you weren't flying?
It's a difficult question to answer for the simple reason that there weren't many things to do, because Digri was in quite an isolated location. We didn't even have to wash our clothes, as there was a native laundry team for that – called 'dhobi wallahs'. There was a village in the immediate area, but that was it, really. A lot of our time was spent writing letters, playing cards and also playing badminton, and occasionally my wireless operator, Jock Balnaves, and I would go out on bicycle rides. The squadron, however, did organise various activities to stimulate body and mind, as the positive benefits of engaging the brains and bodies of men stationed off the beaten path in an often-challenging environment, like Digri, was well-recognised. My crew and I were fortunate in that our time on 159 Squadron coincided with the dry season, when temperature and humidity were bearable.

Sometimes I would have to take a Liberator up for an air test to confirm that it was able to go on operations. Whether or not any of my crew would come up with me would depend on what it was being tested for.

How important was the camaraderie between you and your crew when you were flying operations, and to what extent did it contribute to your operations being successful?

It was very important. A crew functioning smoothly aboard a plane like a Liberator was like a well-oiled machine working successfully. Every piece has to do its job to keep a machine working, and it was like that with a Liberator crew. Every crew member had a specific role to play to make the flight 'successful', whether it was a combat operation or just an air test back at Digri. Communication between everyone was vital to ensure this, and if two or more people didn't get on, then that could affect the entire atmosphere inside the aircraft. Potentially negative consequences, like low morale, could lead to a disastrous outcome.

Fortunately, my crew got on very well, and to the best of my knowledge so did the other crews. However, I didn't really get on with Len Upjohn when I first met him. As I have mentioned, I lost my first navigator, as his drunken brawls and antics in Palestine became too much for his superiors, so he was taken off flying and returned to the UK. On another crew, the pilot, who was from New Zealand, became seriously ill and was returned home. Consequently, I gained the navigator from his crew; it was Len, who was twenty-four at the time. The reason why we didn't immediately get on is because Len was full of praise for his previous pilot, who was also twenty-four, and obviously Len thought that as I was only age twenty, I still had a lot to learn.

But a chance remark, however, soon improved our feelings towards each other. I had asked Len about his job prior to being called up, and his reply was that he was, 'learning the ropes,' with a firm known as 'South East Essex Electrical Supply Co'. By coincidence, I was learning the ropes with a firm known as 'North West Kent Electrical Supply Co'. Both of our firms were under the umbrella of a larger firm and were only separated by the River Thames.

Talk me through your crew. What were they like as people?

They were nice chaps, and we all got on very well. For example, Jock Balnaves, my wireless operator, was from Scotland; he was a classic example of how generous the Scots are. Len Upjohn was an

154

excellent navigator; he had outstanding accuracy and could quickly recalculate if anything went wrong, such as on my twenty-first operation, on the night of the 20th-21st of January 1945, when he recalculated dropping the mines at Victoria Point. My front turret gunner, Blondie Whittle, was excellent, as he was very accurate and really enjoyed shooting at targets. Lance Williamson, my co-pilot, was a nice chap, not fat, but heavily built - the type of guy you would want by your side in a fight. As for Sammy, my rear gunner, to this day I'm still not sure about him, as his guns did not once work when they were needed. I never heard him fire a shot at an operational target, only when the guns had to be cleared. He was thirty-one when he joined the crew, the oldest one of us all, and eleven years older than myself. Also, I am still slightly suspicious of my flight engineer. I was never happy about what happened on the way to bomb Bangkok, on the 4th of November 1944, so for the rest of the tour, I kept an eye on matters myself, via an instrument in the cockpit.

What became of your crew after the war? I know you kept in touch with Len Upjohn and Jock Balnaves.
Lance Williamson was killed in July 1945, not long after returning to the UK, when a Tiger Moth he was flying crashed. I never kept in touch with my flight engineer, but I did with Len and Jock. I met them quite a few times, and I became the godfather to Len's daughter. However, he was promoted within his job and moved to Wales, and I lost touch with him after that. I didn't remain in contact with Blondie or Sammy. Jock and I were in touch up until he passed away, which I believe was only a few years ago. I visited him in Scotland, and he visited me in Kent. He was from a town named Stanley, which is around ten miles outside of Perth.

Let's talk about Carl Fristrom, nicknamed 'Frizzy', a man who you said was your best friend during your years in the Far East. You have mentioned him quite a few times already.
He was confident, easy-going, and he had a couldn't-care-less attitude about him. Frizzy was the type of chap who one never forgets. He was so easy to get on with. I cannot think of Cox's Bazar,

on the eastern side of the Bay of Bengal, without remembering him. The only time he ran into any trouble was when he had a disagreement with George Livingstone, my post-159 Squadron co-pilot in the Far East, which resulted in Frizzy being put in a headlock. Frizzy's co-pilot and I had to pull them apart. Although Frizzy and I had been friends since meeting in Palestine, it wasn't until after operations, when we were posted to Baigachi, 24 miles northeast of Calcutta, and later to Cox's Bazar, that our friendship really became strong. During operational flying on 159 Squadron, we were each preoccupied with the responsibilities of leading our own crews on flying duties, but we would socialise in the Mess or join in activities together, such as sports.

The Penang operations were great feats. A lot of the planning and the success in mining Penang was due to W/Cdr Blackburn. What are your thoughts about these operations now, over seventy years later?
The first, on the 27th-28th of October 1944, was a great success. The second, on the 26th-27th of November 1944, was a washout, and the third, on the 23rd-24th of January 1945, was basically a repeat of the first. The organisation behind the three raids was huge. I remember W/Cdr Blackburn telling me years later that he had received very little support from senior RAF officers, or the Americans, who were convinced that it couldn't be done with Liberators. They were right, at least with the way that the Americans flew Liberators. W/Cdr Blackburn, on the other hand, had worked hard to revolutionise the Liberator's performance by reducing weight and radically altering the way the aircraft was flown. As a result, both the range of the Liberator and the payload capacity had been raised to record levels. Penang, 1,500 miles away, was a key port in the Japanese supply line and also the primary base of operations for both Japanese and German submarines in the Indian Ocean. Because of his vision, W/Cdr Blackburn saw Penang as a viable target, though his sceptics were many.

The Americans carried a larger crew than we did, which meant added weight. Our Liberators had their armoured plating removed from behind the pilots' seats, as well as all guns and turrets, except for the front and rear guns. Each RAF Liberator, stripped of excess weight, could carry the extra fuel necessary for the record-setting round-trip flights to Penang and back.

The first Penang raid, only my third operational flight, was quite a baptism of fire for me.

Honestly, I highly doubt that Penang would have happened without W/Cdr Blackburn. He had to do so much pre-planning, and a lot of the resulting success must be put down purely to his sheer force of personality. He had a forward-thinking brain and seemed to anticipate the problems we would face and to come up with solutions for them; our short runway at Digri and the extra fuel needed for round-trip flights of roughly 3,000 miles are two examples of that.

What sticks out in my mind now is that I can so vividly remember the last half an hour of our approach on the first trip. It was getting more tense by the second. As it was a completely new target, we knew little about their defensive capabilities, and we didn't even know for certain if they had radar.

The Americans were so impressed with the raid, and how it was planned and executed, that they awarded W/Cdr Blackburn their Distinguished Flying Cross. In fact, they wanted to award every crew member who took part in the operation their DFC. The RAF, however, vetoed it, so W/Cdr Blackburn accepted his DFC on behalf of the Squadron.

Why did the RAF veto it?
Quite simply, it wasn't in the nature of the RAF to hand out medals like that; they never awarded medals easily. Non-commissioned officers couldn't be awarded the British DFC; it was only for commissioned officers. Non-commissioned officers could only receive the Distinguished Flying Medal, the DFM.

How did W/Cdr Blackburn commemorate the awarding of his American DFC?
He threw a party in Calcutta, but I don't know much about it, as I wasn't able to go. I had been posted to Baigachi by that point.

In the years preceding your first meeting with him, W/Cdr Blackburn had been through a lot in his RAF career. Did he ever talk to you about any of it?

On the flying side, no. When he was on the *Laconia*, he described how close he was to being sucked down into the sea by the drag of the sinking ship. He said that he had to swim really hard that night. He never spoke about his time as a prisoner of war or being freed, either. Years later, I exchanged letters with Gordon Drain, his former navigator on 159 Squadron. In one letter, I wrote to Gordon about our squadron dropping napalm, and he told me that he remembered it due to the fact that it was the pilots who dropped it and not the navigators themselves.

While we are on the subject of medals and the DFC, weren't you supposed to be awarded the British DFC, but it never happened?

Frizzy was, too. As far as I know, each squadron on frontline duty was allowed to award one or two pilots the DFC, for things like outstanding service, outstanding flying and things like that. W/Cdr Blackburn told me after the war, when we met in Malta, that he had put both mine and Frizzy's name down for the DFC before he left for Calcutta, but that the Canadian CO who took over 159 Squadron scrubbed our names and replaced them with those of two Canadian pilots.

That's unbelievable.

Yes, and W/Cdr Blackburn was quite annoyed about it, too. At first, I was quite rankled about it, as well, as I had screened one of those Canadian pilots, but eventually I realised that there wasn't anything I could do about it. Now, it doesn't bother me.

Your willingness to take risks and to throw caution to the wind during your operational flying has been mentioned a few times already. How do you look back on it now?

I suppose I look back on it as a manifestation of a period of excitement and novelty. One story which symbolises this was when I was taxiing around the perimeter track at Digri, and I noticed that two trees were exactly opposite each other on either side of the perimeter track, which was unusual. I started to weigh up in my mind if I could fly between them and estimated that I could, just about. I asked Len Upjohn if he thought a Liberator could fit through the gap, but he saw right through me and said, 'Don't you dare, Denis! I have a wife back home!' Another one that springs to mind is when I was at Baigachi. The CO called me into his office and asked if I had been low flying again. When I said that I had not, he asked me how I accounted for all the twigs and leaves around the tail wheel.

I had a ground crew member ask me if I ever felt nervous about flying an aircraft, especially taking off and landing. 'No,' I replied; to me, it was simple and fun.

Looking back on it now, though, I can't see myself doing half the things I did back then. However, I would love to go back into the air again, I really would.

What is your standout memory from your operational flying?
The night when we bombed the railway bridge which crossed the Nakhon Chaisi River, when we escaped death so many times, both over the target and then at Chittagong, where we miraculously landed unscathed. How we made it through a balloon barrage covered in fog and then avoided a steamroller on the runway is just down to pure luck. It's unbelievable, really.

What are your thoughts on the Liberator?
The Liberator at first sight frightened me, because it looked so big. In actual fact, however, I found the controls quite easy to manipulate, and I took quite a liking to it. It did handle well. One problem I experienced was that if the autopilot was on, a blown fuse could completely throw off the autopilot, and the aircraft could end up in any position. It happened to me three times. The first two times we ended up in a half-roll before I managed to turn off the master switch that controlled the autopilot. On the third occasion, we almost ended up on our tail before I managed to turn the master switch off and fly the plane manually.

To many people, autopilot is a very modern concept, and not something that many think of as being in a Second World War aircraft. How did it work?
It had all to do with the control column and the trim of the aircraft. However the pilot had set the plane to fly, the autopilot would lock in that position. If the pilot had been flying straight-and-level, then by engaging the autopilot, that balance would be maintained. If the pilot got it wrong and turned on the autopilot when banking the aircraft, it would maintain that position.

What are the final figures for your operational flying?
I joined 159 Squadron on the 15th of October 1944, and I left on the 10th of February 1945. In that time, I did a grand total of 325 hours and 40 minutes of flying, of which 314 hours and 10 minutes were on operations. Within those operational hours, 73 hours and 50 minutes took place during daylight, and the other 240 hours and 20 minutes were flown at night. The 11 hours and 30 minutes of non-operational flying included air tests, bombing practice and taking W/Cdr Blackburn to Calcutta.

CHAPTER TEN

FLYING IN INDIA, CEYLON AND THE FAR EAST AFTER 159 SQUADRON, FEBRUARY – OCTOBER 1945

Converting to the Warwick at Baigachi, flying troops and freight from Cox's Bazar, saved by a dog, flying a Sentinel around the perimeter of the Bay of Bengal, further Warwick adventures, Dakota flying from Yelahanka, a spell in hospital, the war with Japan ends, meeting old friends and Singapore experiences

You mentioned that after finishing operational flying with 159 Squadron, you were posted to Baigachi. Though you were no longer flying on operations, the war was still going on. What was the nature of your flying during that time?
Frizzy and I were both posted to Baigachi. The aim was for us to eventually go on to Cox's Bazar and begin a system of flying passengers and freight, mainly between Cox's Bazar and Akyab. On occasion, the task would also be to fly soldiers across the Bay of Bengal to Calcutta, or to be more accurate, to Alipore, for a week's leave. However, we needed to first learn to fly the twin-engine Warwick, the main aircraft which would be used for ferrying the men and freight. Baigachi, not Cox's Bazar, was the RAF airfield where Warwick conversion training took place. The Warwick, a slightly larger version of the Wellington bomber, was primarily used for transporting supplies and military personnel.

What surprised both Frizzy and myself was a public flying display put on one day. The highlight of the display was planned to be the bombing by six Mosquito aircraft of an old Anson that was no longer being flown due to age. The Mosquitos were to shallow-dive bomb the Anson, but only with eleven-pound practice bombs.

When the time came, the first four Mosquitos released their bombs and missed the target. The fifth Mosquito came in at a steeper dive but failed to pull out and flew straight into the ground, killing both men onboard. The last Mosquito, being flown by their CO, went ahead with the 'attack', and the Anson exploded, so it seemed like he was successful with his bombing. Either that, or else the Anson was detonated from the control tower with explosives connected by wires. Who knows? I have no idea why that display was put on.

Your time at Baigachi must have been very different from your prior training at conversion units in Palestine and then at Kolar, in India, where entire crews were transitioning to a new type of aircraft. At Baigachi, it was just you and Frizzy, pilots, converting to the Warwick. In addition, at Baigachi, you were much more experienced and had completed a tour of operations. Quite right. I arrived at Baigachi with 683 hours and 45 minutes of total time in the air, including the 314 hours and 10 minutes of operational piloting on 159 Squadron. I would say that any pilot with those numbers in the book could be classified as 'experienced'. Frizzy's numbers would have been similar. We didn't have any classroom exercises at all at Baigachi. The first time I ever saw a Warwick was with Frizzy and our instructor, and we immediately began flying it. The instructor did a circuit and landing, then Frizzy followed suit and finally I did one. Frizzy and I actually began our Warwick flying on the same day as we arrived at Baigachi, the 11th of February 1945.

How did the Warwick compare to the Wellington and Liberator?
I didn't like the Warwick. It was meant to have Bristol Centaurus engines, but because of engine development and delivery problems, American Pratt & Whitney Double Wasp engines were fitted to many Warwicks, including the Mk III versions at Baigachi. The Pratt & Whitney engines, which were less powerful than the Bristol Centaurus engines, required longer propeller blades to generate the power needed for flight. This meant that when taking off, the propeller blades were only eight inches or so from the ground. Because of this, if the pilot hit a runway bump, the blades could

strike the ground and ruin the engines, in some cases, but definitely bend the blades, in all cases. On top of this, I didn't like how the Warwick handled. It's hard to describe why; I either took to a plane or I didn't.

What came next?
We were there for nine days, and in that time we just learnt how to fly the Warwick, which was the sole objective of our stay there. However, on the eighth day, with Frizzy and me at the controls, we flew our first freight run.

How many other pilots were converting to the Warwick with you?
Believe it or not, there were no other pilots there for conversion training; it was just the two of us.

What happened once the two of you had learnt to fly the Warwick?
We were posted to Cox's Bazar, where we joined 224 Group Communications Squadron. Frizzy and I each had our own Warwick. Cox's Bazar only had one runway, of around 2,000 yards in length. It was operated by the RAF and the US Army Airforce. There were no hangars; all the planes were kept out in the open. The Americans had P-51 Mustangs, P-47 Thunderbolts and six small single-engine Sentinel aircraft, which could carry three people. The RAF had our two Warwicks and three single-engine Argus aircraft, which were slightly bigger than the Sentinel and could carry four. The six Sentinels there were flown by the RAF, as we had leased them from the Americans.

From the end of March 1945 until the end of April, Frizzy and I, based at Cox's Bazar, piloted our separate Warwicks on many flights carrying freight and passengers to and fro, with Akyab being our most frequent destination. Some of the other airfields we landed at were Alipore (the destination when bringing troops on leave in Calcutta), Double Moorings and Chittagong. Although I didn't care for the Warwick, I enjoyed this opportunity to fly.

Did the British and the Americans get on well?
Yes. We socialised, though no Americans were my personal friends. The American units were situated to the north end of the runway, and our facilities were near the southern end. We would go to the US cinema and watch gun camera footage of American Mustangs shooting down Japanese planes in air combat, but regular feature films would be shown too. The Americans also had a store where we could buy just about anything we would need or could use, within reason. An establishment like this American shop really illustrated the differences in the standards of living between us and them. The Americans definitely had a lot more money and a greater opportunity to spend it, though they only had coffee, while we had tea.

During that time of transporting troops and freight, did you experience any hair-raising moments like you did on operations?
Nowhere near to the same extent as on operations, but once, the Japanese sent four Mitsubishi bombers to attack Cox's Bazar. They were each carrying a single 100-pound bomb, but their method of aiming and releasing their bombs was all wrong. They forgot that when a bomb is dropped, it doesn't fall straight down. Instead, it carries on moving forward as it falls. As a result of all this, only one bomb hit the runway, and that was on the northern end, the American side. The other three bombs went into the sea. The Americans sent up Mustangs, which shot down all four Japanese bombers. What little damage was done was repaired within a few hours, and life carried on as normal.

On another occasion, I was preparing to land at Akyab. At the time, Akyab was a busy RAF base, also used by the Americans as a staging post. There was a paved runway and a dirt runway, which were parallel to each other. We had to land on the dirt runway, as three Mustangs had crashed on the paved one. From what I heard, the three P-51s were landing one after the other, in close succession, when one of the wheels on the first Mustang came off. This resulted in the Mustang 'collapsing' and ground looping. The second crashed into the first, and the third went into the second. Fortunately, all three pilots were okay.

We came in to land on the dirt runway. I was on my final approach when for some reason I could not slow the plane, at least according to the indicated airspeed on the control panel. I went through the normal procedures but ended up landing with a big thud and at a greater speed than I should have. Once I hit the ground, I slammed on the brakes, and though I knew that the aircraft was slowing down, I was still travelling at a higher speed than I should have been at that point down the runway. I feared that we would overshoot the runway and wind up coming to a halt in the gully beyond the end of the runway. Fortunately, our speed continued to reduce, but I noticed a Dakota pulling out of the area where the planes were parked. Once I reached that area, the space was free, and I performed a manoeuvre that is the aircraft version of a handbrake turn in a car. I applied full power on the port engine while applying the brakes to the starboard engine and somehow made it into the gap and safely stopped. Completing that manoeuvre without pranging was pure luck.

Did you find out what the problem was with the speed dial?
Yes, a bird had been impaled onto the pitot tube, which resulted in a false reading on the airspeed indicator. There was nothing wrong with the dial itself; the impaled bird just resulted in a false reading.

There are two incidents I forgot to mention, which I believe took place on the 20th and 21st of March 1945. The first was when I beat up Digri, my old operational airfield, after I had volunteered to deliver a parcel there. A 'beat up' is when a pilot flies in low across an airfield. As I approached Digri, I came down to around 300 feet and roared over the airfield, but then my starboard engine failed, causing me no problems in the air. I came around and landed without incident, but taxiing proved more difficult, as I had to open up the functioning port engine to move forward and then steer against the resulting turn to starboard; in this manner, the Warwick proceeded in a zig-zagging motion. The ground crew managed to fix the starboard engine, I returned to base and fortunately I didn't face any punishment.

The next day, I was returning to Cox's Bazar from Akyab with freight when for some reason I decided it would be fun to come in on my final approach from a really low height. I ended up flying below tree height; I know this, as I couldn't see the runway. At the last second I hopped over the trees, and it was then that I saw a crashed P-47 Thunderbolt on the runway, with the ground crew trying to extract the pilot. I said some explicit words and went into a steep climb, up to circuit height, and waited for the Thunderbolt to be cleared off the runway before landing.

You must have faced serious repercussions for that incident.
Yes, as soon as I landed I knew I was in serious trouble. In fact, the CO came right up to the aircraft; he was furious. When my crew and I came out of the aircraft, he immediately asked who was piloting it. I told him it was me, and he proceeded to tell me of the repercussions I could face and how he could easily strip me of my rank. He then told me to report to his house that evening in my 'best blue', which meant that my official uniform had to be spotless. His house, which was a bungalow, was around two miles away.

That evening, I went to his bungalow. It was dark, I had no torch and I was quite nervous. I arrived and knocked on the door, and he told me to enter. I saluted him, and it was at this point that I noticed he had a dog, an Alsatian. I gestured to it, and it started to wag its tail. When the dog came over to me, I began to pat its head. The CO told me that the dog obviously liked me and asked me if I had one back home. This turned into a conversation about dogs, which lasted for quite a while.

Eventually though, the incident was brought up. I told him that I had no idea that the Thunderbolt was there, and had I known, I would never have done what I did. He gave me some stern warnings, and that was that. Looking back on it now, I'm sure that what worked in my favour was the dog liking me, the conversation about dogs and the fact that I looked so young. Even now, I can't really get over it; I went there to be reprimanded and ended up talking about dogs.

Though the number of hair-raising situations was significantly less than on operational flying, didn't you actually fly one operational flight during your time at Cox's Bazar?
Yes, it took place on the 23rd of March 1945. Frizzy and I had to deliver chemicals to Imphal, in India, but he opted out of it. I was

entitled to have an escort there and back, because we were told that we would be flying into airspace that was still within range of Japanese fighters.

As I climbed away from Cox's Bazar, a Hurricane joined me on my starboard side, but after about ten minutes, the pilot called me up on the radio to tell me that he was running low on fuel and so was going to return to base.

Also, this Warwick had a turbo fitted to each engine. This was a system designed to boost engine power. A dial in the cockpit, when activated, would gradually close off a pipe carrying the engine exhaust gases, and those gasses would be diverted back to the engine for added power. The dial went from one to ten, depending on how much extra power the pilot wanted. The reason for the turbo being fitted to this Warwick was that the aircraft would have to climb to 10,000 feet to cross over a range of mountains, and the engines needed the turbo boost to gain the necessary altitude. Most, if not all, of our flying during this stage took place at around 1,000 feet or so, where a turbo was not needed.

Did the set-up of transporting troops operate smoothly?

As I have mentioned, our instructions were, in part, to set up a system for getting front-line soldiers to India for a week's leave, and then to return them to their unit. Frizzy and I would both depart from Cox's Bazar, but we would fly to different airfields. Frizzy would fly to Chittagong, and I would fly to Akyab. Our final destination on some of these flights was Alipore. During any stopovers, Frizzy and I were free to do as we wished, as long as we transported the troops on time.

The system worked quite well for a few weeks, during which time we got several hundred battle-weary soldiers away from the front line. But, as you can imagine, the inevitable happened when Frizzy's Warwick became unserviceable through engine failure. The replacement had to come from the UK, but no Warwick was immediately available. At the beginning of our Warwick assignment, Frizzy and I agreed that if one of our aircraft became unserviceable, its pilot would not harass the other pilot to fly his aircraft. Therefore, I continued flying my Warwick while Frizzy was stuck on the ground, only able to fly the single-engine planes that were available. Eventually, Frizzy begged me to let him do a run in my Warwick. Fortunately for him, I was assigned a trip to take non-military passengers to Akyab but to return to Cox's Bazar empty, so I suggested to Frizzy that he be my co-pilot on the way there, and then on the way back he would fly the plane with me as his co-pilot.

The war in Burma was a hard and brutal conflict. Did you ever speak to any of the soldiers that you transported?
No, aside from the odd chit chat as they were getting on and off the aircraft. But the topic of the war was never mentioned.

What was life like for you in the few months that you were stationed at Cox's Bazar?
I enjoyed myself. There was a really relaxed atmosphere; it lacked strict formality.

Frizzy and I were the only ones who were allowed to fly the Warwick. In forty-three days, between the 17th of March and the 28th of April 1945, I made thirty-three Warwick flights over twenty-one days of flying. On nine dates, I made two separate flights, and once I made three flights in a single day.

When I wasn't flying, I spent a lot of time playing cards, relaxing on the beach (which was very close by), watching films in the cinema, socialising, and things like that. One amusing event that stands out is the time when nurses being transported along the beach in a jeep whistled at me as I sunbathed.

Strangely, I was the only one I can remember who enjoyed swimming in the sea. Very few of the other chaps ever went in, and if they did, it was just for a quick dip.

With Frizzy's plane stuck on the ground as a result of its engine failure, what happened to the troop transportation service?
It still operated, but the service was reduced. I took up some of the slack before my plane became unserviceable due to it having to have its fabric surfaces recovered and sprayed with a chemical, which stopped insects from eating away at it.

What did the two of you do, seeing as there were no big planes to fly?

I took the Warwick to Cawnpore on the 4th of May, for the fabric maintenance work to be carried out, but there was no aircraft to take me back, so I was stuck in Cawnpore for a few days. A random Dakota showed up, and I hitched a lift. We stopped in Calcutta, so I checked in to accommodation at the Salvation Army, and there Frizzy was, but he looked ill, all shaken up, and he wasn't himself. He proceeded to tell me that while I was away a new Warwick had been sent to Cox's Bazar to replace his. He allowed his co-pilot to do the acceptance test, with himself aboard, but on landing his co-pilot crashed straight into stanchions, which were big iron pillars embedded in front of the control tower to protect it. The plane was a write-off, and the co-pilot was seriously injured and needed several weeks of hospital treatment. Frizzy came away from it with minor injuries, but he was suffering from complete shock. He had been sent to Kathmandu, Nepal, to a place where they dealt with cases involving a loss of nerve and other psychological issues. But when I met him in Calcutta, he was awaiting a plane which would take him back to Australia.

I could not believe that all of this had happened in the short time I was away. At Alipore, a small plane had been sent from Cox's Bazar to get me back there, and Frizzy came with me to sort out his belongings. A few of us threw him a small going-away party. One memory that really sticks out in my mind is that George Livingstone, my co-pilot who had previously held Frizzy in that headlock, poured him a drink and the two of them made up. I was really happy to see that. The next day, I accompanied Frizzy back to Calcutta. In Calcutta, he was to await his flight, which would be the beginning of his journey back to Australia. We both knew that we would probably never meet again, so it was quite emotional. Both of us were almost in tears.

Did you keep in contact with Frizzy?

We kept in touch for a while. He soon left the Royal Australian Air Force, got married and began working as a pilot, flying small planes that sprayed crops. We eventually lost touch. But a few years ago, around 2010, a chap was writing a book on notable figures from the war, and W/Cdr Blackburn was one of them. He put adverts in newspapers and on the Internet, and Frizzy saw this, wrote in with what he knew about W/Cdr Blackburn and mentioned me. A few years later, a chap who lived on the same street as I did saw that Frizzy had mentioned me and brought it to my attention. I managed to acquire Frizzy's phone number, but when I rang, his wife answered and told me that he had died the previous year. That really upset me.

How did you spend your time in Calcutta, it seems like you spent a good amount of time there?
I would check into my Salvation Army accommodation, which back then was one rupee a night, at a time when the exchange rate was fourteen point something rupees to the pound. By the way, in the Calcutta Salvation Army, they had quite a set-up of single rooms, and they served breakfast. Non-military personnel could stay there too. If the guest couldn't stump up the rupee, he could still get a single room without breakfast for a cheaper price. If he couldn't afford the room, then he could pay an even cheaper rate for a shared accommodation, with many others in the same room and on the floor; each would get a cup of tea and a biscuit with that arrangement, as well. But if he couldn't afford that, then the cheapest option was to pay for a spot on one of the support beams, which were situated on the bottom floor. There, it was possible to sleep by draping one's arms over a beam and leaning on it. During the monsoon season the Salvation Army lodging was absolutely packed, especially the bottom floor, where the beams were situated.

When I wasn't there, I mainly spent my time relaxing and shopping, buying clothes and whatnot. While I certainly saw others in uniform, I didn't really sense a big military presence in Calcutta at the time.

Soon after you had dropped Frizzy off, you had to fly all the way around the Bay of the Bengal.
A signal came through to Cox's Bazar saying that our six Sentinels and three Argus aircraft had to be taken to Yelahanka, in southern

India, along a route around the northern edge of the Bay of Bengal, then southward down the east coast of India before ultimately ending in south central India. On the 21st of May 1945, the day before these flights were scheduled to begin, I had flown a doctor to Akyab in an Argus, and I didn't know anything about the signal until I returned to Cox's the next day, the 22nd.

The first leg of the 1,400-mile journey was to Chittagong, and the second leg was from Chittagong to Alipore, in Calcutta. The ensuing legs were from Alipore to Cuttack, Cuttack to Vizagapatam, Vizagapatam to Gannavaram, onward to Donakonda, then to Madras and finally due west, inland, from Madras to Yelahanka, on the north side of Bangalore in the interior of southern India. It was a lot of flying.

On the 23rd, on the leg to Vizagapatam, while flying a Sentinel solo, I started getting light-headed from heatstroke and knew I had to get down quickly. I remembered that several airfields had been built in the region, but the one I could see was covered with cattle. I remembered a salt flat that I had seen from the air, so I flew there and carefully landed. I taxied close to a small bungalow that I had seen, and then passed out.

A while later, I awoke to noise - a load of angry men had appeared, brandishing big sticks. When I saw this, I restarted the engine and started spinning the plane at full throttle with the right rudder pedal pushed as far as it could go. This caused the plane to spin in a circle, kicking up dust and salt and keeping everyone away. At that point, an Anglo-Indian chap, an inspector type of person, stepped forward and calmed everyone down. He invited me to his house and told me that I should lie down and sleep. When we arrived at his bungalow, he offered me a drink of whisky or brandy, or something like that, and I was quickly asleep. When I woke up, I was in a lovely bed, and in pyjamas that his servants had put me in. I got dressed and went to speak with the chap. He let me phone Madras, which was where the big regional RAF offices were. I gave them my position and informed them that I needed fuel to replace what I had lost while searching for a landing site.

That night, we sat down and ended up talking about the future of India. He told me that it was inevitable that the British would have to pull out of India within a few years, and that the British occupation of India was unsustainable. What also became apparent was that he didn't like the British system of rule. He made intelligent arguments, and what he said made a lot of sense. He had a way of making his point without insulting people and was capable of strong arguments regarding the British leaving India, which in time proved to be quite accurate. I liked him and recognised that he was an intelligent man.

The next day, word came from Madras that a plane would be coming in with a five-gallon fuel drum. I decided to make life easier for the incoming plane, so I laid out around twelve turbans in the shape of a runway. Before the plane arrived, however, the wind changed direction, so I had to move them all to align with the wind.

When the Sentinel landed, I was surprised to see that there were two pilots. The idea was that the second pilot would take over my plane and I would be the passenger. I strongly objected, and it was agreed that I would carry on flying my Sentenel. Once the plane was refuelled, I took off and headed for Vizagapatam. I started to feel dizzy again but managed to reach the airfield and land, but there was not a soul to be found. I exited the aircraft, walked into town and went to the hospital. I was there for three days. They wanted me to stay longer, but I left and walked alone back to the airfield. From there, I conducted a pre-flight inspection of the plane and found that a bird's nest had begun to be built in the air intake. I cleared that and took off for Gannavaram, and from there I continued on to Donakonda, where I stopped to refuel. I continued to St. Thomas Mount, which was the airfield that serviced Madras. I was there for two days, where I spent most of my time swimming. I then finally made it to Yelahanka on the 29th of May.

What was the objective of this flight path?
That puzzled all of us taking part. Those aircraft were intended to be used as air ambulances to get injured people out of the jungle. Yelahanka, being in the centre of southern India near Bangalore, was nowhere near the jungle or the war zone. As it turned out, there was a miscommunication somewhere along the line, as those aircraft were supposed to go to Rangoon, which by that stage had been liberated from the Japanese.

On the 5th of June 1945, I began the 1,400-mile flight back to Cox's Bazar in the same Sentinel I had delivered to Yelahanka. The flightpath was identical to the outward-bound journey, minus my unintended emergency stopover between Cuttack and Vizagapatam on the 23rd of May. I arrived back at Cox's Bazar on the 9th.

It was quite an adventure, flying all the way around the Bay of Bengal, then back again, along the same route. I was supposed to go on to Rangoon, but I stayed at Cox's Bazar.

Why didn't you go all the way to Rangoon?
The reason is that another Warwick had been delivered to Cox's Bazar, with instructions that as the only pilot available to fly it, I was to do the acceptance test. The aircraft had to pass before it could be 'taken on strength' onto the squadron – that is, officially added to our flying roster. So, while all the other aircraft and personnel from our unit were on the way to Rangoon, I stayed behind to do the acceptance testing on the 9th of June 1945.

At the end of the actual flight test, after being given permission to land, I lowered the undercarriage lever, presuming that the landing gear would drop, in preparation to land. However, there was a problem. Three green indicators were supposed to light up, showing that the undercarriage had dropped and locked in place, but they didn't light up. Also, a loud horn sounded to signal that the undercarriage had not come down. Therefore, I aborted the landing, raised the undercarriage lever, did another circuit, and once again went through the preparations to land, but the same thing happened - the undercarriage wouldn't register as being properly lowered.

I contacted the control tower and told them that I wanted to slowly fly past with my undercarriage lever down, so that they could see if the landing gear appeared fully extended, partially deployed or still in the 'up' position. They agreed to my plan, and following my pass, they told me that the wheels appeared to be down, but that they couldn't be certain.

I then asked for permission to do a 'fast landing', in which I would come in fast, with the undercarriage supposedly down, then purposefully hit the wheels hard on the runway, the idea being that the bump would dislodge anything that might be interfering with the electrical system. Permission was given. It was a dangerous manoeuvre, especially as the tips of the propellers were so close to the ground, as I have already mentioned. I decided to do it anyway. As I approached the runway, I lowered the undercarriage lever to the down position, but once again no green lights were showing and the horn was blaring. However, when I banged the wheels on the runway, the green lights lit up and the horn stopped blowing, so I did another circuit and landed, and the plane was accepted onto the squadron.

Was there anyone else on board that Warwick with you?
It wasn't just me on that Warwick. There was also an RAF corporal and a young chap who had only recently been called up. The corporal was apparently quite the boxer. When the horn was going off and it became apparent that something was going wrong, the young chap completely panicked and tried to open the door in order to jump out. The corporal ended up knocking him out.

The day after the acceptance test, you flew to Ramree Island, which is on the coast of Burma and about 170 miles southeast of Cox's Bazar. It was on this island that you had the most unbelievable encounter.
Oh, yes. On the 10th of June 1945, I took passengers to Kyaukpyu airfield on Ramree Island for a meeting. I was to wait at Ramree until another plane arrived, and then it was planned that I would take its passengers back to Cox's Bazar. However, the monsoon weather had other ideas. We managed to land just as the monsoon broke. The runway, which was built from coconut matting and PSP, interlocking segments of pierced steel planking, was obviously hit by a lot of rain, which caused it to flood, and as a result it became lumpy and uneven. It also caused the PSP to buckle.

So we were stuck at Kyaukpyu airfield, and it was there that I had the most unlikely of encounters. The fact that I met this person on that tiny island was so improbable that it's almost the stuff of fiction. One day, I heard a voice asking if he could come in the aircraft and have a look around, as he had never seen a Warwick before. My head shot up as I recognised his voice. It was Clive Woods, a man I had worked with in the electrical showrooms back in Kent. We had not seen each other in four years, since I was sixteen. A lot had changed since then. It must have been quite a sight for him, as I was just in my underwear due to the fact that it was so hot and humid. He asked me if I was named Elliott, which I confirmed. This conversation took place in the cockpit. He proceeded to ask me if I was the wireless operator, and I said no. Then he went through all of the positions one can have in an aircraft before finally arriving at pilot. He didn't believe that I was a pilot, so I told him that when he got the runway fixed I would show him who flew the plane. He declined my offer.

He was an airfield engineer. Originally, he was an air gunner, but a nasty leg injury on an operational flight put an end to that.

Even now, I find it unbelievable that I met him on a small island on the coast of Burma.

How long were you there?
We were there for four days. We arrived on the 10th of June and left on the 14th. The passengers we had arrived with were taken to accommodation, and we were stuck in our Warwick for four days. Clive was kind enough to keep us supplied with food, water, books and things like that during our time stuck there. We read the books, played cards and just tried to find ways to pass the time. There wasn't much else to do, as it was monsoon weather, which meant heavy rain and strong winds. After four days, the rains eased off, so the PSP was replaced, and we were able to take off. I never saw Clive again.

What happened with the two groups of passengers?
The ones who were coming from Rangoon were taken directly to Cox's Bazar, in a Dakota. The passengers we took to Ramree Island stayed there. I flew with an empty plane back to Cox's Bazar to pick up passengers to take to Akyab.

During your time flying Warwicks, Germany surrendered. Were there any celebrations where you were?
No, the war with Japan was still raging, so everything carried on as normal for us.

After Ramree Island, your time with the Warwick was coming to an end.

I only flew the Warwick three more times after leaving Ramree Island: Cox's Bazar to Akyab, and back, covered the first two, on the 16th of June, and the last time was a big trip going to Alipore, starting at Cox's, which was on the 21st of June. We flew from Cox's Bazar to Chittagong, only around 55 miles north of Cox's Bazar. From Chittagong, we flew to an American airfield in Calcutta named Dum Dum, and then on to Alipore, also in Calcutta. Once at Alipore, I handed over the Warwick to another British pilot, who was taking it to Cawnpore. From Alipore, we took a train on a two-day journey to Bangalore, in the centre of southern India. An RAF vehicle met us there and then took us to Yelahanka, on the northern outskirts of Bangalore.

Until mid-October 1945, I was stationed at Yelahanka. On the 7th of July, Flying Officer Horler, with myself as co-pilot, set out from Yelahanka to fly a Dakota to Santa Cruz, in Bombay, but the flight was aborted due to bad weather, and we returned to Yelahanka. We tried the next day, but once again bad weather forced us to abort the journey. We finally completed the flight to Santa Cruz on the 11th. On the way, I asked the navigator what the date was, and he told me that it was the 11th of July. I realised that it was my twenty-first birthday. The navigator insisted that we celebrate, and fortunately there was a crate of canned beer on board. Everyone in the crew got a can, but when we opened them, beer sprayed everywhere. Still, we managed to drink the beer that remained in the cans.

On the 14th, we came back to Yelahanka with an important passenger, Air Commodore the Earl of Bandon. To my surprise, W/Cdr Blackburn had sent me a very nice fountain pen, which was waiting for me upon my return to base. Knowing that he was still in Calcutta, I was able to write to him to express my thanks.

Our next trip was the following day, the 15th of July. We took the Earl of Bandon from Yelahanka to Kandy, in Ceylon, to meet Lord Louis Mountbatten, then an Admiral and also Supreme Allied Commander South East Asia Command. I didn't fly the aircraft though; Flying Officer Horler did. The Earl of Bandon was in the co-pilot's seat, and I was in the third seat. Approaching Kandy, from my vantage point, I noticed that both had forgotten to put the undercarriage down, so I leaned forward without saying a word and pushed the lever down that lowered the undercarriage, and then I pushed the small lever that locked the undercarriage in place; they didn't notice. If I had not done so, then we would have crash-landed. Imagine the sight, had that happened: the Earl of Bandon arriving to meet Lord Mountbatten, and the aircraft the Earl is in crash-lands!

What did you do during the duration of the meeting?
Leaving the Earl to his duties, we left Kandy on the same day to fly passengers to Ratmalana, also on Ceylon, and then returned to Kandy the next day to collect the Earl.

On the 17th of July, with the Earl of Bandon again in the co-pilot's seat, we flew the 250 miles from Kandy to Madurai, in India. From Madurai we flew to Chettinad, a journey of 50 miles, and then returned to Madurai. I can only assume that the flight to Chettinad was to take passengers. The next day we took the Earl 225 miles northward, back to Yelahanka.

The rest of July was taken up with three round trips from base to Santa Cruz and back, a little over 500 miles in each direction. It doesn't sound too eventful, but on the 19th I was scheduled to captain a Dakota for the first time, because a second Dakota had been delivered to base. On the same day, FO Horler was detailed to take fourteen officers to Santa Cruz, while I was to take fourteen non-commissioned officers to Santa Cruz. We had heard that there was a storm on our route, so I decided to fly out over the Arabian sea and approach Bombay from the sea. Horler's Dakota, however, had become unserviceable, so the CO put all of his passengers onto my plane, leaving me with twenty-eight passengers, instead of the fourteen that I was meant to carry. As a result, some of them had to sit on the floor. On every flight in a Dakota, so far, I had only been the co-pilot; I had not flown, landed or taken off once in a Dakota. I went to see the CO and told him all of this. In a calm and laid back manner, and showing incredible faith in my abilities, he looked me in the eye and said, 'Oh, you'll manage.' I don't know why he didn't just order FO Horler to fly my Dakota.

How did the flight go?

Before I left, FO Horler told me not to forget to set the elevator trim to number four. That positioned the tab on the tail at the correct angle for take-off. One thing I do recall is that after all of the passengers were onboard, while I was walking down the length of the plane checking the passengers off against my list, a squadron leader asked me if I would be flying the plane, which I confirmed. He then asked me my age, and I replied that I was twenty-one. The squadron leader then wished to know how many hours I had flown. I told him the number, and he turned to the chap sitting next to him and said something like, 'He has already flown more hours than I have in my entire career.' Fortunately, the flight went well and was a complete success.

The rest of July just involved flying to Santa Cruz and back three times and was without incident.

Was August as uneventful as the second half of July was?

August was a busy month that involved criss-crossing India, but the flying, with me as captain, was largely routine.

However, one thing did happen. I previously mentioned the time that I flew a Sentinel around the Bay of Bengal and had to perform an emergency landing on a salt flat due to the onset of heatstroke. Well, the same thing happened again on the 8th of August. I was taking fourteen passengers to Santa Cruz from Hakimpet, just north of Hyderabad in the interior of the country. We were cruising along nicely, when I started feeling off. My co-pilot, George Livingstone, who had fought and then made up with Frizzy, took over the controls. I went and sat next to the navigator and promptly passed out. When I awoke, I made my way back to the cockpit, sat down in the co-pilot's seat and discovered that George was preparing to land. He could fly an aircraft well but had never actually landed a Dakota. I noticed that he was rounding out at too high an altitude, so I leaned over, took over the controls, landed the aircraft and then promptly passed out again.

What happened once you had landed?

An ambulance was called, and I was taken to Bombay Military Hospital, where I spent several days. During that time my health improved. I was eating good food, and the hospital itself was of high quality. What happened next is that a brigadier general in charge came and spoke to me; he was furious. He told me that I had been doing too much flying, had not been eating enough and that he was going to contact my CO and tell him that I was not to fly at all until I had passed a full RAF medical. He did have a point, as I was no more than eight-and-a-half stone and had been flying extensively, and without a break, for months, since my 159 Squadron tour of operations had finished.

Did the medical take place at the hospital?
No, once I was discharged from the hospital, I was taken as a passenger back to Yelahanka and was then taken into Bangalore to have the medical.

Another Dakota had been delivered, and it needed to be air tested. I wanted to do the testing, so I nagged and nagged my CO, but he said that I couldn't fly until the results of my medical came through. So I told him that I had passed and that the results were in the post, when in actual fact I had no idea if I had passed or not. He relented and on the 19th of August told me that I had twenty minutes to complete the air test, but I went up for nearly two-and-a-half-hours. Fortunately, the letter confirming that I had passed my medical arrived while I was in the air.

Did you face any punishment for exceeding the twenty-minute limit by nearly two hours?
No, fortunately I didn't. My CO during that time only really cared about the paperwork side. Flying didn't interest him; he hated it, though he did know how to fly aircraft.

Two events took place on the 6th and 9th of August 1945 that changed the world forever, the dropping of two nuclear bombs, 'Little Boy' and 'Fat Man', on Hiroshima and Nagasaki, respectively. Do you remember where you were when news came through of these new weapons, and the effect the news had on everyone?
During that time, I was here, there, and everywhere, so I can't remember exactly where I was when the first bomb was dropped, though I was in hospital when the second atomic bomb was dropped.

Although the bombs had been dropped thousands of miles away, they affected all of us, as their devastating impact virtually brought the war to a close. In our minds, the end of the war was a forgone conclusion after the atomic bombs were dropped, even before the Japanese surrender was announced, as there was no way that the Japanese could carry on after that.

Prior to the bombs being dropped and the subsequent surrender announcement, the Japanese were still waging war in the Far East, with no end in sight, and it was in the backs of our minds that we could be dragged into that with all the risks that it would have entailed. In fact, before the surrender, I received a signal via the adjutant of 224 Group Communications Squadron giving me instructions to report to another Liberator squadron for a second tour of duty. However, that was soon followed by another signal informing me to ignore the first signal and to await further instructions. I was relieved that I wouldn't have to face a second tour of Liberator combat flying, with its inherent dangers. About a week after both atomic bombs had been dropped, word came through that Japan had surrendered.

In September, purely by chance, a funny thing occurred. At Yelahanka, there was a long table in the Mess where we ate our meals. At breakfast time, I said to a chap that I wanted porridge, as opposed to cornflakes. Then I heard a voice a few feet away say, 'Are you sure you don't want cornflakes?' It was my friend, Ron, from Southern Rhodesia pilot training days. After Southern Rhodesia, he had gone on to a Spitfire training unit at the same time as I was on Wellingtons. Anyway, I had an air test that day, so I took him up in my Dakota. He was amazed at its speed.

Later on, Ron and I were in the cinema when a message appeared on the screen, telling me that I had to go to the foyer. So I went with Ron and was met by the CO. He told me that I had to go pick up four airmen at the Sergeants' Mess and drive them to the airfield in an RAF vehicle, the British equivalent of a US jeep. I apologised and told him that I couldn't do it, as I had never driven a car before. He looked at me and said, 'Oh, you'll manage' - his exact response after I had expressed my concerns at captaining a Dakota for the first time.

Of the few vehicles parked and available, the CO didn't exactly remember which one he wanted me to drive, but he told me that the second half of the number plate began with 7. So Ron and I went to the Mess, found what we thought was the correct vehicle and then picked up the airmen, but except when I managed to reach third gear at the end of the short trip, I didn't get above first gear. My driving was bad. Whilst we were stuck in first gear, one of the airmen said something like, 'Does this thing only have one bloody gear?' My reply was something like, 'Well do any of you know how to drive?' As it transpired, none of us knew how to drive. Between us, we could fly a wide variety of aircraft, but we couldn't drive a car. It was quite amusing, really.

How did the car hold up? Gears weren't synchronised back then. It transpired that I did damage the gearbox. I know this, because the next day the station engineer complained that someone had damaged the gears in his car. Not only that, but it wasn't even his car that I was supposed to drive.

It's quite amusing that you had completed a tour of operations and had flown a good number of aircraft, many times in quite demanding conditions, yet you didn't know how to drive a car. Yes, I know, but the flying by this stage was much the same: crossing India, with a few stops in some other countries in the region. For example, we did have a few stops in a place called Morib, which is in Malaya, not long after the Japanese surrendered.

The most exciting thing in the first part of September as far as flying was concerned was when a tyre blew up upon landing at Mingaladon, the airfield that serviced Rangoon. We ended up swerving off the runway. No one was injured, and the aircraft was fine, but the whole wheel had to be replaced.

Anyway, the war was over at this point. The Japanese had surrendered, including in Malaya, and there were not any wild celebrations after the Japanese surrender from what I saw; things carried on as normal.

Didn't you also meet Laurie, your friend from the troopship to South Africa in 1942?

Yes. Since we had parted ways when I disembarked from the troopship in Durban, we had kept in touch via letters. He had become a tank commander and had fought in North Africa. By this stage, he had been posted to Delhi, in India, so we arranged to meet. At Yelahanka, there was an urgent parcel that needed transporting to Delhi, so I volunteered to deliver it. Dakotas also had autopilot, so for the much of the flight I had it on, and my crew and I sat in the back and played cards. Every once in a while I would go into the cockpit to make sure that the slight oil leak in the starboard engine wasn't causing any problems. As long as the oil pressure remained within limits, I could just carry on. Of course, if it had dropped, I would have needed to land somewhere, but fortunately, it remained within limits.

I was so determined to reach Delhi while Laurie was there that I contacted the airfield we were supposed to stop at for refuelling and told them that I was going to continue on to Delhi. I made it to Delhi with not much fuel to spare. Once there, I found a mechanical fault, so the plane would be down for maintenance, giving us another day in Delhi. Afterwards, I went to the army camp, which was quite large, and was told where to find Laurie, but he wasn't to be found in the Nissen hut where he was billeted. Another chap told me that he had gone to the cinema, so I left a note saying that I would be in Delhi until tomorrow and that he should come to the airfield. He read my note, and we met up the next day and went to the cinema. All of this happened between the 30th of August and the 1st of September, only a day before the Japanese officially surrendered.

Laurie and I met after the war too; we returned to Britain at roughly the same time and met up in Farnborough.

Not long after meeting up with Laurie in Delhi, I became the co-pilot of a F/Lt Stephens, who became our flight commander. I flew in the co-pilot's seat on seven trips with F/Lt Stephens between the 7th and 16th of September 1945, although the only reason I was in the co-pilot's position, and not the captain's seat, was because he held a higher rank than me.

Before we move on from your time in India, I would like to ask you something. You left India in 1945, and in 1947 India gained independence from Britain and went through a period of horrific violence as Pakistan became an independent country. During your time in India, did you notice anything that gave an indication of what was to come?

The name Gandhi comes to mind. He and other Indian leaders had stirred up quite a lot of anti-British sentiment during the war period. There was definitely an anti-British feeling in India at the time. I got the feeling that it was worse in southern India, such as in Bangalore, and that sort of area. However, I never felt unsafe.

The violence in India, once it erupted, was generally along religious lines, though I can't say that I sensed any ill-feeling or witnessed violence between people of different religions.

As you mentioned, the Japanese officially surrendered on the 2nd of September 1945. Without a war to fight, did the role of the RAF in the Far East change, and if so, how did it affect you?

Although I was only in the region for a few months after the war, the discipline, adherence to hierarchy and formality seemed to continue. However, without the need to help fight a war, or to supply a war, things changed in the sense that I was carrying passengers to places like Burma, Sumatra, Java, Malaya and Singapore as part of the plan to reclaim control of our colonies and reinstate our influence in the region.

For example, British troops arrived at Morib, Malaya, to reclaim control and to either fight or take the surrender of the Japanese troops stationed there. I do have strong memories of that. On the 11th of September, we flew from Rangoon to Morib. Before going there, we were issued with pistols, while the ground crew were armed with rifles. When we were coming in to land, we had to have our pistols ready, as we had no idea what reception we were going to receive. Even though the Japanese at Morbid had already surrendered, they completely outnumbered the British personnel, so it was always in the back of our minds that they could revolt. Fortunately, everything worked out okay.

We were later told that when British forces landed on the beach closest to Morib, the Japanese had four divisions there.

Thirteen days after the Japanese officially surrendered, you flew to Kallang airfield in Singapore for the first time.

I believe we went there to deliver mail and spent most of the day there. We delivered mail across the region a few times.

The city wasn't bombed out, though there was damage in places. Still, despite that, it was very noticeable that Singapore was an opulent city, but one thing I noticed was that morale was very low among the local people. My only theory to explain this was that they realised that they had an awkward few years of rebuilding ahead of them.

What was outstanding right from the start was the high cost of living in Singapore. We were issued with tins of cigarettes, and many of the men would sell theirs or exchange them for other goods. In a way, cigarettes were a form of currency.

The standout memory of my first time in Singapore was when four of us went into the bar at the famous Raffles Hotel and asked what they were serving for drinks. Just then, a young man appeared and told us that we couldn't be served. I asked why. He looked us up and down and informed us that because we were wearing jungle greens, we were not suitably attired and therefore wouldn't be served. I then asked if we could get a glass of water, but we were told that we couldn't. What was amazing about it was that as this was going on, Japanese prisoners of war were being marched past outside.

The flight sergeant in charge of the ground crew asked me if I liked boxing, and I told him that I enjoyed watching it. He informed me that there were three fairgrounds in Singapore, one of which specialised in boxing, so if we had time and boxing fights were scheduled, we would go and watch. There would always be a few fights of different weight classes. One bout which stands out was a heavyweight contest, two big chaps. One had the other against the ropes and threw an uppercut from the waist with such power that it launched his opponent out of the ring.

What was happening with the Japanese prisoners of war during your time in the region?

They were slowly being shipped back to Japan. They were also used as manual labour. Morib had a dirt airstrip, and the first time I landed there was after heavy rains; we sank into the mud. It was Japanese prisoners of war who dug out our Dakota.

After being extricated from the mud, we were shown to our accommodation, which was very bare, so a few of us went to look for furniture. We had come out of a hut and were walking back when we came face-to-face with a king cobra that was coming from the opposite direction. Once it saw us, it reared up, so we started to throw things at it, which caused it to seek shelter in a shed. An army chap then marched past with a group of Japanese prisoners of war. One of our party asked him if we could borrow his rifle, to which he obliged. The rest of us took shelter behind trees as he went into the shed and blindly shot into the area where he heard movement, and by sheer luck he blew the snake's head off. The bullet ended up embedded in the tree I was hiding behind.

Were there any interactions with the Japanese prisoners?
Not by me. The only time I saw any Japanese prisoners was when they got our Dakota out of the mud, on the occasion with the king cobra and when we were in the Raffles Hotel. But on the occasion when we first landed at Morib, when we were dug out by Japanese prisoners of war, a funny thing did occur. Upon surrendering, the Japanese had handed over the tools and items that they had been issued with. From this collection, we could take whatever we wanted. One of the officers in our group took a counterweight scale and exclaimed, 'I have always wondered how much my testicles weigh,' and then and there he got them out and weighed them.

What a sight that must have been.
There was a ring of us standing around him and watching, we were really surprised. It was quite funny; a lot of us were in stitches. When he had finished, he asked if anyone else wanted a go, but we all declined.

For a very short time, before being stationed in Malaya, you were based at Kallang, in Singapore.
Yes. I arrived at Kallang on the 1st of October 1945 and was there until the 14th of October. An air test on the 8th of October was the

only flight I did during that two-week period, so a lot of time was spent exploring Singapore and watching the boxing matches at the fairground whenever they were on, as I mentioned earlier. We didn't visit all three fairgrounds that were in Singapore, just two: the one with the boxing and another, which I believe was run by Chinese, or maybe Malayans. They put on plays in their own language. There was one time when we misinterpreted something and began to applaud, which drew the attention of the crowd, as we had been applauding at the wrong time.

I just want to clarify something before we move on. You have spoken about transporting passengers during that period of flying. Can I assume that they were all armed forces personnel and not civilians?
Yes. The passengers were armed forces personnel, with the overwhelming majority being from the RAF; the rest were from the army. The only exception was a civilian doctor I took to Akyab.

CHAPTER ELEVEN

STATIONED IN MALAYA, OCTOBER 1945 – MARCH 1946

Kuala Lumpur, flying wounded personnel out of Batavia, perceptions of personal danger, a murder, Denis's challenging last flight in the Far East and an assessment of the Dakota

In mid-October 1945, you were posted to Kuala Lumpur, in Malaya. What state was the city in so soon after the war had ended?
Officially, as of the 15th of October 1945, my unit, stationed in Kuala Lumpur, was a detachment of Air Headquarters Malaya Communication Squadron. The headquarters of the squadron were situated at Kallang, with detachments at Batavia, in Java, which was controlled by the Dutch, and Kuala Lumpur. However, the headquarters were moved to Kuala Lumpur in early November. In Kuala Lumpur itself, I wouldn't call the atmosphere normal, but neither did it seem terribly abnormal; I can only speak for Kuala Lumpur, not for the country as a whole.

When I had first touched down at Kuala Lumpur back on the 15th of September, the airfield was in a very bad state. It didn't have any runways. Instead, there was a soaking wet field, which served as the landing ground, though this problem was quickly solved.

When we arrived at Kuala Lumpur, we were surprised to be told to go and find our own accommodation. We ended up staying in a large house, which didn't have much furniture, close to the airfield. Speaking about furniture, a rat had burrowed its way into the sofa and came popping out one day. The cook in the house saw it and threw a knife, killing it outright. During our time in the house, we had to keep guard; we were issued with and taught how to use .303 rifles for that purpose.

What was the role of your flying while based in Malaya?
It remained the same as it had been prior to going there: primarily taking passengers around the region. The reason why my flying duties were mostly taken up with passengers is because so many people were being posted home as their tours had come to an end, or they were being promoted or for additional reasons were being moved around the region to reclaim control of the colonies, and the like. However, we weren't always moving personnel. One time we had to collect a lawnmower.

You had to collect a lawnmower?
Yes, a group captain had seen a Japanese lawnmower in Kota Bharu that he coveted. He wanted it transported to Kuala Lumpur, where he was stationed. So, on the 13th of November, we went and picked it up.

Are there any other standout moments from your flying while in Malaya?
The weather was quite volatile while we were there, so on more than one occasion we had to abort a trip.

On the 16th of November, we travelled by Dakota to Batavia to pick up wounded personnel and take them to Singapore. We were there for one night, so checked into a hotel close to the airfield. The atmosphere in Java was very unstable; the hotel manager warned us not to go out because of the violence. During the night, we heard gunfire going off throughout the city. The airfield itself was very close to a canal, in which dead bodies were seen floating.

The next day, we were tasked with transporting the wounded men back to Singapore. As the Dakota in front of me took off, it came under machine gun fire. This resulted in several of the wounded passengers being killed, and the doctor on board being wounded.

So what did you do?
I took off and kept as low as possible, just skimming the boundary hedge, still on full power, and then I waited until I was well clear of the airfield before climbing.

Even though the twelve-year Malayan Emergency would not begin until 1948, the building tension with the Communists in Malaya added to the general turmoil in a country beginning its recovery from war and Japanese occupation. With this in mind, what were relations like between the local populace and the British?

Relations seemed pretty normal, actually. I suppose a good indicator of my perception of personal threat was when on one occasion my wireless operator and I walked into the city centre, as he wanted some clothing; we carried no weapons. It was quite a relaxed walk, without looking over our shoulders. On that journey into the city, we saw a group of children kicking a ball around on a school playing field. It was little things like that which made me think that things were beginning to return to normal. But of course, armed conflict would erupt once more, in 1948.

Additionally, a lot of British personnel were coming down with venereal disease, so I guess one could say that relations with the local women were good. I didn't realise how widespread venereal disease was until I walked into a bathroom and saw an army chap, who was in quite a state, cutting off a strip of carbolic soap and trying to force it down into his penis through his urethra. It transpired that he was a married man with a child. Not only would his wife have questions about why he wasn't expressing his interest in her, to put it in a nice way, but back then venereal disease was quite a serious thing, as antibiotics were not easily available. Also, if one went to the medical officer to receive treatment, then everything would be put down into the patient's medical record, which could prove embarrassing, or it might even impact an RAF career.

However, living in Malaya wasn't all rosy for me. My crew and I had an arrangement with a garage owner that in exchange for a few tins of our cigarettes and half a bottle of whisky or whatever, we could use his car, running costs included, for as long as we were in Malaya. We took quite a few trips in his car. On one occasion, we were returning from a dance about ten miles outside of Kuala Lumpur. The dances practised there were the waltz and foxtrot. There were two of us in the car, George Livingstone and I, and the axle caught fire. We pulled over and stopped, and luckily the fire went out. A short while later, as we were debating who was going to walk into Kuala Lumpur, another vehicle came past and pulled over ahead of us. Four men with bad intentions came out, brandishing guns. George and I got behind the doors of our car for protection. Luckily, we carried pistols, which we drew in preparation for a gunfight.

What a frightening situation that must have been.
I can't speak for George, but I was scared. Fortunately, we heard another vehicle approaching, and thankfully it was a British Army lorry full of soldiers. Once the four men with guns realised this, they got in their car and sped away, pursued by the army lorry.

George got a lift into Kuala Lumpur to tell the garage owner what had happened with the car, and I was left on my own. Despite what had just happened, I wasn't scared at being left there. Besides, at that stage it was starting to get light.

George and the brother of the garage owner returned, and it was then that I learnt that the garage owner was missing. We later learnt that he had been murdered. Apparently, a group of men had asked for a test drive, and the garage owner had agreed. At some point during the drive, he had been shot and left in the back seat. I know this, because a search party had been organised. I did not participate in the search, as I had to do an air test. However, George took part, and that's how I know that the owner was found as I described: lying dead in the back seat, having been shot.

Did anyone know why he had been murdered?
It was believed that he was murdered by the Communists because of his views on the British, his actions towards us and possibly for holding anti-Communist views.

Not long after he was murdered, your last ever flight in the Far East took place, and it was quite eventful. What happened?
On the 17th of December, I had flown from Kuala Lumpur to Mingaladon, Rangoon's airfield, with a different co-pilot, as George was assisting in the search for the missing garage owner. We carried nine passengers, made up of army and air force personnel,

who were going Christmas shopping in Calcutta on behalf of their units. We continued to Calcutta the following day. I landed at Dum Dum, Calcutta, as it had an extra-long runway, which was needed as we ended up carrying a 7,000-pound load on the way back. In addition to myself, the navigator and the co-pilot, we also carried nine passengers on the return leg: the personnel returning from their holiday shopping. On the 21st, after a three-day stay in Calcutta, we began our journey back and made it to Mingaladon airfield, Rangoon, without incident.

I had intended to refuel and carry on to Kuala Lumpur, but we stayed the night at Mingaladon, as a meteorologist had warned me that a tropical storm was on our flight path. The next day, the 22nd, was when things went wrong. An hour or so after take-off from Mingaladon, we hit a violent chain of storms that took about half an hour to get through. Soon after we were out of them, I handed over control of the Dakota to my co-pilot, telling him that he only had to maintain the altitude I had set, and I went back to chat with the navigator to confirm our position.

It was at that point that a cylinder exploded on the starboard engine. I noticed that the cylinder affected was receiving fuel that was still being ignited. I knew this because I could see a little flame shooting out of the engine. I realised that I wouldn't get any power from that cylinder, but I knew I could get some from the rest of the engine, but to lower the risk of fire I would have to reduce the revolutions. My co-pilot was terrified; he had only flown Spitfires prior to this, and never a big aircraft.

I put the aircraft into climbing power on the port engine and kept the starboard engine going on much lower power. I climbed to a height of 900 feet, knowing that it would get us over the coastal hills. Once we had cleared the hills, I feathered the starboard engine, secure in the knowledge that we wouldn't have to climb anymore. After that, I deliberately turned north to head to an old Japanese airfield near Tavoy. I knew there was an airfield there, as we had been warned about it, and others, while on wartime operations.

Once near Tavoy, I steadily descended but came into a layer of low cloud, which was really fog, caused by the sun heating the soaked ground. At 400 feet, I saw that the airstrip was only a few hundred yards away, but we were much too high, so I went into a falling leaf manoeuvre to reduce height much more quickly. At the airfield boundary, I was still about fifteen feet too high, but I forced the plane down with a heavy landing and immediately brought the brakes into use. When we finally came to a stop, I was almost in tears due to the relief. A few of the passengers actually got out and kissed the ground.

What was the aftermath of it all for everyone involved? To survive something like that must have elicited strong emotions in people.
We had to spend the night at Tavoy. There was a four-man meteorology unit stationed there, so it wasn't an abandoned airfield. That night, everyone involved had a celebration in the mess, and it was the only time in my life that people sang, 'For he's a jolly good fellow' to me. During the celebration, I asked my co-pilot what he would have done if I had not able to fly the plane when the event occurred, and he admitted that he had no idea. Metal fatigue was the reason given for the cylinder exploding.

The next day, six Beech Expeditors, American-built twin-engine planes, were sent to transport us, the passengers and the freight to Kuala Lumpur, nearly 800 miles to the south. Three of the Expeditors had to make a second trip in order to ensure that all of the freight had been recovered. Even the radio and cockpit instruments were removed from the Dakota and taken back to Kuala Lumpur, to ensure that the Communists didn't get their hands on them.

An army chap told me that I had been very fortunate. At Tavoy, he said, there were two landing strips, one running north-to-south, and a shorter one running east-to-west. I had landed on the north-to-south strip, but according to the army chap the east-to-west strip was still mined.

Many years later, in an RAF magazine that I receive four times a year, I read an article by a chap asking if anyone had any information on Tavoy airfield. I then wrote in with the story I have just told you, and the sergeant who was there at the time it took place saw my article and replied to my letter. He remembered the incident.

What you did was quite a feat. I'm surprised you didn't receive an award for it.
I received a Green Endorsement in my log book from the group captain, praising me for what I managed to do; he was the same group captain for whom I had picked up the lawnmower with in Kota Bharu for delivery to Kuala Lumpur. Funnily enough, when he was talking to me about my landing at Tavoy, he looked at me and said, 'Aren't you glad that I taught you how to fly a Dakota?' 'Bloody cheek,' was my response, which could have put me in trouble, as I had technically sworn at an officer. Luckily, he saw the funny side to it.

So why was that flight your last one in the Far East?
Because that Dakota was the only one we had in the unit. I have no idea why another one wasn't sent. By the time I left the Far East in late March 1946, it still had not been replaced, to the best of my knowledge.

Your last flight in the Far East took place in late December 1945, and you left the Far East three months later, near the end of March 1946. In that time, you did no flying, so what did you do?
I would have been in Kuala Lumpur during that time, still attached to Air Headquarters Malaya Communication Squadron. I was stationed with a communications squadron. Honestly, I don't remember a lot from that period, so it must have been uneventful. The atmosphere was more relaxed, and we had the freedom to go into Kuala Lumpur itself. The only story which really sticks out is quite random: for a joke, a chap and I tried to whip each other with wet towels. Why that stands out so vividly I don't know.

What's your opinion on the Dakota? It's a plane that is held in high regard by many. Do you agree?
Yes, it was a lovely plane. It handled really well and was a reliable aircraft that could do long flights. It was also built very well and could fly in all conditions, anywhere in the world. It was a great plane, it really was, and in some places it still is!

CHAPTER TWELVE

BACK IN BRITAIN, APRIL 1946 – NOVEMBER 1949

Sailing back to the UK, at home on leave, Swannington, becoming a commissioned officer and an adjutant, driving a car and obtaining a licence, a letter from W/Cdr Blackburn, leaving the RAF, adjusting to civilian life, rejoining the RAF and learning to fly Lancasters

On the 27th of March 1946, you boarded the troopship SS *Capetown Castle* to begin your journey home. When did you find out that you were going home, and were you happy to receive the news?
No, I was not happy. I was in Kuala Lumpur. I was called into the adjutant's office. He looked up and said, 'Good news Denis, you're going home.' I looked at him and said, 'Home? I don't want to go home,' but it had been decided; I was going home. I was having such a good time out in the Far East. It really was an adventure, while the updates from home told me that Britain was going through a bad winter and that rationing was still going on. However, a new rule had set the period for an overseas tour at two-and-a-half years, and by that stage I had been overseas for well over three years.

I went back to the billet and packed my things. I then boarded a night train to Singapore, which was absolutely packed with people. The only place I could find to sit was between the carriages, so that's where I slumped with all of my gear. At first, I sat on my large pack and put my smaller pack and suitcase on each side of me, but when the movement of people between the carriages stopped, I rearranged my things so that the smaller pack acted as a pillow; this enabled me to lie down. During the night, I was partly woken up by the sounds of rattling, which I assumed was the train in normal transit along the rail line. But when I woke up in the morning, I became aware of a draught coming into my back, which turned out to be wind rushing through a bullet hole. I found the bullet itself on the floor and threw it away in disgust. I soon learned that the train had come under machine gun fire overnight, presumably by the Communists.

Once in Singapore, I dropped off my luggage and went shopping. I bought a tea set made of pewter for my foster mother, and for Bert, her biological son, I purchased a smoking set which consisted of a specially-decorated cigarette tin and a small frame into which one could slide a box of matches. There was also a gap in the frame that was covered with the rough coating used to strike matches.

What feelings did you have knowing that you would probably never see the Far East again?
I was quite sad. I felt a greater sense of freedom out in the Far East, as opposed to the stiff air of authority back home. If there had been a way that I could have avoided going home, I would have done it; the longer I could have stayed out there, the better. At the same time, though, it wasn't that bad, because in my mind I was not going to leave the RAF, so there was always the possibility that I would be posted back overseas, and potentially back to the Far East, in the future.

What were conditions like on the SS *Capetown Castle?*
The conditions onboard were really good. The food was excellent; it was typical British food. I could have cereals, porridge, or something like bacon and eggs for breakfast. Stews and roasts were the types of food that were served for lunch and dinner. With a library onboard, there were plenty of books to read, but in all honesty, I was just happy looking out to sea. The mood among the passengers was quite joyful as well. I think that many of them were looking forward to going home.

I will tell you what made the voyage really good. Onboard were men of a wide variety of ranks, including officers. Around twenty of us were warrant officers, which is the highest rank one could hold without being commissioned. Each commissioned officer had duties aboard the ship, as did all other ranks, but for whatever reason, we warrant officers did not. So for our small group of warrant officers, it was three weeks of relaxation.

Many of us had been on Mepacrine tablets for the duration of our time in the Far East, in order to combat malaria. We chucked them overboard, thinking we wouldn't need them anymore. For me, it was a big mistake. Once I was back home, I started getting one cold after another. When I went to the family doctor, he noted my yellow skin and asked if I had been on Mepacrine and if I still had any. I told him that I had none, which was unfortunate, as anyone who took Mepacrine tablets was supposed to gradually come off them. The doctor gave me some more, and I decreased my dosage over the course of ninety days, until I was no longer taking any.

Anyway, on the same day that we left Singapore, a troopship departed Bombay, also destined for the UK. We caught up with it just before reaching the Suez Canal, in an area known as the Great Bitter Lake. Our captain tried to overtake the other troopship but ran aground on sandbanks. Our fuel tanks had to be emptied before we could be refloated on the next high tide, after which the tanks were refilled. By this time, the other troopship was well ahead.

While on the voyage home, I got to know another warrant officer, who was in a bunk on the next row. He had also flown Liberators, but on a maritime, not bombing, squadron. He got his 300 hours of operational flying by patrolling the Bay of Bengal. According to him, during his tour, his gunners never once had to fire a shot in defence, and they never dropped a single bomb or depth charge, but their 300 hours still qualified as a tour of operations.

After we exited the Suez Canal, we made our way across the length of the Mediterranean, over which I would fly within four years while on patrols in conjunction with the Royal Navy.

Eventually, we reached the Bay of Biscay, which was cloaked in dense fog. The SS *Capetown Castle* had to crawl through the thick fog with its foghorn blaring every few minutes.

How did it feel to be back on British soil?
I disembarked on the 16th of April 1946 at Southampton, and honestly, I wasn't too happy. One can imagine what it was like, with a troopship load of men and a few women trying to disembark with all their kit and cases.

I arrived in London at nine at night. It was dark and foggy, and there were no buses to Farnborough at that hour, though I managed to persuade a taxi driver to take me the fifteen miles home; he charged me a lot. I arrived home at half past ten, rang the doorbell and heard my foster mother say, 'Who can that be at this time of night?' My younger foster brother, Billy, answered the door and called back, 'It's Denis.' My foster mother replied, 'It can't be.' One sees these images of parents being overjoyed at being reunited with their children who have been serving overseas, but despite having been away for over three years, I didn't experience any of that; my foster mother was as stern and emotionless as ever, and of course my foster father had passed away while I was overseas. So in all honesty, I wasn't too pleased to be back. I would have much preferred to have stayed overseas.

After about half an hour, Billy, who must have been around seventeen at that time, went to bed. I tried to get my foster mother to open up, but to no avail. I looked around the walls, expecting to see geckos, like I had been so used to seeing in the Far East. I then made a comment about how small the room seemed, which it was, after what I had experienced. Still, it took her by surprise. In the end, well after midnight, she told me that she would put a hot water bottle in my bed, and that was that.

What was it like adjusting to life back home after being away for so long?
It was sort of halfway between civilian life and forces life, in the sense that I was at home and had all this free time, as I was on leave during that period, but at the same time I was still in the RAF.

All of that leave meant that I had a period of great relaxation. I spent a lot of time with the dog, but when I first arrived home I don't think he recognised me. Then, on our first walk, he was off the lead, and I whistled to him in the same way I used to. He stopped dead in his tracks, turned around, and after a second or two bounded towards me at full sprint. He jumped up and wouldn't stop licking me.

My foster mother had also complained to me about her gas oven, so I took her into Bromley, and into a gas showroom for kitchen appliances, and I asked her which one she liked. She pointed out which one, and I took out my cheque book and bought it for her on the spot. They came and fitted it the next day and showed her how to use it, but, still, she didn't show me any gratitude; there were no hugs or anything like that.

The standout event of this leave was a visit by Laurie, from my troopship out to South Africa in 1942. I had last met him in Delhi. Laurie was from East London, so the distance to my home wasn't too far a journey for him. We had lunch and then went out for a walk and caught up on events. While stationed in the Far East, we had played chess by post, though due to the time it took for each other's letters to arrive, we had only completed about three moves each. Consequently, we set up the chessboard at the same stage as it was in the last letter, and he proceeded to wipe the floor with me.

I also got back into cycling. Before passing away, my foster father had taken apart my bicycle, lubricated everything and put it in the loft. I got it downstairs and reassembled it. One day, when I was out riding, I came across a bicycle shop, and in the window there was a racing bike. I bought it on the spot and gave my old bike to Billy, with whom I spent a lot of time until he was called up for national service; in his case it was the army.

I went out with Joan a few times. Our guardians were still dead against it, so we would meet in public and go to the cinema, the swimming baths or places like that. In fact, once when I was at the swimming baths with her, I ran into my first set of foster parents. Unbeknownst to me, they worked there, and the look on their faces when I showed up in uniform was quite something. They had not seen me in well over a decade, since I was a child, and there I was, twenty-one and in full battle dress.

What came next for you after your leave was over?
On the 14th of June 1946, I was posted to 274 Maintenance Unit at Swannington, an airfield in Norfolk, where I worked in administration. I was there for a little over a year, until I left the RAF in September 1947. Sitting in an office bored me to tears. I told each successive CO that I wanted to go back onto flying, and every single one told me that he would organise it, but with the armed forces still going through a period of mass demobilisation, we had a high turnover of COs. I continued flying a desk.

While I was at Swannington, I was notified that my commission had come through. I had completely forgotten about it, and it wasn't until I went to London for a final interview with senior officers that I learnt that the original application was dated from December 1944 and had been signed by a 'Wing Commander Blackburn' of 159 Squadron! W/Cdr Blackburn had encouraged me to put in for an officer's commission and had even filled in a large number of the forms on my behalf.

Why he was so personally interested in my promotion to officer, I don't know for certain, but I suspect one clue may be an operational flight when I took off with bombs on board and successfully did what is known as a 'rate four turn'. Such a manoeuvre is where the pilot executes a tight turn by banking the aircraft at a severe angle of, say 60°, instead of making a much wider turn at a lesser angle.

W/Cdr Blackburn had not taken part in this operation but was most likely watching from the ground. The next day, he called me into his office. I saluted, and he then asked me if I wanted a commission. I told him that I wasn't really interested, and his reply was something like, 'Well, if you're not up to taking the responsibilities of an officer, then we'll forget about it.' That really riled me, as I knew that I was just as good as officers were, so I agreed to apply for a commission. W/Cdr Blackburn told me that he would even do most of the paperwork for me.

In a 'Record of Service' summary document I received from the RAF in 1967, I was allegedly 'granted an Emergency Commission as Pilot Officer' on the 8th of January 1945. Furthermore, the note said that I was 'promoted Flying Officer' on the 8th of July 1945. Not true, either one; I did not receive a commission until I was at Swannington in 1946. Or, I should add, if those statements were true, and I was granted a commission in the month after W/Cdr Blackburn filled out paperwork for my commission, then I was never notified, and my pay was not increased, either. Furthermore, the 159 Squadron Operations Record Book and the Green Endorsement, dated in January 1946, which I received after my one-engine emergency Dakota landing at Tavoy, in Burma, on the 22nd of December 1945 both list me as a warrant officer. That 1967 letter's information is incorrect.

Anyway, my commission had finally been granted in 1946, but in order for me to accept it, I had to sign on for another year. I passed the interview and the medical, but I very clearly stated that I would only sign on if I was put back onto flying. This was agreed to, and I signed on, now as a commissioned officer. But still, I was not put back onto flying.

You will recall that my previous promotion in December 1944 jumped me the unusual two steps from sergeant to warrant officer, completely bypassing the rank of flight sergeant. I put that down to W/Cdr Blackburn's influence. When I gained my commission in 1946, the jump in rank was again essentially two grades, from warrant officer to flying officer, but the reasoning in 1946 was to ensure that a promotion brought me more money. I was told that my bump up to flying officer was due to the fact that a pilot officer earned less than a warrant officer. Thus, I advanced from the NCO rank of warrant officer to the commissioned rank of flying officer, but first I was a pilot officer for one day.

Now that you were a commissioned officer, how did things change for you?

I was given a cheque to cover the cost of the uniform change, and then it was back to Norfolk. As a flying officer, I replaced an adjutant who was demobilised a few days after I returned. The sergeant in charge of the admin staff was a great help in those early days of 'learning the ropes', as was the CO, so imagine my shock when a message came from the Air Ministry stating that the CO was to be demobilised.

On the same day, another message came in, informing us that an Anson aircraft would be bringing previously ordered equipment. The CO jumped into his vehicle and went out to inspect the runway, which was officially out of use. He was at the far end of the runway when I received news that the delivery would be the next day. I needed to pass this message to him, but there were no mobile phones or anything like that in those days. I spotted a Verey pistol and took it to the outside platform and let off a shot to get his attention. I had allowed for the wind, but a gust took the shell further than I had anticipated, so it only landed a few feet from the CO, who via the vehicle was back within minutes. In a frightful temper, he roared, 'Were you trying to kill me?' I showed him the message concerning his demobilisation and the one regarding the Anson, which calmed him down.

The next day, the sound of distant Anson engines filled the air. I quickly contacted the senior equipment officer, who was expecting the equipment that he had ordered, and he took me in a vehicle to the control tower. However, en route, our view of the bend was disrupted by big banks of earth, which were designed to protect our aircraft from enemy fighters; Swannington airfield was still set up as it had been during the war. Just as we reached the bend, so, too, did the Anson. The pilot had landed it in the wrong direction, diverted onto the perimeter track and just headed for the control tower. At quite a speed, he reached the bend just as we did. Sitting in the passenger's seat, I was suddenly confronted by the Anson's port propeller heading straight for my head. Fortunately, the pilot cut off power to that engine and my driver slammed on the brakes, so the two machines finished up only a couple of feet apart. It was just as well; otherwise, it could have been my head cut to pieces or even cut off! The pilot never did explain why he had landed downwind. The ground signal board was showing the correct wind direction, plus there was, of course, the windsock.

What was your role as an adjutant?

As an adjutant, I was like a secretary to the CO, to put it in civilian terms. I basically assisted him and dealt with any mail that came to him. An adjutant was a commissioned rank, so I was also in a position to give orders. I didn't really like being in a position of authority; it was unnatural to me. Not to mention that I was now moving in circles that were unfamiliar to me.

Swannington, at that time, had around 250 airmen. Officers consisted of the temporary CO, his junior assistant, a senior equipment officer, also with a junior assistant, an admin officer, an accounts officer and me. Like myself, the junior officers were in their early to mid-twenties.

So was there really no flying at all for you during your time as an adjutant?

There were two occasions when I flew. The first was a quick air test of a twin-engine Anson on the 18th of January 1947 with a S/Ldr Pinkham taking the pilot's position, while I sat alongside of him as his co-pilot. Though it was only of twenty minutes' duration, I was fortunate for this opportunity, as S/Ldr Pinkham granted me a chance to fly the Anson for part of the flight. Then again, on the 22nd of January, a visiting FO Guile offered me a slightly longer chance to fly an aircraft, this time his single-engine Proctor. Once more from the co-pilot's seat, I was given the honour of taking the controls for part of this one-hour flight. We performed circuits and bumps and then did some local flying. It was great; at that time flying any aircraft was joyful. I don't know the purpose of FO Guile's visit to Swannington, but he did stay the night.

I am sure it was during your time at Swannington that you bought your first car and acquired your driving licence.
Out of the junior officers at Swannington, none of us could drive, but I did learn during my time in Norfolk.

One of our officers at Swannington was an Argentinian who had rented a local cottage. He soon got accommodation in our own officers' quarters, so he no longer needed the car to get to and from the cottage. At breakfast one morning, he asked if anyone would like to buy his car. I immediately put my hand up and said that I would. He remarked that I couldn't drive, to which I replied that he could teach me. So I became the owner of his Ford 8, a three-geared car with a reverse gear, too. At the traffic-free airfield, I soon got the hang of driving, but further afield on actual roads L plates and insurance were required. Proof of taxation was also required, so the Argentinian chap and I settled up the tax bill, and I had the correct paperwork to present to the authorities.

Then it was off to Norwich, where Woolworths sold L plates, and then to Norwich Union Insurance Co. The motor section was not in one of the high-rise offices of later days but was up a narrow staircase to a single office, where an individual soon dealt with my needs. So there I was, taxed, insured and ready for the high road.

The Argentinian officer and I spent most of that day in Norwich. Parking was no problem back then, and I soon passed my driving test. I took an instant liking to Norwich; lots of changes to modernise it were already taking place. There were numerous shops and stores staffed by helpful and friendly people and a marvellous market. I liked the city so much that in 1974 my wife and I bought a little terraced house there. Nearby there was a swimming pool, a great attraction to me as I am someone who loves swimming. We moved into the house in 1979, which was five years after ABBA won the Eurovision Song Contest with 'Waterloo', which by coincidence was the name of our road.

I assume you passed your driving test in Norwich?
No, I took my test in South London during leave, when I went home to Kent. A corporal was also on leave and wanted to get to London, so I agreed to drive down with him, before then heading home to Farnborough. He would drive through the towns, and I would be behind the wheel on the country roads. Our plan was going well until we reached London and parted ways at the Underground station in Tottenham. He gave me directions, but before long I was lost, as I did not know that part of London. I soon ended up in a cul-de-sac and performed a horrible three-point turn trying to get out of it, with gears crunching. I then asked a policeman who was standing nearby if he knew the directions to Bromley, which back then was a part of Kent. He advised me to follow some tram lines, which terminated at Herne Hill. Fortunately, I knew the way home from there.

Bert, my foster parents' biological son, was there, so I went out with him in the car a few times, and he gave me some advice and tips on how to pass the driving test.

The day of my test came. The test centre was in Catford. I went with Bert, as he was expecting to be able to come round with me on the test, but the examiner told him that he wasn't allowed to. From there, it was just a case of following the examiner's instructions. I remember that we came to a crossroads where a policeman was standing on a plinth directing traffic. I didn't even see the policeman, so I just drove right past him. The instructor said to me, 'Do you always drive past a policeman who is giving stop signals?' I honestly had not seen him. Later on, the instructor told me to take the next left, which I did, but too sharply, causing the wheels on the left side to bounce over the curb.

Not long after that, he told me to do an emergency stop, which I did, so efficiently using both the brake pedal and the handbrake that the instructor almost went through the windscreen. I had stopped so sharply that the braking system seized up. The examiner turned to me and said, 'I suppose that one of us will have to get out and rock the car, and I suppose that will be me.' He did it, and the brakes returned to their normal positions. He got back in the car, and we returned to the test centre, where he reviewed his notes and commented on my RAF uniform. I'm not kidding, he said these exact words: 'I see you can fly aircraft, so you must be able to drive a car. We'll put it down as a pass.'

I can't believe that he actually passed you.
I know; it could never happen now.

Before long, I was back at Swannington in my adjutant position, a role I have already explained.

Wasn't it during this time that a very interesting letter arrived?
After I had become an adjutant following my commission, a letter arrived for me, from W/Cdr Blackburn. I have mentioned how when we were on operations he asked us all what we were going to do after the war had finished. He had said that he was going to buy a yacht and sail it around the world and asked if any of us wanted to join him, to which I said that I would. This letter was regarding that. In the letter he told me that he now had a yacht and was in Marseille, France. He had also written detailed instructions on how to reach him. Unfortunately, as I had already signed on again I was unable to take him up on his offer.

Looking back on it, do you regret that circumstances meant that you were unable to go to Marseille?
Yes, very much so. The mental image of being out at sea, on a yacht, had even more appeal than flying; I really loved the sea. If I had not signed on again, I would have been off to Marseille in a flash.

Once your year was up, you actually came out of the RAF.
Yes, I came out in September 1947, because I wasn't flying. I wanted to fly; that was the entire reason I joined the Air Training Corps

and went into the RAF. Once I was out, I did a number of jobs, but I couldn't take to any of them. I applied to be a bus driver, but they had stipulations about age, height and weight, none of which I met, although I was offered an inspector's job. Back then, there were strict rules regarding bus punctuality, so I would have had to visit random bus stops and see if the buses came on time. The job, however, never materialised, as it meant having to do a period as a conductor, which I had no interest in doing.

I also had an interview for a job with an engineering firm that worked on the London Underground, but that opportunity didn't pan out either.

I applied for a job with British South American Airways, and I thought that I had an excellent chance of being hired, having accumulated over 1,000 hours of flying, but at the interview it transpired that they wanted all of their pilots to have at least 5,000 hours of flying. So I was turned down on that.

Honestly, it was a period of odd jobs, and once my RAF enlistment had concluded, of trying to adjust back into civilian life. I think that challenge is something that all ex-service people face, and for some it is a major, ongoing struggle. You see it with those who return from the Middle East campaigns today.

The Berlin Airlift soon started in late June of 1948, which for you was a potential opportunity to start flying again.
I thought so. My desire to fly was why I re-applied to join the RAF, but the application process took so long that by the time I had passed through the flying schools, the Berlin Airlift had been over for quite a while.

My foster mother was not happy at all about me going back into the RAF and told me that I should not do it. She was quite angry about it and said that she was going to write to the Air Ministry herself and put a stop to it. She had an inflated ego and seriously thought that her words and wishes carried such weight that she could influence things like that. I told her that I had reenlisted, and there was nothing that she could do about it.

My application was eventually processed, and I was accepted back into the RAF, after about a year-and-a-half as a civilian. On the 19th of April 1949, I was posted to RAF Cardington, in Bedfordshire, to be kitted out. I no longer retained my commission; I went back in as a non-commissioned officer, with the rank of flight sergeant.

From Cardington, I was posted to 1 Pilots Refresher Flying Unit (PRFU) at RAF Finningley, then in Nottinghamshire but now in South Yorkshire, on the 27th of April 1949, to fly Wellingtons. I was the happiest man alive, having returned to flying. I took to it like a duck to water once I got back behind the controls of a Wellington. There wasn't any dust to shake off, so to speak. The unit was made up of all sorts of men, including many on national service. For me at least, there were no exams to go through. It started off with circuits and landings, then eventually it turned to cross country exercises and bombing practice.

On the 6th of June 1949, I was posted to 236 Operational Conversion Unit at RAF Kinloss, in Scotland, for three-and-a-half months of training on the legendary Lancaster bomber. Having never piloted the Lancaster before, I was fortunate in taking to this aircraft straight away without any problems.

I became familiar with the layout of the cockpit, the effects of controls, taxiing, straight and level flying, climbing on an even heading, climbing turns, medium turns, descending, stalling, gliding, taking off into wind, approaching and landing. Then I moved on to my first solo, followed by steep turns and then instrument flying. The training increased in complexity the further along I progressed, so that I was prepared for nearly every possibility.

One thing I had to do with the instructor was to practise low-level flying, over the sea. I came down to fifty feet, then twenty, and then the instructor asked me to perform a sharp turn to port, which I did. The manoeuvre revealed a wake being blasted behind us, like a ship at sea, all caused by the slipstream, of course.

I liked instrument flying. The added training I received carried tremendous value, as flying in fog and other inclement conditions was not unusual, especially over the British Isles.

I did have to take exams while I was at Kinloss, on things like the inner workings of a Lancaster.

There was one scary incident while I was there, where the air traffic controller saved us from catastrophe. While in a Lancaster with my instructor at the controls, we were coming in to land in fog so heavy that we couldn't see the other end of the runway, when the air traffic controller suddenly called out, 'Aircraft just landed, turn right immediately!' My instructor promptly followed the directions, and a few seconds later another Lancaster appeared from the fog, also turning right. What had happened was that as we were landing, another Lancaster was also landing, but from the other direction. In the thick fog, neither aircraft was visible to the other on approach to land, and since there was no wind, a landing could be made from either direction. Both Lancasters came off the runway, but there were no injuries.

I passed all of the exams and was cleared to fly Lancasters. I then left Kinloss on the 27th of September 1949, and following just over five weeks of leave, I was posted to Malta on the 4th of November. I would serve there with Coastal Command on 38 Squadron for the next two-and-a-half years.

CHAPTER THIRTEEN

MALTA, NOVEMBER 1949 – MARCH 1952, PART ONE

Arriving on 38 Squadron in Malta, the role of the RAF,
air-sea rescue searches, ageing Lancaster bombers, removing
the end of a five-year-old's thumb, exploring Malta, meeting
up with W/Cdr Blackburn and rubbing shoulders with royalty

After you had finished at Kinloss, you had five weeks of leave before being posted to Malta.
The RAF gave me just over five weeks leave prior to my departure. Knowing that I was headed back overseas, the first thing I did was sell my car. I sold it to an old friend from my choirboy days, Reg Pattison. Aside from that, the five weeks were mainly taken up with getting ready to head out to Malta.

We were taken to RAF Luqa on Malta in a basic Dakota. By basic, I mean it did not have any cushioned seats or anything like that.

I made two friends on the way out there, and once we arrived we noticed that the *Times of Malta* printed the temperature of the sea. It didn't bother us that it was November; the apparent water temperature was enough to take a swim, so the three of us went to Sliema harbour, dived in and then promptly came out within a few seconds. The water was too cold to swim in.

What was the role of the RAF in Malta at the time?
I arrived on the 4th of November 1949. At the time, our main role was to work with the Royal Navy. During numerous dual exercises, the RAF honed its skills in cooperating with the navy. The Cold War was in its infancy, and the powers that be seemed to believe that

the Russians would flood the Mediterranean with submarines, so learning and practicing how to hunt and destroy submarines was the focus of many exercises.

We were also tasked with air-sea rescue duties. The two RAF Lancaster squadrons stationed in Malta at the time, 37 and my 38 Squadron, were on standby for air-sea rescue work on alternating weeks.

As part of our air-sea rescue instruction, I took part in a training programme which taught me how to drop a lifeboat by parachute from a Lancaster. The release height depended on the wind direction, aircraft speed and wind speed. Ideally, the elevation was 400 feet, the indicated airspeed was 120 miles per hour, and the drop was upwind from the targeted victims in the water so that the lifeboat would drift towards them. The boat itself could carry eleven people and had enough supplies to last eleven days. When the lifeboat hit the water, flotation lines would shoot out from each side for fifty yards, offering those in the water means by which they could pull themselves towards the boat. The difficulty for the air-sea rescue pilot was in adhering to the drop parameters, as indicated by the cockpit instruments.

However, my first flight in Malta did not involve the Royal Navy, anti-submarine activity or air-sea rescue. Freshly arrived pilots had to go through the 'Flight Commander's Check', which was a formality more than anything. It was just to make sure that the pilot could handle the Lancaster efficiently.

My check flight turned out to be quite eventful. I was flying the plane, with the flight commander in the co-pilot's seat. At RAF Luqa, there were two runways, north-east to south-west and north-west to south-east. Although the north-east to south-west runway was the most used, I landed from south-east to north-west, owing to the wind direction. I didn't then know it, but there was quite a bump on the south-eastern end of the runway, where a bomb crater from the war had been filled-in. While landing, just as I pulled back on the control column to settle with the nose up and on all three wheels, the aircraft hit the bump, which launched it about four feet or so into the air. When landing a Lancaster, the pilot set the throttle, but for the last bit of a landing the co-pilot controlled the throttle; this was because both of the pilot's hands were on the control column.

After that bump threw us into the air, I knew that we would come back down, nose first, if I didn't do anything. As this would have been disastrous, I just knocked the flight commander's hand off the throttle and put on maximum power so I could land the Lancaster with the nose up. From then on, I knew about the bump, so I would always allow for it whenever I landed there.

What examples can you give of the types of exercises that you flew, in cooperation with the Royal Navy?
All of our exercises were carried out as though we were at war. The waters around Malta were divided into boxes, each of which was identified by a number and letter. These boxes stretched a long way out from Malta, even to the area around Cyprus, 1,000 miles to the east. On the way to its assigned box, my Lancaster would make contact with the relevant naval vessels, which were acting as though they were in a convoy of ships. Our aircraft would give our estimated time of arrival. Then, once there, the aircraft would be given its coded exercise number by the fleet commander. We would then carry out that exercise.

As part of the exercise, we would pretend that Russian submarines were shadowing the convoy. The navy liked having aircraft around the convoy, to watch for submarines; they called us their 'eyes in the sky'. As aircraft travel at much higher speeds than ships, after overflying the convoy, we would circle back and end up again approaching the convoy from the same direction as on our previous overflight.

British submarines also took part in these exercises, acting as Russian submarines, so we would 'hunt' them, so to speak. Once a submarine was located, we would circle it and drop a smoke float, or a flame float at night, at the submarine's last known location. Then we would drop sonobuoys to track the submarine's movement within a one-mile radius around a circle centred on the smoke float or flame float.

Sonobuoys were portable sonar systems that, when dropped from an aircraft or a ship, would help in detecting submarines. Each sonobuoy had its own radio frequency and colour. If a submarine's location was picked up via, say, the red sonobuoy, the strength of the signal received by that sonobuoy, monitored aboard the aircraft, would be used to work out the submarine's latitude and longitude. In addition, the submarine's direction of travel could also be worked out by analysing the signals from other deployed sonobuoys; each sonobuoy would broadcast a unique signal strength. The wireless operator would determine the direction and speed of the submarine and then the navigator would plot details on a chart. This plotted information would then be passed by wireless from the aircraft to the navy, who would then head towards that position.

Eventually, the navy would pick up signals from the submarine on their own hydrophones. In this type of exercise, the 'destruction' of the submarine would be left to the navy. If the submarine reached the end of the sonobuoy's mile-radius circle undetected, then we would drop another sonobuoy, or more than one, to continue tracking it, and so on. I believe we carried eighteen sonobuoys, so we could keep this up for quite a while.

During my time in Malta, we must have carried out six of those big exercises with the navy, and all of them involved convoys and submarines. The American Sixth Fleet also took part in some of those exercises, which could last for several days.

Another example of the flying I did involved 'WT homings'; WT stood for 'Wireless Telegraphy'. Our assignment on such an exercise was to home in on transmissions from a ship while flying far out to sea and then to navigate to the ship to assist if needed.

I remember that we also went on photography exercises, where we would fly over a site and photograph the area.

We also had to do exercises to keep our flying skills up-to-date. Once a month we practiced landing on three engines, which meant shutting down one engine in flight. These exercises took place both during the day and night and had nothing to do with the navy.

You mentioned the big exercises that you took part in with the Royal Navy, but I assume that smaller-scale exercises took place too?
Yes, they were basically scaled down versions of the big exercises, ensuring that our navy vessels could safely avoid being torpedoed by submarines. They would involve one aircraft, one ship and one submarine.

In fact, it was on one of those small exercises that I helped to save the lives of six men. I'm jumping ahead to the 23rd of January 1952, when I was still on 38 Squadron Lancasters out of RAF Luqa on Malta. Prior to the incident, I had gone to the control tower to receive orders for my scheduled low-level bombing exercise. While I was there, another Lancaster crew was receiving 'WT homing instructions; they were tasked with homing in on a submarine. I previously mentioned how the sea surrounding Malta was divided up into boxes, each with its own letter code and number. During my briefing, I had heard a box code being given to the other crew.

Our own exercise had taken us to the south of Malta, and it was on the way back that I was sure I heard a very brief one-word emergency call of 'MAYDAY' on the radio. I queried my crew, but no one else had noticed it. I then called the control tower, but they had not heard a distress broadcast, either. I asked the officials in the control tower for orders but was told to carry on as normal, so I did, initially.

But after a few minutes of pondering, I decided to act upon my intuition, because I was sure I had heard that MAYDAY call. Ignoring orders from my own base, I asked my navigator to set a course for the box number that I knew I had heard being given to the other crew in the control tower. As captain of the aircraft, I could make that decision, but I would be in serious trouble if I was wrong.

We reached the area and soon enough spotted a dinghy. We were fortunate to have caught sight of them as they crested a wave in very rough seas. Once their dinghy was pinpointed, I informed a destroyer in the area, and the survivors were soon picked up. I asked the destroyer how many were on the dinghy, and the response came back that there were six crewmen recovered, but that two were missing.

I started circling away from the oil slick, from where their aircraft had crashed, in case there was anyone else in the water. After a while, we saw a body floating in a Mae West, an inflatable life preserver named after the famous Hollywood star. It looked as though the man was waving. Informed of our find, the destroyer put out a longboat to pick up the guy, who, it was determined, was a national serviceman. As he was in a really bad state, the destroyer headed for Malta as fast as it could, but unfortunately the lad died on the way. The other missing person, a ground engineer, was never found.

It transpired that the crew I had helped to rescue was the same one I had overheard in the control tower receiving their instructions. I was lucky to have overheard them. When I was mulling over the apparent MAYDAY call, I knew it would most likely have been broadcast from the section of the sea assigned to that Lancaster. If I had not overheard them, I wouldn't have known where to begin our search.

I spoke to the pilot soon afterwards, and he told me that the reason the Lancaster crashed was because part of the starboard wing had fallen off. When the plane hit the water, the flight engineer hit the button to release the dinghy, but it wouldn't come out of its storage compartment; he had to manually hack it out. The truth is, Lancasters were getting so old by this time that incident rates were on the rise. I had quite a few incidents while flying Lancasters, some of which were quite dangerous. The pilot also told me that losing the section of the starboard wingtip heavily impacted the flying characteristics of the aircraft and called for all the effort he could muster to keep from violently losing the aircraft and killing the entire crew. Concentrating upon ditching the Lancaster, he only managed to transmit his shouted MAYDAY once before he had to vacate his seat and exit the sinking aircraft. That was the one MAYDAY that I heard.

I also met up in the Mess with the flight engineer from that crew. He told me that the Lancaster had been flown to Malta from Britain, and that he had said in the dinghy that if 38 Squadron were on air-sea rescue, they would be awaiting discovery 'for bloody days.' He had said it not long before we showed up.

After the flight, I had to speak to the CO in charge, and while I did not face any repercussions for ignoring orders, he told me that if anything like that ever happened again, then I had to obey orders. He was the sort of chap who applied the rules to the letter.

A non-flying incident also comes to mind from this period in Malta. A woman named Elsie, who used to wash our dirty laundry, was sitting on the wall outside our accommodation when a three-ton lorry came swerving around the corner. The driver, only a young chap on national service, crashed into the wall. Elsie was crushed under the lorry. Those of us who were there tried to lift the lorry off her, but we couldn't move it. She screamed and made a lot of noise, but slowly her screams and movements quietened and she died. I watched her die in front of me. It's the sort of thing that sticks in your mind forever.

What were the consequences of that tragedy?
The driver was immediately arrested and taken into a cell that we had on-site. He was eventually shipped back to the UK, but I'm not sure what happened to him after that.

I imagine that your time on standby for air-sea rescue must have been quite active considering the military and non-military activity that was taking place in and around Malta and the Mediterranean as a whole?
When our squadron was on standby, an aircraft was always put on readiness. If an emergency signal came in, then the engines would be immediately started up to minimise the time needed to get airborne.

However, our first rescue mission, on the 20th of February 1950, led to a disagreement with my flight commander regarding meals denied to my crew and myself. While the incident was unpleasant at the time, it seemed to have blown over without negatively impacting my career. To this day, I feel justified in my actions.

On the 20th, I captained a Lancaster on a navigation exercise which amounted to three hours and five minutes in the air. It was customary to have a meal after a flight of that length, and so, having planned to be fed after the exercise, my crew and I were hungry. To our surprise, this meal was denied to us; this did not sit well with me. Instead, we were immediately sent across the Mediterranean Sea to Libya in order to search for a Vampire that had crashed somewhere in the North African desert. Our aircraft departed RAF Luqa and travelled to El Adem, 15 miles south of Tobruk, Libya, where the people in charge of the search were based. Once there, we were given a Lancaster and were told what had actually happened. A 73 Squadron Vampire pilot had baled out of his aircraft west of El Adem. The goal was to find this pilot.

Yes, we were military men who were expected to perform our duties, and most certainly, I understood that our flying experiences were valuable assets for the search, but I objected to being sent out without the meal that my crew and I expected – and needed to best perform our duties.

When the flight commander turned this rescue mission into an order, I told him to record in the squadron records that I was flying under duress.

We flew successively for three straight days, including long searches of over ten hours on the 21st and over seven-and-a-half hours on the 22nd. Then, after a search of two-hours-and-five minutes on the 23rd, we made the return flight to Luqa on that same day.

On arrival at Malta, I decided to have it out with the flight commander. First of all, I had to see the adjutant, who asked what it was all about. I replied that it was in regard to the entry in the flight log book. After retrieving the book, he told me that the notation about my flying under duress wasn't entered. I asked to see the flight commander but was informed that he had been given compassionate leave, as his father was apparently seriously ill. If I had been able to see the flight commander, then I would have demanded that the statement be written into the squadron records.

Nothing more came of it.

The good news – and it was most satisfying to my colleagues and I – was that the uninjured Vampire pilot had been picked up by Bedouins, put onto a camel and taken into the nearest town. A desert rescue party then reached him. I was told that the pilot received a strong telling-off for abandoning his aircraft.

What amazed me about that search was that from the air, even though the wartime fighting in the Western Desert campaign in North Africa had been over for roughly seven years, we could still identify the wreckage of burnt-out tanks and lorries. Unfortunately, mines from the war were still buried in the sand, and camels would occasionally step on them and blow themselves up.

A little over two months later, on the 28th of April 1950, an incident occurred where a twin-engine Meteor of 1 Overseas Ferry Unit was lost on an exercise somewhere between Tunis and Tripoli, possibly due to engine failure. It had disappeared without trace after last being seen climbing through cloud. The hope was that its two-man crew, consisting of a pilot and his navigator, had baled out and were awaiting rescue in the waters of the Mediterranean.

My crew and I were on standby when the call came in, and for the first time I took off on an actual air-sea rescue operation loaded with a lifeboat. When we reached our assigned search box, in an area estimated to be where the plane had crashed, we spent perhaps four hours searching the area. We found no clues before eventually having to return to Malta; our time in the air amounted to five hours and fifty minutes, all but the last hour being daylight. Following a short air test on the 29th, we again headed out to search on the 30th, this time with four passengers serving as extra eyes. This search was longer, amounting to nearly eleven hours by the time we returned to Luqa. Sadly, the Meteor pilot and navigator were never seen again, and no remains were recovered.

I was involved with four more air-sea rescue searches until my tour with 38 Squadron was completed in March 1952. I already mentioned the 23rd of January 1952, when a Lancaster ditched in the Mediterranean south of Malta, and I had followed my intuition after seemingly hearing 'MAYDAY' once.

The three other searches, all in 1951, are worthy of mention.

On the 1st of April 1951, my crew and I were diverted from a daylight exercise to participate in a search for the pilot of a ditched American aircraft at a position approximately 100 miles east of Delimara Point in Malta. We saw nothing on this flight of four hours and forty-five minutes, but we were happy to learn that the pilot was picked up by an American destroyer in the vicinity of the crash and returned safely to his base.

Then came another search, on the 5th of May 1951, when we were called upon to search for a missing French Vampire thirty miles south of Sardinia. Despite our best efforts on a flight of eight hours and forty minutes, we did not find the pilot.

On our way back to Luqa, we flew through a big storm. Suddenly there was a flash and an instant bang was heard, which signalled that our Lancaster had been struck by lightning. We arrived back at base without any issues, but when we landed one of the other pilots on the squadron saw a huge spark shoot out of the tail of our Lancaster, indicating that static electricity in the bonding wire had been released. Bonding wire was put in the frame of the aircraft to absorb static. The aircraft, RE187, had to be taken out of service to ensure that all the static electricity had dissipated and to recalibrate the instruments. I next flew aboard RE187 for nearly ten hours on the 11th of June, without issue; the aircraft was in excellent working order.

My third and final air-sea rescue flight of 1951 was on the 12th of October 1951, when my crew and I were diverted from a long night navigation exercise to participate in a search. We spent over eleven hours in the air. I vaguely recall that this search was off the coast of Cyprus, though my log book gives no geographic detail.

Earlier on, you mentioned a crew whose Lancaster had part of its starboard wing fall off in flight. You also mentioned that you had quite a few incidents while flying Lancasters. What happened on those occasions?

Not all of these incidents took place while I was in Malta, but a few did. On one occasion, on the 4th of October 1951, we were on an exercise when the propeller on number two engine, the inboard engine on the port wing, started to increase in revolutions and spin out of control, even though I had pushed the revolution control lever straight down. Still, the propeller's spin carried on rising in speed due to the oncoming rush of air flowing over the blades, which now were uncontrolled by engine power. Not knowing if the problem was with number two engine or its propeller mechanism, I shut down that engine completely and immediately feathered the propeller to rotate the propeller blades, presenting knife-like edges to the onrushing air. This minimised drag in order to reduce, and hopefully to halt, the life-threatening windmilling. The risk of a runaway propeller breaking away from the shaft attaching it to the engine was real, and very dangerous; breakaway propellers were known to tear into the fuselage or to otherwise cause severe damage, with dire results.

I pulled back on the control column to put the Lancaster into a steep climb but with the three working engines purposely set for minimum power, but the plane stalled. As we were falling, I increased power to the good engines to regain flight control and repeated what I had done before, but this time the climb was even steeper. Fortunately, there was a loud noise as the number two engine's propeller slid back into place on its shaft. I still had three perfectly-functioning propellers and their engines, so I was able to fly onward.

Air traffic control told me that they couldn't give me permission to land due to stormy weather conditions at Luqa, my intended destination. I was told by the CO to fly to Libya and land at an RAF airfield named Castel Benito, so we changed course and headed there. When we were in wireless range of Castel Benito, I radioed them to explain what had happened, but they told us that they couldn't help as they were experiencing sandstorms, which we could see from the aircraft. They recommended us to go to an American airfield named Wheelus Field, near Tripoli, Libya, and to get there as soon as possible, as sandstorms were forecasted to head in their direction.

We arrived at Wheelus Field, and I received instructions on my approach to land from south-to-north. The flight engineer looked out of the window and saw that around six rescue vehicles were assembled for an emergency response, but I landed smoothly and taxied to our dispersal, in front of the control tower. The Americans were surprised that only four of us made up the crew. I repositioned the aircraft so that debris from the sandstorm wouldn't enter the air intakes.

Behind our Lancaster on the approach to land, there was a Skymaster with an engine on fire. Behind that, another aircraft, an American jet, was coming in. The Skymaster landed without any problems, but the pilot of the American jet forgot to put down his undercarriage. Consequently, the jet landed on its belly and sparks shot out everywhere as metal scraped along the runway. Eventually, it slid to a stop without further harm, and no injuries.

We were there for two days, waiting for replacement parts to be brought out from Malta, to fix the engine or propeller assembly, or possibly both. In fact, the Americans actually made the necessary parts themselves. Also, I'm sure it was on the second night there that a huge meal was put on, and it was excellent.

On another occasion, I was flying from Malta to join the Mediterranean Fleet off the coast of Cyprus. It took around four hours to arrive there. Once I was within visual range, I radioed the

Fleet Commander for instructions. He replied by telling me that my number four engine, the outer engine on the starboard wing, was on fire. Indeed, there were big flames shooting out of the engine, but luckily the fire extinguishers that were built into the engine or nacelle worked and the fire was put out, after which we returned to base. We were told that once an engine caught fire, one had thirty seconds to put it out before it reached the fuel tank.

One incident I heard about but didn't see was the death of the instructor who had converted me onto Lancasters. He was captaining a Lancaster when it suddenly exploded on take-off, killing everyone. It was thought that fuel vapours had leaked into the aircraft, and that when the wireless operator flicked a switch the resulting spark caused the explosion.

I believe that all of my other incidents with Lancasters happened when I was with Coastal Command in the UK.

One non-Lancaster incident at RAF Luqa is worth mentioning; I wasn't there when this happened, either, but was told about it later on. At the end of one of the runways at Luqa was a row of Nissen huts. Apparently, during the Blitz of Malta in the Second World War a heavy bomb had fallen on the same end of the runway, leaving a large crater. The crater was filled in with tarmacadam, resulting in the bump that I came to know when I joined 38 Squadron. Tarmacadam is quite flammable, and apparently someone thought it would be a good idea to set it on fire. Before long, the fire had grown out of control, endangering the Nissen huts. The result was that the civilian fire crew had to be brought in, alongside the airfield fire crew stationed there, to help extinguish the flames.

One other incident I experienced with a Lancaster in Malta was when I removed the end of a five-year-old boy's thumb.

You removed the end of a five-year-old's thumb?
Let me explain. After landing one day, I was called in to see the CO and was told that a five-year-old boy had been flying a kite in the overshoot area, which is rough ground beyond the runway for aircraft unable to stop before the runway ends. The string of the kite was wrapped around his thumb. Apparently, as I was taking off, and I flew above the overshoot area, the kite became entangled in the

aircraft, which resulted in the end of the boy's thumb being severed. From what I later gathered, the boy went to hospital for treatment, but I don't know if anything else came of it. Why the boy had been in the overshoot area flying a kite is beyond me.

You almost lost your sight on one occasion.
One of my ground duties was to check the fire extinguishers, to ensure that there were no faults with them. I would take the top off of each to check for leakage. Inside was a small container filled with a chemical which upon contact with water created foam. On about the third or fourth extinguisher, the container exploded, resulting in some of the chemical splashing onto my face. I immediately rinsed my face with water from the cylinder to get the chemical off. From there, I made a beeline for the sickbay and received treatment. The medical officer told me that by splashing water on my face I had probably saved my sight.

How did you spend your free time?
When the water was warm enough, my free time was mostly spent swimming. During my entire time in Malta, I leased a car, so I or anyone else who wanted to come with me would often drive down to a favourite swimming point, named Delimara Point. Another place we often went to was named Ghajn Tuffieha, and it was there that a fair-haired and light-skinned chap we were with died of sunstroke. He was sunbathing, which didn't seem abnormal, but when someone went over to check on him he was unconscious. Most of us were in the sea and had not taken any notice of him. We just assumed he was sunbathing and maybe having a nap. He was taken by ambulance to a naval hospital and from there put on a flight back home, and it was during the flight that he died.

Speaking of sunbathing, we had a flat roof on our accommodation block. I used to occasionally sunbathe there with nothing on. One day, a member of my crew thought it would be funny to photograph me as I sunbathed in the nude. The skin that was usually covered by trunks was so white, while the rest of me was so brown, that when the photograph was developed it looked as though I had swimming trunks on.

I also had a bicycle while in Malta, so I would often cycle around the island, taking photographs and enjoying the scenery. Some parts of Malta were really photogenic, but it did surprise me how much of the northern half of the island was used for farming.

Once, on a hot and beautiful day, I wanted to see more of the northern part of the island. During that period I was doing a lot of photography. Off I went on my bike, sometime after I had finished breakfast. I first headed to the beach at Ghajn Tuffieha, where the fair-haired chap had caught sunstroke. After a swim, I took some photographs of the area and then cycled across the island to a place called St Paul's Bay, which is where St Paul supposedly came ashore after his shipwreck.

During the afternoon, in a little town named Paola, I cycled towards a policeman standing on a plinth to ask for the time. He looked me up and down and started talking away in Maltese until I asked him to repeat it in English. 'Oh, you're English,' he said in surprise. I had black hair and was so brown that he thought I was Maltese.

On the south side of the island were some very old ruins named Hagar Qim, and near to there was a wonderful place to swim, though one had to be prepared to go down some steep cliffs to reach it. Over the course of my visits there, I became friends with the owner of a café close to the swimming spot. When the café was closed or he was away, he would rig up two rifles in such a way as to shoot anyone trying to break into the premises. Behind his café was a wall, around 100 yards long, along which he grew grapes. I got to know him so well that I became one of the lucky few who could help myself to the grapes whenever I wanted them.

Valletta was quite a busy city, which I liked. It had a nice atmosphere and a good range of shops. In fact, it was in Valletta that I had a chance meeting with W/Cdr Blackburn, now a civilian. My crew and I were walking down the main street when I felt a pat on my back and heard the phrase, 'Don't I know you?' I turned around, and it was W/Cdr Blackburn. Although surprised, I was glad to see him. We had a chat, and then my crew and I drove around with him in his rented car for a while, eventually stopping off at a horseracing track on the outskirts of Valletta, which I hadn't known to exist until

W/Cdr Blackburn showed it to us. It wasn't a traditional track, as the horses pulled carriages. For each race, I predicted a winner and was right for the first five races, which led everyone to put a bet on my recommendation for the sixth race. The horse I chose didn't win, so W/Cdr Blackburn and my crew, who had bet on my prediction, all lost money. Ironically, the horse I had chosen came in last.

After watching six races, we all made plans to have an evening meal. Earlier, W/Cdr Blackburn had told us that he had bought his first yacht and was sailing all over the place, and during the meal I drank cherry brandy for the first time; it went straight to my head. Once the meal was over, we got into W/Cdr Blackburn's car and went down to Delimara Point, where I proceeded to strip down and dive into the sea. Most of us swam, but W/Cdr Blackburn didn't. After a while, everyone went back to the car, and W/Cdr Blackburn dropped us off at our base before heading off to wherever he was staying.

I met him for a second time in Malta. He had given me a telephone number during our first meeting, and on one occasion I phoned and asked for 'Wing Commander Blackburn'. He came to the phone and told me not to use his rank anymore, as he was just a civilian now. When we met up, we just had a walk along the beach, and during the walk he mentioned the letter that he had sent me regarding Marseille. He told me that I was a 'bloody fool' for signing on with the RAF and not joining him. He also told me that he had bought a new boat, a German E-boat from the war. The problem was that neither engine was working. To solve the problem, he organised the removal of one engine, which was put on a York aircraft and flown to Germany for repair, and from there it was flown back and refitted into the boat. Then he had the same done with the other engine. He must have called upon high-ranking contacts to pull that off.

I didn't see W/Cdr Blackburn again in Malta after our second meeting.

It wasn't just W/Cdr Blackburn you met while you were there. You also rubbed shoulders with royalty.

Yes, briefly. My crew and I had gone down to Sliema to see if an air-sea rescue boat could be reconditioned to use for our pleasure. The next building harboured Prince Philip's yacht. As he happened to be there at the time, he wandered over to ask us what our intentions were. We told him about the boat that we hoped to recondition and had a chat with him, and he then told us to follow him to where his yacht was stored. When he opened the doors and led us inside, we saw, up close, his stunning yacht, which was so polished that we could see our reflections.

I liked Prince Philip. He was quite chatty and came across as one of the boys. He didn't have a chip on his shoulder or an attitude based on his social standing. That was my first instance of meeting him, early on in my tenure in Malta. The next time I saw him was after a major exercise that took place off the coast of Gibraltar. Afterwards, by chance, I ended up sitting three or four rows behind him at a bullfight in La Línea de la Concepción, in Spain. I didn't speak to him, but a photograph was taken and published in a British newspaper; I think it was a Sunday edition, and I can be seen sitting a few rows behind him. For what it's worth, I did not enjoy the bullfight at all. It came across as barbaric, and the bulls looked drugged to me. I would never go to a bullfight again.

On another occasion, our present Queen Elizabeth, at that time Princess Elizabeth, inspected our squadron. All of the aircraft on the squadron and their crews were assembled in dispersal, and she came past with her entourage. No words were exchanged or anything like that. In fact, we were told to avoid eye contact with her and to not speak to her unless spoken to. It was in such stark contrast to my interaction with Prince Philip in Malta.

CHAPTER FOURTEEN

MALTA, NOVEMBER 1949 – MARCH 1952, PART TWO, PLUS SHORT ASSIGNMENTS IN NORTHERN IRELAND, WALES, GIBRALTAR AND CYPRUS

Malta postings, RAF Ballykelly in Northern Ireland, RAF Valley in Wales, a major exercise in Gibraltar, 'killing' a submarine for the third time, meeting W/Cdr Blackburn in Gibraltar, a trip aboard a submarine, another Northern Ireland detachment, a Battle of Britain display over Gibraltar, becoming a commissioned officer again, Cyprus and Denis's 38 Squadron posting draws to a close

Not all of your time with 38 Squadron was spent in Malta. You were also posted to Northern Ireland, where you spent around six weeks, followed by nearly three weeks at RAF Valley in Wales. Please tell me about your time in Northern Ireland.
We were sent on detachment to the Joint Anti-Submarine School – JASS – at RAF Ballykelly, near Londonderry, Northern Ireland, for several weeks, between the 27th of October and the 9th of December 1950. We were there for exercises involving the Royal Navy's Home Fleet. As in the Mediterranean, submarine hunting and protecting convoys were the focus.

On one occasion, we had to test a new device called the Autolycus. It was believed that by using this device, it was possible to detect the fumes from submerged submarines, which used diesel fuel at the time. Once the fumes had been picked up, the submarine could be located more easily. I only tested it once. I was with the flight commander, and we had to ascend to 10,000 feet to start with, on the principle that the fumes would be carried upwards. We then had to gradually descend, going into the fumes, which would then lead us to a submarine. Amazingly, we actually located a submarine, which was estimated to be 500 miles away. This didn't mean much, as by the time we would have arrived there the submarine would have been long gone. Our trial worked out by sheer luck, but because the Autolycus couldn't be relied upon, it was quickly withdrawn.

Looking through my log book, I see that some of the flying I did was recorded in code. I can't remember what the codes stood for, so I can't really say what happened on these flights. I assume that they were exercises of some sort, though only short ones, as they were mostly noted as lasting less than three hours. Most of the flying at Ballykelly was conducted during daylight.

Did your flying in Northern Ireland differ from Malta in any way?
JASS was a specialty school centred upon anti-submarine naval defence exercises, though many of my 38 Squadron flights from Malta were similar in scope. However, at Ballykelly there was no air-sea rescue component to our flying, as there was on Malta. The only other real difference between the flying in Ballykelly and Malta was that the weather was much worse in Northern Ireland than in Malta.

One new experience was that I went down into a submarine for the first time. Some of us on the 38 Squadron detachment who wanted to go into a submarine joined our squadron leader in this opportunity. The thinking was that because we were working with submariners so much, we should see what it was like on their side. The submarine didn't leave port but did submerge, so we were able to experience what that was like.

What was it like being down in a submarine and seeing the inner workings of one?
On that occasion, I didn't get the chance to see how the submarine fully operated, as it was docked in port. We were not in there for long, but I did get a claustrophobic feeling being stuck inside a metal

tube and a sense of fear and helplessness should anything go wrong. After so many hours flying aircraft, I had begun to learn what sorts of things go wrong and how to fix them, but in a submarine I had the impression that if something went wrong, then there wasn't much that could be done. It was the fear of drowning, I suppose. I love the open ocean and being at sea, but not under it; being under the sea felt unnatural to me.

What did you do during your free time at Ballykelly?
There was only one place of interest to me, and that was the city of Londonderry, only six miles away. It was from Londonderry that my navigator at the time and I took a day trip into the Republic of Ireland. We didn't go far into Ireland, only to the first town over the border. I remember that when we were in that town, it was clear that the atmosphere towards us was less than friendly, though to me, at least, the same atmosphere existed in Londonderry.

On the 9th of December you arrived by Lancaster at RAF Valley on the island of Anglesey, Wales, and spent the next twenty days there. What can you tell me about your time there?
I have no recollections of RAF Valley, so certainly nothing that happened there was ingrained upon my mind. It must have been classroom training of some sort, because not a single flight was made during my time there. Most likely, the subject was tied to maritime convoys and anti-submarine methods and duties.

On the 29th of December 1950 you returned to Malta.
Yes, and for just short of two months I was back at RAF Luqa in Malta. The flying was mostly taken up with exercises. The training during that period included a low-level bombing exercise on the 5th of January 1951. Also, there was an instrument flying exercise, which meant that I could fly the aircraft only using the dials in front of me. I wasn't allowed to look out of the windows. The other exercises that I have in my log book are coded, though I can see that there was a navigational exercise to Benina.

On the 20th of February 1951, you flew to Gibraltar to take part in a big exercise that involved the Americans and in which Prince Philip commanded a frigate.

Yes, four 38 Squadron Lancasters were sent to Gibraltar. My Lancaster flew there on the 20th, the second and third Lancasters arrived on the 23rd, and the fourth Lancaster arrived on the 24th. My crew and I transported thirteen ground crew passengers, plus W/Cdr G.B. Warner; he officially flew as the aircraft's captain. Before the exercise took place, I had to take W/Cdr Warner to Port Lyautey, in Morocco, on the 22nd of February. Of the four 38 Squadron Lancasters in Gibraltar before the exercise began, three were unserviceable. The one in which I had flown to Gibraltar was able to fly, but it had no instruments; every single cockpit instrument had been removed for servicing after we had arrived on the Rock. I reported this to W/Cdr Warner, but he countered by saying, 'Look, there is not a cloud in the sky. What do you need instruments for?' And that was that.

Consequently, we went to Port Lyautey and came back on the same day in that Lancaster. It was the only time that I have ever flown without a single instrument. When we arrived at our Moroccan destination, the wing commander went off to watch a film, and my crew and I had to stay with the aircraft, so we didn't even get a chance to see anything of the country.

Next came the major exercise, in which you flew day and night on four separate days within a week.

The exercise, named 'Straits One', began on the 26th of February 1951. The purpose of the exercise was to ensure that convoys could safely come in and out of the Mediterranean via the Straits of Gibraltar without being torpedoed by submarines.

I remember on the first day of the exercise, while flying at night, we were given a patrol assignment to carry out. It could have been a 'square' search or a north-south 'creeping line ahead' search. A north-south creeping line is when the aircraft conducting the search flies from north-to-south in its search zone, turns 180 degrees at the southern end of the zone and then flies northward again, on a slightly different longitudinal track that is parallel to the first leg. At the northern limit of the zone, another 180-degree turn is made, and a new, parallel south-facing longitudinal track is flown. This back-and-forth 'creeping line' eventually covers the entire area of the search box. A square search is when the aircraft starts in the middle of its assigned search box and expands outward, covering the area. These are two examples of search patterns; there are more.

On the first night, I had a bust-up with a pilot over the radio after he ordered me to change the altitude at which I was flying. I remember him coming out with something like, 'Hey buddy, what height are you flying at?' I was at 1,000 feet, so that's what I told him. 'I want you to go to 2,000 feet,' came his reply. 'Negative,' was my response. He asked me for my rank, which was flight sergeant at that stage. He told me his rank, which was higher than mine, and then ordered me to go to 2,000 feet. My reply was that I was captain of my aircraft, and the only person I took orders from was my own commanding officer.

Was that exchange mentioned in the wash-up afterwards?
Yes, every captain gave his version of events. Eventually, it was my turn to stand up. I proceeded to explain how this pilot had ordered me to change my height, which I had refused to do, and I explained why I refused. W/Cdr Warner of my squadron then stood up and said that what I had done was right, that I was the captain of the aircraft, and that I had obeyed the orders of my CO.

Were the next three flying days as eventful as the first?
No. The only submarine I came across was on the first night. The submarine was on the surface, and its commander was clever; he had stopped close to a group of fishing boats which were not supposed to be there, and which had also turned their lights on to attract fish. The submarine commander had turned on his submarine's navigation lights to try and blend in, but to me it didn't look right. So I came in low without any navigation lights on and circled around, in order to confirm that it was a submarine. Once I had done so, I ascended and came in a second time. I didn't drop sonobuoys around the submarine, as I had done during the previous big exercise, off the coast of Malta. This time, I had to try and 'kill' any submarine I

found, so when I came in on the second approach, I opened the bomb doors and claimed the so-called 'kill'. Cameras attached to the aircraft captured the whole event.

At the wash-up afterwards, the submarine commander got up and gave his version of events. I then got up and gave my account. Once he realised that it was me who had 'killed' him, he uttered, 'Bloody hell, not you again.' The reason for this is that I had by pure coincidence 'killed' his submarine twice in the past.

The first time, we had been going from Malta to an exercise off the south of Cyprus. There was a rule at the time that if you saw a submarine, even between exercises, you could claim it as a 'kill'. On that occasion, it was on the surface heading due east.

The second time was when we were on our way from Malta to Gibraltar for the exercise. I was south of him, heading due west. I had him on radar but didn't know if it was a submarine, as it appeared as just a blip, but it was down to sheer luck that we spotted his submarine on the surface; it was lit up by moonlight.

I became friends with that submarine commander, and when I was back in Malta he invited me down into his submarine on an exercise. During the Gibraltar exercise, however, that particular submarine was the only one I found; not much of note happened on my other flights.

Wasn't it during this big exercise that your crew revolted?
Yes, during that period we were doing quite a lot of flying, day and night, as has already been mentioned. Sometime during the exercise my crew came and informed me that they were rebelling because of the amount of flying that we were doing. They wanted me to be their spokesperson, but I wanted nothing to do with it. In fact, I cautioned them that they would be looking at a court-martial if they went ahead with it.

Still, they were undeterred. They went to see the wing commander and announced that they were revolting, but he either misunderstood or misheard them and replied that if they were vomiting then they should go to the sickbay, as there was nothing that he could do about it. My crew didn't follow it up and just left. They were very lucky that he had responded as he did.

Did you come into contact with Prince Philip again during the exercise?

No, not during the exercise. The only time I saw him was during the wash-ups, which were debriefings. I found it interesting that whenever he got up to speak, whoever was speaking would sit down straight away regardless of his own rank. I don't believe it was a rule, just courtesy.

Following that exercise, you had a week in Gibraltar. What was your impression of it?

I really liked Gibraltar and would return during my later time with 38 Squadron. The people were very friendly, the food was delicious, the weather was wonderful and the atmosphere of the place was great. I liked it so much that I asked people I knew if they could purchase property on my behalf, though it never happened.

While in Gibraltar, I actually met W/Cdr Blackburn for the last time, though I can't exactly remember if it was on this occasion or another, as I visited Gibraltar quite a few times. When I did meet him this final time, he no longer had the German E-boat. He told me he was transporting the yachts of rich Americans across the Atlantic and into the Mediterranean. The owners would fly over and then have a sailing holiday in the Med. After they were finished they would fly back home, and he would sail their yachts back across the Atlantic to America. During our meeting we went to Europa Point. A photo of us was taken there, though I don't know where the photo is. But that was the last time I saw W/Cdr Blackburn. He ended up settling in Antigua.

After the week in Gibraltar following the exercise, I returned by air to Malta, on the 10th of March, in the same Lancaster that I had flown out in; the instruments which had been removed on arrival in Gibraltar had been reinstalled. Flying with my crew and I once again was W/Cdr Warner, the same 38 Squadron senior officer we had taken to Gibraltar on the 20th of February, and then, on the 22nd, to Morocco and back to Gibraltar. In addition, as on the flight from Luqa to Gibraltar, we carried thirteen ground crew as our passengers.

After returning from Gibraltar you had just under four months in Malta before heading back to Northern Ireland for a little over five weeks. How was your time in Malta spent?

The weeks were mainly spent on exercises, many with coded names which I can no longer decipher. Some were navigational, and most were in cooperation with the navy. My crew practiced bombing and gunnery skills, and, as usual, there were air tests to conduct. We flew to Nicosia, Cyprus, twice in this period, prior to our second deployment to Northern Ireland, each time returning to Luqa two days later. Only twice were we needed for air-sea rescue work, which I spoke about earlier.

Earlier, you mentioned that after becoming friends with its commander, you went down in the submarine that you had 'killed' three times.

After the Gibraltar exercise he and I became quite good friends. Out there at least, there was an agreement that if an airman wanted to go aboard a naval vessel or if a seaman wanted to go up in the air, then it could be organised. So I arranged to accompany the submarine commander out to sea on a short exercise.

The first thing I noticed upon entering the submarine was the smell of boiled cabbage.

I certainly sensed my uneasiness when the submarine left port; I was out of my element in an environment which felt unnatural, but I had expected this, and so it was of little concern to me. I was very interested to see how an exercise worked on their side, and I quickly noticed that the submarine crew worked like a well-oiled machine. What I also became aware of was the immediate change in internal pressure when a dummy torpedo was fired.

On the 5th of July you travelled to RAF Aldergrove, eleven miles west of Belfast, Northern Ireland, for your second stint there, associated with the Joint Anti-Submarine School. This stay lasted just over five weeks.

The day before we left, I fractured my wrist in a swimming accident. As it was July, with wonderful weather, a group of us had gone to Delimara Point for a swim before our departure. Everyone else had finished and was heading to the car, but I decided to stay in for a few more minutes. One of the others called out that they were going to leave without me, so I got out of the water, gathered my things and made a dash for the car. It was then that I tripped, and the landing resulted in a fractured wrist. Back at base, I was seen by the medical officer, who bandaged my wrist. Fortunately, it didn't inhibit my flying of the aircraft. The only thing I couldn't do was apply the brakes, so the co-pilot did that for me.

Regarding Northern Ireland, it was more exercises, though in my log book they are written in code, which I can no longer decipher. I only made five flights while I was there. It was quite an uneventful five weeks.

You returned to Malta on the 11th of August and would remain there for another four months and nearly three weeks. What happened during that time?
The first month was business as usual, including practice in instrument flying, two long night and one lengthy daylight exercises, radar homings, training in low-level bombing and even a trip from Luqa to Castel Benito, Libya, and back. Then, in the second week of September 1951, the CO notified me in his office that I was chosen to participate in a flying display to commemorate the Battle of Britain. I assumed it would be in Malta, but, in fact, it was to be in Gibraltar. When I asked the CO for more information, I was informed that I would be flying a Lancaster against a Vampire in what was known as 'fighter affiliation'. In such an exercise, the Lancaster attempted to evade a mock fighter attack by, in this case, a jet-powered Vampire.

On the way to Gibraltar on the 12th of September, I practised my corkscrew flying, as it's the way one throws off an attacking fighter. On the 14th I practised for the display together with the Vampire, and we performed it the next day.

Keep in mind that I was not alone in my Lancaster; my crew was with me during the display. From five miles out we kept aligned with the runway and began our display, finishing up when over the runway. During the display I corkscrewed the Lancaster violently to present as difficult a target as possible to the 'attacking' Vampire, whose pilot was attempting to mock-shoot me down. During the actual flying I couldn't see the Vampire behind me, so I just focused on trying to throw it off. The air traffic controller called up to say how impressive the display appeared to those watching and asked if we would do it again, to which we both agreed.

The Vampire pilot turned to the south over the Bay of Gibraltar to avoid the over-3.5-mile long linear north-south-aligned Rock of Gibraltar, and when clear of the Rock itself, he turned eastward over open water to bring himself back to the starting point. I took a more dramatic route and went into a rate four turn. In the narrow window in which I was flying, the Rock of Gibraltar was on my immediate left at the finish of our first display. In order to turn back without having to follow the Vampire's route south to avoid the Rock before turning east, I opted for the incredibly tight 180 degree rate four turn, virtually standing the plane on its side, returning my Lancaster over the airfield, this time with the Rock on my right.

Looking back, I still sometimes can't believe I did that manoeuvre because that turn was done within the limits of the runway and the Rock itself. It was a crazy manoeuvre; I would never do that type of turn again.

Once we were back at the starting point, the Vampire and my Lancaster repeated what we had done on the first pass, but afterwards we both flew out over the Bay of Gibraltar, which was roughly four miles across. I can't speak for the Vampire's whereabouts from that point on, but I circled around for about an hour until the remainder of the Battle of Britain display was over; this was because other aircraft were taking part, and I didn't want to be in the wrong place at the wrong time.

After the display was all over and I had landed, the group captain in charge of RAF Gibraltar told me that when I performed the rate four turn, he could see the top of my cockpit. In fact, he seemed quite annoyed about it. The Vampire pilot told me that he was unable to get me in his gunsight and would most likely have been unable to shoot me down.

Both my Lancaster and the Vampire had cameras fitted, and it was also filmed and photographed from the ground, so footage of this must exist somewhere.

After I returned to Malta on the 17th, I only flew once more in September: a short coded night exercise of one hour and forty-five minutes on the 26th. Even when we weren't flying, there were still duties to perform. I already mentioned one, with the fire extinguisher, where I nearly lost my eyesight. Another example of a necessary duty was in assisting the officers on their rounds. On any days where no duties had to be completed, I was free to leave the airfield, as long as I had permission from the CO.

How did October compare to September?
I flew seven times for a total of twenty-eight hours and forty-five minutes in September, and seven times for twenty-two hours in October. In fact, the 4th of October was when the propeller started to come off, which resulted in me diverting to Wheelus Field, the American air base near Tripoli, Libya. On the 8th, we had to do a simulated lifeboat drop exercise. We didn't actually drop the lifeboat; instead, we just practiced maintaining the correct height and speed. The rest of the month consisted of more exercises and, on the 12th, the one air-sea rescue call out off the coast of Cyprus, which I briefly mentioned earlier.

November carried on in a similar vein. The problem with November was that by then it was much colder, and the sea was too chilly for swimming, so the seasonal change limited the things that one could do outdoors. I started playing a lot of squash, as RAF Luqa had its own squash court.

One noteworthy event that happened in November was that a disagreement I had been having with my CO regarding my rank concluded. For a few months prior, he had been pressuring me into becoming a commissioned officer again; I had been flying as a flight sergeant. He claimed that the RAF wanted all aircraft captains to be commissioned officers. However, I had no interest in becoming a commissioned officer; I had been one before and didn't have any interest in becoming one again. The reason for this is that life as a commissioned officer was more formal, rigid and expensive; expensive in the sense that an officer had to pay for things like mess fees, garden fees, the CO's charity, formal occasions and things like that. While if you were non-commissioned, you didn't have to pay for any of that. This dispute with my CO lasted several months, until it came to the surface when he called me into his office and said that it was now official RAF policy that all pilots had to be commissioned. Consequently, I relented and agreed to become a commissioned officer, for the second time.

A special plane, a twin-engine Valetta, was put on to take me to Fayid airfield in Egypt on the 19th of November 1951. I underwent an interview and a full medical before returning to Luqa on the 24th. I passed, the results were sent to my CO and, after the bureaucratic side was sorted, I became a commissioned officer once again in March 1952. My promotion advanced me from flight sergeant all the way to flying officer, bypassing warrant officer and pilot officer ranks completely. I had previously skipped one rank when being promoted, back in both 1944 (sergeant to warrant officer) and again in 1946 (warrant officer to flying officer), and now I was jumping two ranks.

The reason for me skipping two ranks was based upon money, like in 1946; the pay of a pilot officer, the lowest commissioned rank, was lower than that of a flight sergeant.

December was more eventful. The first three days were spent in Tunisia, flying to Bizerte and El Aouina. On the night of the 3rd of December, an engine caught fire not far off the coast of Cyprus, just as we were going to join the Mediterranean Fleet for a combined exercise. When I told you about this event earlier, I failed to mention that I was not even the pilot on that occasion. The CO had told me that my co-pilot should captain the aircraft, to 'gain further experience', and that's what happened. My co-pilot-turned-pilot took off from Luqa and flew to Cyprus. Just before the engine caught fire he went to use the lavatory, so I sat in the pilot's seat during his brief time away from the cockpit. While I was in his seat, the engine caught fire, which turned out to be fortunate, as my co-pilot told me that he would not have known what to do if he had been in the pilot's seat when it occurred.

He landed the aircraft upon our return to Malta. Afterwards, the CO told me that in the flight log book I should write that I was the captain, not co-pilot, as it would look ridiculous that a captain had only 100 hours or so of flying and the co-pilot had well over 1,700 hours of flying. I agreed with him that it looked ridiculous, but I refused to enter it into the flight log book as he wished, resulting in quite a dispute. I faced no punishment for it.

The first few days of 1952 were spent in Cyprus.
Yes, we flew to Cyprus on the 31st of December and were there for about four days. We had a set number of exercises to complete and a set amount of time in which to complete them. One exercise was low-level bombing, which we performed on three consecutive days – the 1st, 2nd and 3rd of January 1952. On the first and third days of exercises, we also practiced air-to-air firing. Another Lancaster towed a target sleeve quite a distance behind it, and I had to position our Lancaster within range of the sleeve in order that our gunners could attempt to hit it using live ammunition. Then we swapped roles with the other Lancaster, with my aircraft towing the target sleeve and the other aircraft firing.

We then flew back to Malta on the 4th of January.

The decade of the 1950s was an interesting period of time in the history of Cyprus, a British Crown Colony until independence was gained in 1960. Though the beginning of the Cyprus Emergency was not until the 1st of April 1955, still over three years away when you were there, the majority Greek Cypriot population had made their feelings known; they were against British rule and wanted a union with Greece. Though your time there was limited, what impressions, if any, were you left with?
I can only speak for myself, but fortunately I can't say that I experienced any direct anti-British feelings; in fact, I enjoyed my time there. We would go out to places like cafes where locals would be and they seemed friendly enough. I remember that I used to go swimming in Morphou Bay without incident. It's hard to believe how things would change just a few years later.

Your promotion from flight sergeant to flying officer went into effect in March 1952. How had life changed for you, after you had attained an officer's rank again?
It became more rigid and formal; there were more duties to complete and responsibilities to take on. I just had to adapt from being a non-commissioned flight sergeant to becoming a commissioned flying officer. It was not as hard as it was the first time, back in 1946.

Also, I had so much leave saved up that between flights on the 10th of January and the 14th of March I only flew three times, and none after the 5th of February. Upon my return to Malta from leave, my first flight was a naval/air exercise on the 14th of March. On the 18th of March I flew twice in one day. The first was a simulated sonobuoy exercise homing in on smoke floats acting as sonobuoys, and the second exercise was the same as before but with radar homing added in.

My last flight with 38 Squadron was a cooperative naval/air exercise on the 22nd of March 1952. I was posted back to the UK on the 29th of March and then went on leave until the 15th of May.

Do you have a positive opinion of Malta?
I liked Malta. It was a nice place to be, there were interesting places to visit and the people were generally friendly. My main enjoyment when stationed in Malta was derived from flying when on duty and swimming when not on duty.

Valletta itself was pleasant. It had great cafes, there was a relaxed atmosphere and it was quite visually pleasing. The problem for me was that my posting of over two years and five months was too long for a country of Malta's size. Within time, I felt as though I had seen everything, so I wasn't sad to leave.

CHAPTER FIFTEEN

FLYING FROM BRITAIN, PLUS SUEZ CRISIS ASSIGNMENTS FROM MALTA AND CYPRUS, MAY 1952 – MARCH 1957

The School of Maritime Reconnaissance, the Queen's Coronation Review of the RAF, the Queen and Prince Philip's Commonwealth tour, more comments on ageing Lancasters, the Farnborough Air Show disaster, Denis's promotion to flight lieutenant, the Air/ Sea Warfare Development Unit, 228 Squadron and a new aircraft - the Shackleton, 236 Operational Conversion Unit, back to 228 Squadron, Denis's neck injury, the de Havilland Comet, the Suez Crisis, Denis's final RAF flight and his opinion of the Shackleton

On the 15th of May 1952, you were posted to the School of Maritime Reconnaissance at RAF St Mawgan, Cornwall.
Yes. I was a member of the staff. Qualified aircrew were posted as students to this school in order to learn about air-sea warfare and how to work with the navy on combined navy-air force operations. Whoever was heading the naval side of an exercise would contact the participating Lancasters and explain what he wanted each aircraft to do. For example, the assignment could involve scanning the areas ahead of or to either side of the fleet, or even behind the fleet to check if the ships were being shadowed, but there were many different exercises in which aircrew students were required to participate. All of these exercises were coded in a course syllabus, and I entered these codes into my log book when I took part in the relevant exercise, but over time I have forgotten the meaning of the coded exercises. Each aircraft's navigator at the time had a key to these codes.

On the exercises, all I had to do was fly the plane. The trainee pilot was already a qualified pilot, so he didn't need to learn how to fly the aircraft. He would, however, be at the School of Maritime Reconnaissance to learn the naval side of the patrols so that he could eventually join a squadron. The other trainees would practise their trades. Any mistakes that they made would be corrected afterwards by the chief navigator or chief of whatever skill they were covering. Staff pilots like me had to keep their flying skills up by completing a minimum of thirty hours a month of flying. I usually did a lot more.

Generally, how did the students do?
Quite well, I would say. They had already learnt their respective roles; otherwise they would not have been at St Mawgan. The fundamental reason they were there was to learn how to work with the navy, although there was one instance when a student navigator got it completely wrong.

We were in cloud at 1,000 feet, which was the standard height for flying over the sea. We suddenly experienced turbulence, but I knew from experience that we were over land. There are different types of turbulence depending on upon whether over land or over sea. I quickly realised that we were flying over Ireland, not open water, as expected. Due to the direction that we were travelling in, I put the aircraft into a rapid climb to 10,000 feet, as I knew that we would fly into the Wicklow Mountains if I did not, and also so I could send a transmission to St Mawgan.

I asked the student navigator where he thought we were. He replied that we had to be over Bristol. I then told him to give me a course to get back to St Mawgan, and his response was to plot a southwesterly course. I informed him that if I was to rely upon his navigation, then we would finish up ditching in the sea. The staff navigator took over and plotted a correct course to base.

Later on, I spoke to the trainee navigator, and it transpired that he had completely misjudged the wind as northerly, when it was actually coming from the south. It doesn't sound like much, but it was. For example, say that the wind speed is twenty knots from the north and a navigator works out his course assuming that the wind is twenty knots from the south, then the total error is immense, and the aircraft will end up in a different location to where it was meant to. The chief navigator also went over the charts with the student and showed him where he had gone wrong.

On another occasion, I was captaining a Lancaster with a student pilot and a student navigator on board during a navy cooperation exercise. I had to go to the Elsan, which was the lavatory facility in the aircraft, so I handed the controls to the flight engineer while I was gone. When I returned, I heard the student navigator having words with the flight engineer. The student navigator was complaining to him about not keeping straight and level while I was gone. I pointed out that a slight deviation was acceptable when the flight engineer was at the controls. The student navigator was silent for a few minutes but then he started up again, arguing about the flight engineer. I ordered him to put down his equipment, that I was going to navigate the rest of the way and to consider himself arrested. Once in range, I contacted the control tower and asked for the CO to be available. He was waiting for us when we arrived. I explained the situation to him and left it in his hands. The punishment handed out, as I later learnt, was that the CO gave the student navigator a strict talking to and confined him to his room for the rest of the week.

A navigational exercise that we used to do with student navigators was to take off from St Mawgan, fly due west, then turn in a southeasterly direction and head for another turning point that we used to use north of Spain over the Bay of Biscay. Once there, we would turn north and fly back to base. The exercise's flightpath formed a big triangle, about 1,000 miles in total length.

In what ranges did the navigation exercises take place?
They took place in the Atlantic, mostly down to the coast of northern Spain and back. On three occasions we took weekend trips down to Gibraltar, which was always a nice break, but they were counted as official exercises. On two of those trips, in January 1953 and September 1954, groups of RAF passengers went along. Although it didn't happen on any of my flights, often passengers on similar flights to Gibraltar went mainly to buy thousands of cigarettes. Apparently they were much cheaper in Gibraltar. I remember

hearing that another aircraft had landed back in the UK after a trip to Gibraltar, only to be met by customs officials. So it was something that was known to the authorities.

How did life at the School of Maritime Reconnaissance compare to the squadrons you were on?

There was a difference, but it wasn't so much where I was as what I was. On 159 Squadron and 38 Squadron I wasn't a commissioned officer, aside from the last month or so in Malta, while during my time in Cornwall and Coastal Command I was. I have already spoken about the differences that being commissioned involved.

As a senior staff member, what duties did you have to complete?

They weren't much different from that of my commissioned duties. But on one occasion, the flight commander was posted away, so I took over his role on a temporary basis until someone relieved me. The first thing I did was to order a tool inspection, which I and four other officers conducted. The objective of this was to see if any tools were missing, and if so, why. Upon inspection, several tools were missing. One corporal was missing around five or six items. Some of the excuses were laughable; the main one was to claim that the missing tool had been loaned to someone else. The ground crews, divided into A, B and C Flights, claimed that tools loaned to other flights had not been returned. All I could do was write a report to the CO, who had the power to charge the ground crew for the missing items, but I don't know what came of it. The main objective from my perspective was to keep the ground crew on their toes. If no one checked on them, then they would have taken advantage of it indefinitely.

Aside from exercises with the students, did you have to complete any exercises yourself?

Yes. Checks on the staff were made by the CO or flight commander on a regular basis, to make sure that one was up to standards. The exercises were more rigorous than just basic circuits and landings; we were judged on things like stalling, sharp turns and asymmetric landings. Every month we had to practise landing on three engines, while once a year staff pilots were tested by an examiner from the

241

Central Flying School. With the CFS examiners, skills required of staff pilots at the School of Maritime Reconnaissance were more comprehensive than I had ever previously experienced. In one instance, a staff pilot was grounded because an examiner from the Central Flying School was not happy with his performance. The grounded pilot ended up being posted away to a squadron.

I also earnt my Master Green Instrument Flying Certificate while I was at the school.

What was a Master Green Instrument Flying Certificate?

There were three ratings: White, Green and Master Green. The rating held stated the conditions that one could fly and land in. The reason I had yet to attain a Master Green Test Rating was because during the war things were completely different; we didn't do tests like that. When I went back into the RAF, peacetime rules applied, so I had to take tests, which didn't bother me. I had already earnt my Green rating, in Malta, when I was with 38 Squadron.

For the Master Green test itself, I went up with an examiner, who obviously held a Master Green. During the test I wore a hood that blocked my view out of the windows. The examiner also covered certain dials and instruments, though what was covered up depended on what the examiner was asking of me. If the examiner asked me to do a rate one turn, the instruments which showed how sharply I was turning were visible. All of this was to show that I could perform the exercises without relying on any other instruments. Needless to say, I passed.

I know I have mentioned instrument flying a few times, and while it sounds mad to fly an aircraft without being able to see out of the windows, there are many occasions when it is necessary, like when flying at night or through clouds, where the pilot can't see his surroundings, and must, instead, rely on the instruments.

Even though I was on the staff at the school for a month short of three years, it was quite repetitive in the sense that exercises were repetitive. The objective was to get the students to perform to the same standards as the students who came through the school before. That meant a repeating of exercises for each new group of students.

Your time at the School of Maritime Reconnaissance coincided with the coronation of Queen Elizabeth II, which took place on the 2nd of June 1953, and the RAF Coronation Review, which took place over a month later on the 15th of July 1953. Seeing as you took part in the RAF Coronation Review, what do you remember about it?

Yes. On the 28th of June 1953, my crew and I flew to RAF Odiham for the Queen's Coronation Review of the RAF. For the event itself, there were over 300 static aircraft on display, including four Lancasters; I was the captain of one of them. Over 600 aircraft from the RAF and Commonwealth airforces took part in the flypast. In total, we were there for three weeks, and what I remember is that the weather was terrible; it rained a lot and we had to clean and polish the aircraft every day. Our accommodation was in tents, and we were plagued by earwigs.

One memory that sticks out is when a high-ranking air-official came past my Lancaster with a group of women and told them that my aircraft was a Shackleton. When I corrected him, he looked at me and with a stern voice told me that it was a Shackleton.

On the day of the review itself, the 15th of July 1953, the weather was fine. All the aircraft that were on the ground were lined up wingtip to wingtip, including the four Lancasters. The crews of each aircraft stood in front of their plane, including myself and my crew in front of our Lancaster, and the Queen came past on an open-back vehicle and inspected all the aircraft present. Later that day, the flypast took place, which as I mentioned involved over 600 aircraft.

Two days later, on the 17th of July, we flew back to St Mawgan. I remember that we had a small fire in the radar section, but it didn't cause any trouble and was quickly put out. We landed without any problems.

A few months later, in November, you were on standby for the first leg of the Queen and Prince Philip's Commonwealth tour.

That's right. On the 21st of November 1953, my crew and I flew to St Eval so our Lancaster could be fitted with a lifeboat, and the next day, on the 22nd of November, we flew to RAF Aldergrove, in Northern Ireland, to prepare for the Queen and Prince Philip's departure for their Commonwealth tour. Alongside my crew and I, there was also another pilot and crew on standby; their Lancaster was also fitted with a lifeboat.

The royal couple's first destination was Newfoundland, in Canada, so the area we were to cover was the half of the Atlantic closest to Britain, with the Royal Canadian Airforce taking over once the royal aircraft had crossed into the other half of the Atlantic.

Prior to us going on standby, the CO gave us our instructions, which were that if the royal aircraft went missing, we were to search the area to the limit of our fuel capacity and then ditch beside the closest ship, if there were any in the area.

Fortunately, the Queen and Prince Philip's journey went without incident, and we weren't called to partake in any air-sea rescue operations. We returned to St Eval on the 24th of November.

One amusing thing was that after we received our instructions from the CO, the pilot of the other Lancaster made a quip that if anything happened to the royal aircraft and we had to search for it, would we receive the Victoria Cross before or after taking off. The CO replied with a comment about sarcasm.

When we were talking about your time in Malta, you mentioned that the Lancaster bombers being flown were suffering a high incident rate due to their age, and that you experienced it for yourself during your time with Coastal Command in both Malta and Britain. What incidents occurred while you were at the School of Maritime Reconnaissance?

The first incident that comes to mind was when a new pilot joined the staff. On one of his first flights, he had the misfortune of suffering a double engine failure. As he was making his final approach to land, he completely misjudged the strength of the wind and as a result crashed about half a mile short of the runway. Fortunately, everyone survived, though there were some bad injuries. The Lancaster they were in was completely written off.

On the 15th of December 1954, I was due to fly on an exercise with students, but I just had a bad feeling – a very strong feeling – telling me not to fly. On that night, nothing would have gotten me up in the air. I found a fault with the Lancaster I was due to fly and then did the same with the Lancasters in reserve. I was on B Flight, and I then similarly found fault with two Lancasters from A Flight. Eventually, the CO called the exercise off.

The next day, on the 16th of December, an incident did happen. I went up with students on a daytime exercise in one Lancaster, and later that same day the flight commander of B Flight, also with students, went up in another Lancaster on a nighttime exercise. For the exercise I was on, we went on our familiar route over the Atlantic to the west, turned and proceed down to the usual point near Spain, then turned around and came back to St Mawgan via the Isles of Scilly. It was the same triangle exercise that I already mentioned.

I landed at St Mawgan, went for a post-flight meal and then went to bed. I couldn't have been there for too long when I was awakened and told that I had to take the lifeboat-equipped Lancaster to nearby RAF St Eval airfield, as nothing had been heard from the flight commander's Lancaster. At St Eval, my crew and I were put on standby. We had been there at St Eval for two or three hours when a message came through that a trawler had spotted wreckage and that a body floating in the water had been picked up.

It was found that one wheel had come to the surface still attached to its oleo leg, which is the piston that connects the wheel to the undercarriage. The floating corpse was the flight engineer, with his head caved in. What the authorities concluded was that the flight commander must have left his seat and handed the controls to the flight engineer, who probably stepped on the undercarriage lever by accident. Once the undercarriage was down, drag on the aircraft would have increased, causing the nose to lower and the speed of the aircraft to rise. It was worked out that they must have been doing around 180 miles per hour when they hit the water. Everyone on board was killed. Although there was a bolt that locked the undercarriage lever in place to stop anyone accidentally stepping on and lowering it, Lancasters were getting so old that it was thought that the bolt, probably worn down, had snapped.

Ultimately, the reason why the flight commander's Lancaster crashed was speculative.

The feeling that told you not to fly on that one occasion, could you describe it?
It was an instinct telling me that if I went up in the air something would go dangerously wrong. Yet the next day I didn't have that feeling at all, and everything felt fine.

Let's go back to the incidents that happened with many of the Lancasters.
There was a case of a young chap on another squadron who forgot to put his undercarriage down and just slid along the runway with sparks and flames shooting out. I know this because I saw the whole thing.

On the 25th of October 1954, I lost both inboard engines, one after the other, when around 50 miles from base. After feathering the propeller on number two engine, the first to quit, I called up the control tower at St Mawgan to report that the engine had failed due to a lack of oil pressure. Number three engine then died for the same reason, and I successfully feathered its propeller. I was now coming in on two engines. Able to maintain height on those two engines, I was told by the control tower that the circuit was clear of other aircraft, so I carried out a normal approach at a reduced height and landed safely. There were ambulances and fire engines waiting for me, in case I crash landed. After I exited the runway, I radioed the control tower, where the CO was waiting, and he commended me on a good landing. I replied that my next trick would be to land backwards, which was met with a dry 'Haha.'

What differences occur when you land on two engines, as opposed to four?
You only have half the power, so you have to increase the power on the good engines. Fortunately, we were close to base with only around twenty minutes of flying left when my two engines failed, so I was able to do a low-level circuit and land. If two engines had failed on the same side, then I would have increased power on the two working engines, while also putting on a lot of trim and rudder to compensate for the side where both engines were not functioning.

While on the topic of the problems that many Lancasters experienced and the challenges and sometimes awful consequences that resulted from them, you were in the crowd for Britain's worst air show disaster, at Farnborough on the 6th of September 1952. What do you remember about that tragic event?

Just to be clear, the Farnborough Air Show didn't take place in the Farnborough I grew up in, then in Kent but now in Greater London. Instead, it was in Farnborough, Hampshire.

What I remember is that I had not too long before joined the School of Maritime Reconnaissance. A fellow officer, named Alex, asked if I was going to drive to the Farnborough Air Show, and if so, could I give him a lift, to which I agreed. On arrival there, we were able to park quite close to the main runway, which was fenced off from the public by a post and wire boundary. Alex noticed after a few minutes of standing at the fence that there was a small mound about 100 yards away that would give us a better view. However, it was already quite crowded, so we decided to stay put on the grass verge that ran parallel to the runway. There were also many people where we were; the crowd was quite deep.

The high point of the show that day was going to be a display by a supersonic de Havilland DH.110 aircraft, piloted by a chap named John Derry, who was a test pilot for de Havilland, the aircraft manufacturer. Anthony Richards, a flight test observer, was also aboard. It wasn't long before we heard the aircraft arriving.

After climbing to 40,000 feet, the DH.110 shattered the sound barrier in a supersonic dive towards the airfield, producing a triple boom, immediately followed by a flypast up the runway at about 500 feet and at a speed in excess of 500 miles per hour.

Flying away from the crowd, Derry then banked to the left and flew in a circle so that he was heading back towards the spectators, opposite to the direction he had come in along the runway. Under the stresses of straightening up from the turn and simultaneously pulling into a climb, the wings failed and broke off. The intact cockpit section also broke away from the airframe, but it was one of the two engines, each shooting off like a missile out of the airframe, which caused the worst carnage. This engine ploughed into the crowd of spectators on the mound that Alex and I had almost joined, and the other engine crashed harmlessly, while the cockpit, bouncing along the ground, headed straight towards the crowd that we were in. Fortunately, it stopped about 100 yards away, having injured spectators. We could plainly see John Derry and Anthony Richards inside the cockpit. The main airframe landed on the other side of the airfield.

In no time, rescue vehicles raced towards the cockpit and the mound. Alex and I decided that it would be best for us to leave, to avoid all the rescue activities that were taking place.

We later learnt that twenty-nine people had been killed and many more injured.

What impact did it have on you, considering all your years piloting aircraft and the risky manoeuvres you had performed yourself?
The impact, to use your word, was so strong that I clearly remember the details of the tragic event, even all these years later. It's the kind of memory that can never go away. It was without a doubt the worst crash I have seen in my life.

During your time at the School of Maritime Reconnaissance you were promoted to the rank of flight lieutenant.
The promotion process started in late March 1955 in the latter stages of my tenure at the School of Maritime Reconnaissance, but it was not quick. One of the reasons I applied at this time to sit the exams was to gain the pay increase which accompanied the promotion, alongside it being a stepping stone in case I wanted to advance further in the RAF. At that stage I wasn't sure what I was going to do going forward, so I wanted to keep my options open, and that included the possibility of staying in the RAF.

I had to sit exams on five subjects, only one of which was aeronautical in nature. The five subjects were: Airmanship, Air Force Law, Administration, Queens Regulations, and General Knowledge. Before the exams, I tried to get a copy of the guide to Air Force Law, but so many people were taking exams that there wasn't a copy available, not to mention that I took those exams the day after returning from a navigational exercise in Gibraltar.

The rules were that if you failed on one subject but passed the other four you could retake that one subject six months later, but if you failed on more than one subject you had to retake all the subjects. I passed four out of the five subjects, failing on Air Force Law, but I passed on the second attempt. I then became a flight lieutenant.

After three years at the School of Maritime Reconnaissance, you left.

Yes. I left the school on the 3rd of April 1955. The following day, I was posted to a separate unit, the Air/Sea Warfare Development Unit, located next to the school at St Mawgan. It was an experimental unit where new technologies were tested. I was posted there as an adjutant, but having learnt my lesson from Norfolk, I started to complain straight away. As a result, I was only in that role for just under four months, which was fortunate, as I wasn't very good at it. On one occasion, a squadron leader came in and asked me where the CO was. My reply was something like, 'How am I supposed to know?' 'Ask a silly question,' was his response, and he stormed off in a huff. He could have put me in serious trouble for that remark, but thankfully I escaped disciplining. The adjutant's role was the same as in Norfolk, to basically act as the CO's secretary.

I didn't fly at all from the beginning of March until early August 1955.

The Lancaster was the plane you piloted for 2172 hours, more than any other aircraft, according to your log book. What are your thoughts on the Lancaster?

It was a lovely plane, and my favourite out of every one that I flew. It was highly manoeuvrable and handled very well. I can't fault this excellent plane. The cockpit had a great layout and the bomb bay and doors were really big. The only problem with them was that by the time I flew Lancasters they were getting old. The joke at the time was that they were kept together by string and chewing gum.

However, the Lancaster wasn't the only aircraft I flew during my time at the School of Maritime Reconnaissance. On a few occasions I did some local flying in a Chipmunk, a single-engine trainer plane. Two other officers and I also went up in an Oxford on one occasion, again, for local flying.

The next step for you was being posted to 228 Squadron, and onto a new aircraft, the Shackelton.

On the 27th of July 1955, I was posted to 228 Squadron at St Eval, only a short 2.5 miles north of St Mawgan. I spent the first three weeks in St Eval, not doing a lot; I just waited to be posted to 236 Operational Conversion Unit at Kinloss, in Scotland, in order to be converted onto the four-engine Shackleton. In those three weeks, I only went up in the air three times, all in Shackletons as the co-pilot.

After driving up to Kinloss in my Austin 10, arriving on the 22nd of August, I had to wait two weeks for the course to begin. During that time, on most days I drove the twelve or so miles to Elgin to shop, swim, go to the cinema or have a meal. I really liked Elgin, the pattern of the town and the friendliness of the people. I have always found the Scots to be friendly, generous people; I like Scotland. Even today, when looking through the football scores, I always look out for Elgin City.

Eventually, the course began. The process of learning to fly a Shackleton was basically the same as when I learnt to fly all the previous larger aircraft: understanding what effects the controls had, taxiing, straight and level flying, climbing and descending, stalling the engines while flying and then recovering control, turning (including turns while gliding and climbing), taking off into the wind, approaching the runway and landing. There were no written exams.

As with my earlier Lancaster training, I also had to fly over the sea, drop down to low levels and perform manoeuvres. The Shackleton was designed by Avro as an advanced version of their Lincoln bomber – itself a next-generation Lancaster. Being heavier than the Lancaster and with alternate engines and propellers, its handling and manoeuvrability were considerably different than the Lancaster. The electronics on the Shackleton, among other systems, were more modern, too, and they all had to be learnt. The Mark II Shackleton had a longer nose and longer tail than the Mark I, which affected the flying characteristics. The Mark III Shackleton introduced a nose wheel, unlike the Mark I and II, which had a tail wheel, like the Lancaster. I never flew the Mark III Shackleton, but if I had, it would have taken me back to Liberator days, as the Liberator had a nose wheel too.

After I had completed my training in Kinloss, I was posted back to 228 Squadron at St Eval, where I returned on the 5th of December 1955.

I remember you once telling me that during your time at Kinloss you had the opportunity to be posted back to the Far East.
Yes. During the course in Kinloss, vacancies in Hong Kong, Singapore, Malta and St Eval came up. The idea of going to the Far East really appealed to me, especially to Hong Kong, somewhere I had never been to before. I applied for Hong Kong but finished up being posted to St Eval. This was because two other officers with senior ranks to myself took Singapore and Hong Kong. I had been in Malta for two-and-a-half years, so going back there didn't particularly interest me. The only other place available was St Eval, back in Cornwall, which didn't really bother me since I liked Cornwall.

Judging by your location, I imagine that 228 Squadron spent a lot of time over the sea. Was the role of 228 Squadron similar to 38 Squadron?
Yes, for the most part; we performed many of the same maritime-related flying duties as we had in 38 Squadron, although we only flew on one air-sea rescue assignment, with no results. The clue is in the name 'Coastal Command', under which both 228 and 38 Squadrons fell. On three occasions in 1956, we flew to Malta to participate in exercises there. We also acted as troop carriers, as unlike a Lancaster, a Shackleton could transport troops, with all their kit and equipment in the bomb bay.

It's hard to remember much about the specific exercises we did because a lot of them are coded in my log book. Also, from my return to 228 Squadron on the 5th of December 1955 until the 29th of October 1956, when the Suez Crisis started, I only flew between three and four times a month, and often as co-pilot.

On the 28th of May 1956, a high-ranking government official, someone to do with the Air Ministry, came out on an exercise to experience a long-distance patrol first-hand. After it was over, we dropped him off at London Airport and then continued flying back to St Eval.

On the 8th of June, on the first of my three trips to Luqa while on 228 Squadron, I flew to Malta with my crew to join in a Mediterranean exercise with the Royal Navy that called for our

Shackleton to act as a convoy escort and lookout. We were the Royal Navy's 'eye in the sky'; that was the nickname they gave us. The exercise took place on the 11th of June, and once it was over we spent another month in Malta, where I only flew twice, on the 21st and 25th of June. However, between the 25th of June and the 10th of July, when I returned to St Eval from Malta, I had to recover from a bad neck injury.

What happened?
At the time of the accident on the 25th of June, when I injured my neck, Malta had been going through an unusual period of heavy storms and rough seas, which had ruled out swimming as a possible activity. Knowing that we were flying back to the UK the next day, four of us went to Sliema, to a place that resembled Delimara Point, to take advantage of a last opportunity to sunbathe. I'd had enough of not being able to swim even once during my June deployment in Malta, so despite red flag warnings declaring that swimming was not allowed because of rough sea conditions, I decided to go for a dip. One of our party warned me about the red flags, and I responded with something like, 'You know where you can stick your red flag.' I timed my dive to hit the peak of a wave, but I missed it and fell into the trough behind, which meant that the next high wave came crashing down onto my head at an angle that injured my neck.

I was pulled out of the sea by the other three, unable to move or even support my neck. We went back to where we were billeted, my head being supported the entire way, and then an ambulance was called. From there, I was taken to Bighi Naval Hospital, to a small room offset from the main ward, where I was laid on boards with my head immobilised, clamped either side so I couldn't move my neck at all. The assumption by the doctor was a broken neck. In time, he returned to say that an x-ray had revealed that as a child I had broken my neck, but that the present injury was strained ligaments. When you and I talked about my childhood I mentioned the original neck injury, when I fell backwards and banged my head. This had resulted in the injury missed by our elderly family doctor.

I was in hospital, in that room, for two weeks. There were two of us in the room, myself and a naval officer. We got on very well. On my first night there, we were telling each other jokes that had us in fits of laughter. Eventually we were told off by a nurse, as we were making too much noise. Upon discharge, I flew to St Mawgan, less than three miles south of St Eval, on the 10th of July 1956, the day before my thirty-second birthday.

During August and September I only flew three times in each month. Those flights were basic exercises and also circuits and landings. Nothing else of any note happened during that period.

On the 9th of October 1956, not long before the Suez Crisis, I gained my private flying licence in a twin-engine Anson. Also, I didn't have to take any written exams. I went up with the instructor and did a circuit and landing. The instructor then told me to go up on my own and to keep in sight of the airfield, so I did, for thirty minutes. That's how I got my private pilot's licence. It's funny really; it took me a year of hard work in Southern Rhodesia to get my wings but only thirty minutes to get my private pilot's licence.

Weren't you a passenger on a de Havilland Comet around that time?

Yes. As part of getting troops to Nicosia quickly as a result of the Suez Crisis heating up, we of 228 Squadron, then based at St Eval, were taken to Lyneham, in Wiltshire. On the 31st of October 1956, we boarded a Comet that took us to Luqa, in Malta, so we could transport troops from Malta to Cyprus. At one point, I asked one of the crew what height we were flying at, and he told us 44,000 feet, which amazed me. I had gone from orphan to high-flyer.

Wasn't the Comet at the time facing structural problems which had caused a few to break up in the air?

It had been through that phase, yes. It was public knowledge that in 1953 and 1954 three Comets had been lost due to structural failures, so there was a degree of apprehension among those of us flying as passengers to Malta. At one point during the flight, a bump as we went through an air pocket increased our worry for a while, though the crew told us that it was quite common to experience things like that at such a high altitude.

Though you were only a passenger, what was your impression of the Comet?
That is a difficult question. For one, it was much faster than a propeller-driven aircraft like the Lancaster or Shackleton. It got us to Malta in a little over three hours, whereas a Shackleton would have taken us six to seven hours to reach Malta. I formed the impression that the Comet was an aircraft that was well ahead of its time.

Tell me about your role in the Suez Crisis, which ran from late October 1956 until early March 1957.
It was quite minimal, really. I flew troops from Malta out to Cyprus in a Shackleton on the 2nd of November 1956, and in December I brought troops back to Malta. How it worked was that the troops were flown from St Eval to Luqa, in Malta, and then from Luqa to Nicosia, Cyprus. I didn't fly over Egypt or conduct any raids or anything like that.

My first trip carrying troops to Nicosia was strange in the sense that Nicosia air traffic control would not allow us to land, as there was ice on the runway. Until the ice had been cleared, we circled to the north of Nicosia, around Kyrenia on the coast, but we eventually landed at around four in the morning.

After dropping off the troops, we flew back to Malta and stayed there for a day. Whilst there, we saw one of the V-bombers take off; the noise was tremendous.

One thing we did hear was that apparently a pilot refused to take off to bomb a target, for religious reasons. I don't know the target, but I would guess that it was either Alexandria, an airfield or the Port of Suez itself. Following the pilot's refusal, he was warned that he would either be court-martialled or he could resign his commission; in other words, he could choose to leave the RAF, which he decided to do.

During the crisis itself, did you stay in Malta in case things escalated?
No. On the 3rd of November 1956 we returned to St Eval, one day after dropping off the troops in Cyprus and returning to Malta. In regard to flying, the rest of the month was taken up with instrument flying and exercises, with one exception. On the 11th of December

we flew back to Luqa, then from Luqa to Nicosia on the 13th, to pick up troops. From there, we returned to Luqa, and then the next day we flew back to the UK, to Lyneham, with the troops.

One amazing coincidence happened when we flew troops back to Lyneham via Malta. Billy, my younger foster brother, had been called up for national service in 1946, and then afterwards he had signed on. He had remained in the army during the 1950s, and during the Suez Crisis he was posted out there. What we both didn't realise until the Christmas of 1957, when we compared notes, was that I piloted the Shackleton that he returned to the UK on.

After Billy left the army, he married a Welsh woman and moved to Wales, though we kept in touch until he passed away, which was only a few years ago.

I don't remember too much of the next two months. There was no flying during that time, but I am sure that other than performing ground duties, I used leave I had accumulated. I flew twice in February, and my last-ever flight in the RAF was on the 5th of March 1957, taking Air Training Corps cadets up for some local flying. It's quite symbolic to me now that my first time going up in an aircraft was as a cadet and my last flight was as a pilot taking up cadets.

In the weeks and months prior to your last flight, what were your plans going forward? You must have known that your time in the RAF was coming to an end.

Originally, I planned to go into air traffic control. In my mind, it was a way to get back overseas, and the RAF offered a course on it, to which I applied. Unfortunately, I was turned down on the basis that once I qualified I would just leave the RAF and go overseas, which was true. There was a big demand for air traffic controllers overseas, especially in Africa.

Eventually, I was offered a 'Permanent Commission', which would have been a twenty-two-year contract, once my current contract had ended. I turned it down. I had met the woman who would later become my wife, and in my mind I had to choose one or the other, so I chose her. However, I did receive a letter from the Air Ministry telling me that I could use my rank of flight lieutenant in civilian life, as long as I put 'retired' after it.

Did you know that the flight taking up the cadets would be your last?

Yes, but I didn't really have any feelings about it at all. To me, it was just like any other flight.

What was your opinion of the Shackleton?

I never took a liking to the Shackleton. It was big, noisy and tended to vibrate. It didn't have the manoeuvrability of the Lancaster. In a Shackleton, I could never have done a rate four turn like I did in Gibraltar during the 'Battle of Britain' display in September 1951.

The Shackleton was a powerful plane with a dual purpose, serving as a maritime reconnaissance aircraft and as a troop carrier, although it could also be used as a bomber, if need be. It was an ideal plane for long-range patrols over the oceans, because it could stay in the air for anything up to twenty hours with an overload tank; this was ideal for its maritime reconnaissance role.

The best thing that I can say about the Shackleton was that it was a lot more stable in stormy weather than a Lancaster, which I believe was due to the increased power of the Shackleton; it could just bulldoze its way through the sky.

CHAPTER SIXTEEN

LIFE AFTER THE RAF

*Working in a children's home, a chilling
discovery, Denis's car business, men's outfitter work,
marriage to Ruby in 1962, London opportunities, relocation
to Norfolk, caring for the elderly, relocation to Suffolk as
a widower and Denis's ongoing life as a civilian*

**Your last flight took place on the 5th of March 1957, and you
began terminal leave over a month later, on the 22nd of April,
lasting until the 18th of July. When you finished your full-time
RAF career at this time, didn't you immediately begin a four-
year stint in the Reserves?**
Yes. On the 19th of July 1957, I officially transferred to the Royal
Air Force Reserve of Officers, or RAFRO, where I served until the
18th of July 1961.

**When you left your full-time RAF service in July 1957, did you
have any idea what your next step would be?**
Yes. I had an idea to set up a car delivery-collection service based
in Falmouth, Cornwall, which is where my lady, Ruby, and I were
living at the time. So it wasn't as though I was lost in regard to what
I would do with myself as a civilian. However, I was persuaded to
go into youth work.

In my last few months with 228 Squadron, I had become a PETLO,
which stands for Pre-Entry Training Liaison Officer. The previous
chap had been posted to Gibraltar, and the CO wanted me to take
on the PETLO role. This position was basically the link between
the Air Training Corps and the RAF. When the cadets from the ATC
came to St Mawgan, it was my job to organise their accommodation,
schedule, the contents of their lectures and other activities. They
would occasionally have the opportunity to go up in an aircraft, and

it was my job to organise that. In fact, as I have already mentioned, my last flight was taking up a group of cadets.

The senior officers at St Mawgan believed that I was good at PETLO duties, so they recommended that I make it a career. The education officer arranged two interviews for me; the first was for a juvenile prison type of facility in Surrey, and the second was a place in West Norwood, in London. The main problem with the first facility was the atmosphere; it was horrible. On top of this, there was a handbook filled with things that I would not be allowed to do. There were a lot of restrictions there. When I went in for the interview, I sat in a chair, and in front of me were close to fifteen people, sitting in a semicircle: doctors, social workers, a nurse and other staff. After the interview and a tour of the facility, I was asked if I could return for another interview, but I just told them that I was not interested at all.

The second place, in West Norwood, was completely different to the first, with a much better atmosphere. The main difference from the Surrey opportunity was that I sensed I would have a greater degree of freedom in the West Norwood job, so I agreed to try the position for a month. I ended up becoming a permanent employee.

You were in the RAF for just short of fifteen years, excluding your year and a half of civilian life from 1947 into 1949 and later your four years in the reserves. Was it hard for you to separate from such committed service and adjust back to civilian life after so many years in uniform?
Not at first because I immediately went into youth work, and it was something that I enjoyed.

Tell me about the youth work.
The children themselves were there for a number of reasons. There were cases stemming from divorces or the death of a parent, where whoever had won custody of the child or children couldn't cope with the situation. In other cases, one parent just vanished, abandoning the home in the middle of the night, leaving the other parent unable to manage the responsibilities of rearing a child. The courts often sent us children after deciding a course of action. Things like that.

I found the facilities to be very good. Under the structure devised by superintendent in charge, there were two senior boys' houses, for boys who were thirteen or older. Then there was a junior boys' house, which was for boys from ages five to thirteen. The junior house had a house father and house mother. The two houses for the senior boys each had a house father and house mother and two part-time house mothers. Each house had a cleaner too. The role of the house mother and house father was to be like surrogate parents to the boys. There was also a girls' house on the same site, but it was separated from the boys' houses. The girls' house took in all ages and only had a house mother in charge and an assistant house mother. There was also a nursery type set-up for boys and girls below the age of five, which a nurse oversaw.

A school on-site with its own staff catered to the educational needs of the children. It had been created by converting what had been a junior boys' house into classrooms.

The whole site was quite large. It had its own admin block and a huge meeting hall, including a large kitchen. It also had a gymnasium, its own swimming pool and another hall that would fit all the children for special occasions, such as yearly Christmas activities. Normally, every child ate in his or her own house, with meals having been prepared in the main kitchen and transported to each house via trolleys, which the houses provided.

I was a house father for one of the senior boys' houses. Every Friday, a house mother who worked until 8pm, a psychiatrist and I wrote a report on every boy, noting how he interacted with others, his general behaviour and the like. The reports were then passed on to the superintendent.

Considering that you spent around three-and-a-half to four years in an orphanage as a child, what was it like for you to be back in a similar environment, except this time in a position of authority?

Overall, I found it an interesting job. I definitely had a great deal of empathy towards the children and their situation, about which my experiences during childhood must have had a great influence.

The first thing I did was to appoint prefects among the boys in each dormitory. I did that to lessen the load on myself and to keep the boys well-behaved. Everyone had to be up at half-past seven. It was then up to each boy to choose either a shower or a strip wash, which the prefects dealt with. Next came breakfast, which was brought from the main kitchen on trolleys. After breakfast, I chose two boys to take the trolleys back.

Then the boys went to school, which started at nine. At this time, the school took control of them, and they had lunch in the main hall. At around five, back under my supervision, they ate a light meal. During this meal I would tell them what activities would be available afterwards, things like table tennis, snooker, football and volleyball. One thing I introduced was 'mad hour', which took place every Friday. I told them that they were allowed to use the gymnasium and all its equipment and make as much noise as they liked. If any boys wanted to fight each other, then I would let them do so, as long as it was done with boxing gloves on and under the condition that I would supervise them. There were also wrestling mats that they could use.

How did you keep the boys disciplined? There must have been times where one or two would try and push the boundaries.
I found that the best solution to that problem was to interview every boy there and any new ones who came in; this was routine, anyway. During an interview I asked a boy what his favourite pastime was, and then if he subsequently misbehaved I curtailed that activity. So if the boy liked football, I took that opportunity away from him.

I also had a reward system in place. For example, for the boys who were best-behaved, I organised trips in London or to the countryside. I only took a small group that I could keep a watch over myself. This resulted in the boys behaving well in the hope that they would be chosen to go on one of the trips. Some of the boys who were from London had never seen the countryside before, and they were amazed when they saw fields and farmyard animals.

However, the most successful reward system I had in place was a series of organised dances, where the girls' house was invited.

How did the first dance come to be?
I decided that it would be good for the boys to mix with girls, as they would have if they were raised under normal circumstances. I asked the superintendent, who agreed, and I then went to speak to

the house mother of the girls' house. I said that I would need at least one house mother there, preferably two, and that was agreed to.

Honestly, the first dance was an experiment; I had no idea how it would all work out. I decided to keep it a secret until the last moment. I told the boys that because an official from the Home Office was coming, they had to dress in their best clothes and make the place look spotless, in order to make a good impression. When I eventually told the boys what was actually going to happen, I can tell you, I had never before seen them in such an excited state. They were all trying to get into the showers, all putting on their best clothes, doing their hair and trying to make themselves look as nice as possible for the girls. I told the boys that they could bring along any records that they wanted to dance to.

Did it prove to be successful?
Very much so. It was something that was repeated and that I liked organising. The boys really enjoyed it, and the house mother in charge of the girls told me that the girls really enjoyed it too. Even the superintendent came along with his wife and congratulated me on my idea. It was nice for me to see those boys and girls, with less than ideal backgrounds, enjoying themselves so much.

It appears as though you had a good relationship with the boys under your supervision.
Yes. We were a happy house on the whole. I only had a few bad incidents while I was there. The only example that comes to mind is when one of the boys called one of the house mothers a 'stupid cow'. That really infuriated me. I called him in to see me, with her present, and asked him if he wanted to apologise. His response was something like, 'No, she is a stupid cow.' In a flash of anger, I slapped him on the back of the thighs, which caused him to leave the room crying. It was something I have always regretted doing, and it was the only time I smacked any of the boys. Hitting them was banned anyway. He apologised to her the next day, and, incidentally, those two later became the best of friends.

It seemed like a job you enjoyed, so why did you leave?
I had been considering moving back to Falmouth and setting up the car collection and delivery business that had been in the back of

my mind since my last year in the RAF. However, one incident, in particular, greatly influenced my decision to leave. I was doing some work in the office when one of the boys came in and told me that another lad from my house was having a serious confrontation with a boy from outside the home. This outsider was a known troublemaker who had often come onto the grounds for whatever reason.

I went outside and found them squaring off against each other. The boy from my house was holding a cricket stump, while the other boy was holding a piece of wood. I got between them and just shoved the uninvited boy out of the way, and he scampered off. I told the boy from my house to get back inside.

I thought that was the end of it, but after the uninvited boy spoke to his mother, she contacted the police, telling them that I had smacked her child. A policeman came to interview me, to hear my side of the story. After I had finished recounting what had happened, the policeman went to speak to the mother and boy. Eventually, the policeman came back and told me that after speaking to them, the truth emerged; the mother had smacked her son for misbehaving, causing him pain in his ear. They then tried to pin the blame on me. Fortunately, the police officer had found this all out while speaking to them, so I was told that the matter was closed, and that nothing else would come of it.

However, what really made me decide to leave was that we had a change of superintendent; he was not as helpful to the staff as the previous one had been. The new superintendent called me into his office and told me that if an incident like what happened with the boy and his mother occurred again and it went to court, then I would have to deal with it myself. In other words, the new superintendent was saying that I wouldn't have the support of the home. It was then that I decided to leave and move to Falmouth with Ruby to set up the car collection and delivery service. I don't recall when this occurred, but I think it was in early 1958.

When I told the superintendent of my intention to leave, he told me not to tell the boys until the last possible moment, as it would upset them. When I eventually told them, the reaction was awful. Half of them were in tears and it really tore at my heart. Honestly, I would be lying if I said that I didn't reconsider leaving. It was horrible to see the boys in such a state.

I later found out that the chap who took over from me was unable to control the boys, and that they had run riot. He had to be moved to the junior house, which he also failed to control, resulting in him being asked to find another job.

But there is something else that I must tell you about the children's home.

What is it?

I kept in touch with one of the staff members there, and after Ruby and I moved back to London from Cornwall, I would go and visit him at his office at the children's home to catch up and have a game of cards or something. He had been promoted to superintendent by that point. On one occasion, when he was short of staff, he asked me if I would be willing to look after the boys in the junior house for a few hours as a one-off, because the house father had an appointment he couldn't miss and the house mother was away on holiday.

I agreed to help. During my time working there, I had never even stepped foot in the block where the junior house was. To get there, I had to walk through the dining hall and kitchen area, and something felt strange, but I just couldn't place my finger on what it was. The chap who looked after the boys would usually read them a story, so, temporarily filling his shoes, that's what I did. They were very well-behaved and quickly went to sleep.

I then went for a wander around the building and found myself in the upstairs dormitory; no longer used for housing children, it was now a storage room. When I entered the room, I switched on the light, which emitted a slightly blue hue, and that's when memories started to flood back. I remembered where my bed would have been located, so I began to search for the initials that I knew I had carved into the wall, but I wasn't able to find them. I then remembered that I would have been much shorter, so I crouched down and continued searching.

And there it was, carved into the paint: 'DK', which stood for 'Denis Kimber', my name at the time. That was when I fully realised that I was in the same orphanage I had entered at around the age of three-and-a-half. Other memories started to flood back, like the area where my own mother had visited me on the two occasions I recalled.

At that point I basically froze; I could feel the blood rushing out of my face. I quickly left the room and went back to see my friend. He asked me if I was OK, as to him it looked as though I had seen a ghost. I told him that I had to go, making up a reason why I had to leave. I never went back.

What a harrowing story, and to think that you worked there for a good period of time without realising it was where you spent so much time as a child.
Well, the junior house, where I realised I had spent some of my youth, was in a different part of the orphanage from where I had worked as an adult. During my time working there, I was with the seniors and never went anywhere near the junior block. Nevertheless, that night is a horrible event for me to recall, truly awful.

Why do you think that in your time working there you never realised that it was the site of your orphanage?
I never visited the part of the grounds where the juniors were housed while employed as an adult, and I never went to the senior side of the grounds when I was there as a child. Also, it must be remembered that I was a young boy when I was living there, and that the site itself was very big. I guess that I just blocked out a lot of the memories.

Going back a bit, tell me about the car business.
Setting up the business took longer than anticipated, mainly due to the difficulty in getting insurance for any vehicle and acquiring trade plates for the vehicles that I would be driving. The council wouldn't release the trade plates until I had insurance, and the insurance company wouldn't insure me until I had the trade plates. Eventually, the council gave in.

I started off solely collecting new cars from the Rootes Group in Birmingham and Morris's in Oxford and then driving them back to Cornwall. The return drive would take quite a while, as new engines, requiring a period of breaking-in, could not be driven faster than thirty miles an hour for the first thousand miles.

Eventually, I got to know a chap who transported second-hand cars from the Southwest of the UK to Southampton and Brighton, so I started driving used cars to those places for him. I would then travel to Birmingham or Oxford, pick up a newly-built car and drive it back to

Cornwall. There were two main garages in Falmouth, one which dealt with Hillmans and the other with Austins, and I did business with them both. After a customer put in an order for a new car with a garage, I would take the opportunity to first deliver a used car from the garage to whomever was buying it up country. I would then visit a car manufacturer and drive a new car back to Cornwall, to be delivered either to the buyer or to a garage. Not all transactions were as complete as this, but more often than not I would drive a second-hand car out and a new car back.

What sort of cars were you driving?

I was mainly delivering new Morris and Austin cars from the factories where they were built to Cornwall. On one occasion I delivered a Ford Zephyr, owned by an American chap, to a place in London for shipment to America. As this Zephyr was configured for US driving, the steering wheel was on the left, so I found it somewhat difficult to handle. It was quite a powerful car, and big, too; it could carry six and had a bench seat in the front.

I eventually had a brainwave that some holidaymakers who fell ill while on holiday would need their cars driven back home. With this in mind, I registered with the Automobile Association to be permitted to drive home those who, because of their driver's illness, were unable to drive home themselves. On one occasion, a family had been on holiday in Looe when the father had a heart attack, leaving his wife and two children stranded while he was being treated in hospital. I was contacted by the AA regarding driving the family back to Hull, while the father remained in hospital.

I inspected their car and discovered that the windscreen wipers didn't work. They had to be fixed before we could depart. The lady and her husband ran an insurance company with a few staff members, so it was essential that she get back to Hull. After the windscreen wipers were repaired that day, we set off for Hull. I pointed out that it would be dark for most of the way. She had never been in a car at night and neither had her children, so they were all fascinated with the different lights and signals that they were seeing. We stopped at a café called the Black Horse, in Exeter, to have a light meal and to let everyone use the lavatory. My only other stops were for petrol.

We arrived on the outskirts of Hull at half-past six in the morning.

I had to awaken the mother so she could navigate me to her house. She later phoned to say that her husband had made a full recovery.

Also, in July 1959, while running the car business, I was called in for two weeks of RAF reserve service, which took place at RAF Mount Batten, in Plymouth, and St Mawgan. There was no flying involved; it was all ground work, things like going over the theories associated with our exercises with the navy. I remained in the reserves until the 18th of July 1961, exactly four years after leaving the RAF full-time.

How long did the business last?

About two years. Everything was going well, but then I made a mistake: I took on a partner. He turned out to be a liability to the business.

By the way, it was during this time that my foster mother passed away. I had received a phone call from Bert, her biological son, to say that she was in hospital and didn't have long to live, and that if I didn't come now then I wouldn't have any chance of seeing her again. So I drove back to Kent that same day. She had suffered a stroke, but when I arrived at the hospital and saw her she was able to talk and communicate. After my visit, Bert and I went to her home, which was no longer in Gladstone Road, but in Borkwood Way, which is in Orpington, and not far from the hospital; she had moved house while I was in Malta. It wasn't long after we arrived that one of Bert's colleagues from the hospital came by and told us that my foster mother had passed away.

I stayed in Kent for around five days, helping to organise the funeral and everything else that had to be dealt with. After all of that had been sorted, I went back to Cornwall.

Upon my return, I discovered that while I had been in Kent, a garage owner had made an urgent request for a car that had to be delivered that same day. The garage owner phoned my partner, who said that he could not do the job, as he had a wedding to attend. The result was that the garage owner lost the sale and told me that he never wanted to see my partner again.

Though things like that didn't help, what really killed the business was Falmouth Docks going on strike. As a result, people stopped buying new cars, and so they were no longer selling their old ones. The car business quickly dried up.

So what did you do?

I managed to find a job as a second salesman in a men's outfitter in the spring of 1960, which I held for over two years.

During my time with the outfitter, I married Ruby, in May 1962. Although I had been with her during my time in the RAF, I had not wanted to get married while I was serving or in the reserves. I had seen quite a few pilots enter marriage and then get killed a short while later. I had no interest in tempting fate, so I waited until I was no longer flying or in the reserves before getting married. We were never blessed with any children due to a medical issue that Ruby had. Although Ruby suggested that we foster children, I was against it due to my experiences as a foster child. To me, fostering a child would have constantly brought my childhood to the forefront of my mind, and it wasn't something I wanted to go through.

The big mystery was that not long after our wedding I received a letter of congratulations from W/Cdr Blackburn.

From W/Cdr Blackburn? How did he find out that you were married?

To this day, I have no idea how he found out. He was a wing commander, quite a high rank, and the story I told you about him having the engines repaired and refitted on his German E-Boat suggests that he had contacts in high places. I am sure he could have pulled a few strings to find out my address, especially considering that my wife and I had been living in the same house since relocating from London, and for the majority of my time in the RAF reserves.

However, I was no longer in the reserves when I married Ruby, so my marriage would not have been mentioned in RAF records. How, then, did W/Cdr Blackburn find out about it? He must have kept tabs on me for quite a while. I can't imagine that the first time he checked up on me just so happened to be when I got married; it would have been an amazing coincidence if it had been the first time. Assuming he did check up on me over the years, why did he do it? To this day I can't answer those questions.

Unfortunately, your job with the outfitter was not to last.

The job itself was steady, but during my last summer there it seemed to rain non-stop. This negatively affected sales, as fewer customers, including the many tourists visiting Cornwall, ventured out into the rain to purchase men's clothing. As a result of dwindling sales, the boss cut staff numbers, and he did it on a principle of last in, first out. I was the last staff member to join, so I was the first one out. He was kind enough to give me a suit as a farewell gift. That was in October 1962.

Fortunately, during my time at the outfitter, I had passed a three-month telephone operators course and had taken a part-time job as an operator, so I was still employed.

What was your next step? Being a part-time phone operator could not have been a long-term solution.
At the end of 1962 we moved to Saltash, across the River Tamar from Plymouth. There, I secured a job with the Co-op in their accounts department. I was there for over a year before a large number of staff were let go, including myself. Unfortunately, I wasn't entitled to redundancy, as I had not been with them for two years, the minimum required time to be entitled to it.

What came next?
In the latter half of 1964, Ruby and I moved to Plymouth, in Devon, and I soon found a job at a garage as a petrol pump attendant. We lived in Plymouth for a few years, but due to the lack of employment opportunities, Ruby and I decided to move back to London, where there were many more jobs available. I believe this move took place in around 1968.

Looking back, did you enjoy living in Cornwall?
Oh, yes. It was a nice county to reside in. While living in Falmouth, there were plenty of swimming opportunities. The people, however, were very clannish. Ruby had a friend who came down from London, and once when we were in a shop the friend openly started saying how she was from London, as if it was a badge of honour, and something to be proud of. As a result, she was cold-shouldered, and I told her that boasting about being from London was the worst thing she could have done.

Another example is an ex-navy chap I worked with at the Co-op. On one occasion, he told me that a friend would be visiting him from London. When I enquired about which part, he told me that his friend was coming from Peterborough, a city over 70 miles north of London. 'It's all London on the other side of the Tamar,' was his response, half-jokingly, half-seriously. I don't know if the attitude is the same now; maybe it has changed. Still, Cornwall was a nice county to live in.

London was next for you.
I had gone up ahead of Ruby to London, and by that time the house in Plymouth had been put up for sale. I stayed in a bed and breakfast room in Bromley, which by then had become a part of Greater London, and from the local newspaper I applied for a housekeeper's position on Ruby's behalf, helping to look after a Roman Catholic family's house and children. Ruby was chosen for the job. On top of the pay, the family provided rent-free accommodation, without bills.

I had gained a job with the ESSO petroleum company, near Victoria station, London, in their accounts department, but I was only with ESSO for less than a year. What happened was that I had found the job through an agent. This chap had set up a firm to help people find work. However, the catch was that the new employer gave the worker's wages to the agent, who then took a cut for himself before giving what was left to the worker. Once I found out about this, I promptly quit the job at ESSO and cut all ties with the agent, who ended up being murdered.

Murdered?
Yes. Someone walked into his office and shot him. As my name was on his books, I was questioned by the police regarding the shooting, but only the once.

Where did you go from there?
I went to work for a firm called Ultra Electronics, in their accounts department. Ruby had only lasted three weeks or so with the Roman Catholic family before finding another job that she enjoyed, which was helping to look after a man with Down's syndrome. We had also

found a nice flat in London's West Ealing borough. I was with Ultra Electronics for about four years. They made electrical equipment, things like irons, radios and televisions. They also had a government contract for sonobuoys, which was ironic, as I was dropping them during my time with Coastal Command.

After four years with them, I applied for a job with the accounts department of a company named Metal Box; this was around 1973. The reason was that the terms and pay at Metal Box were better than those at Ultra Electronics.

Metal Box produced cans of various sizes. Including the overseas operations, they had fifty-one factories in total, eleven of which were known as 'open top' manufacturing facilities because they turned flat metal into cans without the tops on. It was done that way so Heinz or whoever could fill each can with whatever it wanted. However, Metal Box also manufactured the tops for the cans, but the topless cans and the tops themselves were produced and delivered to the user separately.

Metal Box factories produced a variety of other products. Some manufactured 'flat sheet' items like trays, biscuit tins and things like that. Others produced paper items, cheque books being a prime example. I was only concerned with the open top factories.

Was it a good place to work?
It was a very good place to work. We had our own accounts office, where I worked with a good team, and we all got on well. It also had its own sports and social club and its own canteen. All of that contributed to a good working atmosphere.

After a few years of working there, I was promoted to 'stock records controller'. In this new position, I had to cost every material coming into the factory and the bits and pieces that would go with it. There were the cost calculations for converting the flat plate to cans and the overall production costs.

The factory manager held a daily meeting with the factory's upper management and myself regarding all of that information. In this meeting, I provided my cost estimates for all the materials and everything else that would be required for the following day's production.

During that time, Ruby was still working with the Down's syndrome man.

Everything went well until around 1978, when labour disputes caused my factory in Acton, London, to close, alongside the open top factories in Glasgow and Liverpool. I was asked to stay on until April of the following year to provide final financial figures.

Towards the end of the year, the mother of the man with Down's syndrome retired, and they moved to her sister's home in Devon. The sister agreed to be his housekeeper, so that put Ruby out of a job.

With both Ruby and yourself facing unemployment, what did you decide to do?
Fortunately, Ruby and I had bought the house in Waterloo Road, Norwich, in 1974, as an investment, so in 1979, when we both lost our jobs, we decided to move into it.

Tell me about your time living in Norwich.
I heard that Norwich Union was looking for two commissionaires; a commissionaire was a person in uniform who directed people to the relevant departments that they were looking for. Additionally, a commissionaire kept out troublemakers. Norwich Union's response was to inform me that both positions had been filled, but that in light of my accounting experience they could offer me a position in their accounts department. I readily accepted.

Fortunately, they were a good company to work for. Unfortunately, I was only there for just under five years, which ruled me out of their pension scheme. The reason I left Norwich Union is because of their policy that everyone, regardless of position, had to retire at the age of sixty. So when July 1984 came along and I turned sixty, it was my turn to retire.

My opinion of Norwich was still the same as it had been when I visited there during my time at Swannington in 1946 and 1947: it was a lovely place. The people were friendly, the atmosphere was great and it offered an excellent market and wonderful shops.

What came after Norwich?
After my job with Norwich Union ended, we sold the house in Norwich

and moved to Dereham, a small Norfolk town about fifteen miles to the west of Norwich. Personally, I never took to Dereham; there was little of interest to me there. When we first arrived, the surrounding area was nice, but within time much of it was built on. There used to be two lovely strawberry fields through which I enjoyed walking the dogs, but one became an industrial estate and the other became a housing development.

Upon moving to Dereham, I took a year off from working, and in 1986 I went back to work, as a carer of the elderly.

It was quite a lengthy career for you.
Yes. It was something I did for around ten years, and as a result I met some interesting people along the way. I was fortunate with my first client because we got on very well. I was with him for three years until he died. He came from quite an affluent background and was a genuinely nice man.

The rest of the clients I had over the years were a mixed bunch; some I liked more than others. Interestingly, one had a brother who, as a Japanese prisoner of war, was put to work on the Burma-Thailand Railway, though the brother never spoke about it.

In 1994 you moved to Suffolk.
Ruby had passed away in 1992. After suffering a severe stroke, she was taken to a hospital in Dereham, which specialised in treating stroke victims. Unfortunately, while she was there she suffered another stroke, which sadly proved to be the end.

Afterwards, I decided to move, but it took two years to sell the house. During that time I was in residence with a client. After the house was sold, I moved into a converted slaughterhouse in a town in Cambridgeshire, but I didn't like the place at all. The first house I found was in east Suffolk, so I moved there. By the time I made this move, I had decided to fully retire, but the care agency managed to convince me to take on one more client, for whom I cared for six months at the most before he died from stomach cancer.

Was it hard to adjust to living on your own in a new area after being married for so long?
No, because I had two dogs who needed to be taken out and a good-

sized garden to attend to. I have always been quite comfortable in my own company, and I had good neighbours, so it wasn't really difficult or anything like that.

How long were you there for?
I was there for twenty-four years, from the age of seventy in 1994 to ninety-three in 2018. During those years a lot changed. For the majority of my time there, until my late eighties, I was quite active with things like walking the dogs, gardening, going into town and meeting with friends. But eventually, I started to slow down, as happens to everyone. In 2005 I sold my last car, to your mother, which was how you and I met.

Even without a car I still kept active, especially with the garden. I walked into town and rode the bus back, went to the beach to swim, walked in the countryside and met up with friends.

By the early 2010s, you, your mother and I had become quite good friends. We would go shopping together, socialise and have days out, which we still do. It was around that time when you started to help me with my garden.

However, in April 2018, after a few days of bad health, I had a serious fall which resulted in me being trapped on the floor for twenty-eight hours, unable to move. During that time, you and your mother became concerned and phoned the paramedics and police, who broke in and released me. During a lengthy hospital stay, you helped organise new accommodation for me, which is where I am now and from where we have been working on this book.

CHAPTER SEVENTEEN

REFLECTIONS ON AN UNBELIEVABLE LIFE

You have lived an extraordinary life. You have experienced and witnessed things both horrific and magnificent that most people will find very difficult to comprehend. What thoughts come to mind when you look back on your life?

What really comes to mind are memories of my mother from when I was around three years old, such as when I was out walking with her, my sister Doris and my brother Harold. I was pulling a toy horse on a lead, and as the toy moved the head bobbed up and down. Another memory that comes to mind is of being near the statue of Queen Victoria outside of Croydon town hall; I was upset and stomping my feet that the pigeons were landing on everyone else's hands except mine and my mother telling me that if I stood still they would come and land on me. On that occasion both Doris and Harold were there.

Considering your childhood, it's impressive that you went on to achieve everything that you did.

I would say it's astonishing how things turned out. Growing up, I always lacked confidence compared to boys my own age, and it wasn't until I joined the Air Defence Cadet Corps (which became the Air Training Corps) in October 1940 that I began to realise that the results I was achieving were just as good as everyone else's, both physically and mentally.

There's no doubt in my mind that despite the obvious dangers and the tragedy that affected so many, World War Two was a positive event for me personally and in some respects for my generation. In a way, it gave us freedom from the old stiff rules of British society and afforded us opportunities that would never have been available otherwise. Even before going overseas, when I was in the ATC, I learnt so much and picked up so many skills.

What positive effects did the ATC have on you?
It made me more confident in myself and in my ability to achieve things. I also met new people and made new friends. There was a strong, positive sense of camaraderie among us. On Saturdays we participated in organised social events, which also included civilian girls. The camaraderie was also reflected in society; people were more open and friendly towards each other. There was this sense that everyone was in the war together, fighting for the common good. The ATC was something I really looked forward to, even the lectures. It became the most important part of my life. Acquiring new skills, and the increase in confidence, led me to look forward to what the future had in store for the first time in my life.

Not only was the ATC enriching my life, but in my day job, in the showrooms, so many of the staff had been called up that I quickly advanced within the business. When I first started I simply swept the floor, but by the time I entered the RAF I was an assistant cashier and was in charge of the storeroom, where things like plugs, fuses and cables were stored. I really enjoyed the responsibility I had. I flourished in my new role, and I actually looked forward to going to work each day, and to the ATC. It was an interesting time. More than once I cycled home to the booming sound of anti-aircraft fire and the sight of searchlights, all in response to the droning of German aircraft overhead.

All of these things would never have happened if it wasn't for the war.

To go from working in a showroom to being stationed on the African continent in less than a year was a huge step, a change in so many ways. How do you look back on that time now?
I look back upon it with the feeling that I had then. I went from feeling that I had not achieved anything to feeling that I was achieving so much. During my time on the African continent I saw, experienced and accomplished so many things. There was a constant sense of eagerness for what lay ahead. Everything in Africa was such a novelty to me, and completely different to Britain in so many ways. I remember being in school and listening to the geography master talk about his travels to Egypt, when he saw things like the Sphinx,

and just a few years later I was standing in front of the same Sphinx and taking photographs of it. Amazing.

The crowning achievement for me during that period was earning my wings. So much went into reaching that spectacular milestone. It was something that in my earlier years of little self-confidence I would never have thought I could reach.

After going solo for the first time in a Tiger Moth, I felt more mature and self-assured. There was a brief period when I even slipped into overconfidence. I was up in an Oxford and was preparing to land at Kumalo, near Bulawayo in Southern Rhodesia. I looked out of the port window and thought to myself that I was the only person on board who could land this aircraft. I then performed a terrible landing, which taught me a lesson about overconfidence and arrogance.

Looking back, Africa was an interesting continent. I grew to like Southern Rhodesia. It was my favourite country on the continent, even though I only really saw one city there, Bulawayo.

Is Palestine, as it was called then, somewhere you look back on fondly?
Yes. Being in such a historically rich area really made me feel that I was a part of that history, which has proven interesting, considering that many people now study that period of the region's past. Jerusalem was such a fascinating city to me. To have read about places in the Bible and then to have visited them and seen them with my own eyes was extraordinary. It's a place where I would have liked more time to explore, with more money available to spend.

How do you look back on India?
On the whole I liked India and its people. As busy as the cities were, and despite the anti-British sentiment, there seemed to be a relaxed feeling at the same time. India is a country I could quite happily visit again. It was a vast contrast to Malaya soon after the Japanese surrender, where there was definite tension in the air. Look at it this way: in India I felt I could walk around any city by myself without any worries, but in Malaya we were told to never go out alone and were even issued with sidearms during our time there. Fortunately, our guns never had to be fired in defence, only brandished once

when returning from a dance one night outside of Kuala Lumpur. However, when we first arrived in Malaya, my crew and I were billeted in an old Nissen hut. We used to take turns turning out the light at night. On one occasion I told my co-pilot that it was his turn to turn off the light. He just grabbed his pistol and shot out the bulb. So at least his firearm was used for something. Another time, a rifle was used to kill a king cobra.

Looking back on my time in India, I don't recall sensing animosity from the populace towards the British, especially in light of how other people felt towards their occupying power. It's amazing how things changed so drastically after the war.

It's quite extraordinary to think that at the age of twenty, you were captaining Liberator aircraft and flying operations.
During that time, I rarely thought about my age. It wasn't until after I had finished my 159 Squadron tour of operations that I thought about it and realised that I had completed a full tour despite not even being twenty-one. To put it into context, the average age of a Liberator captain on the squadron was twenty-four.

To me, it's extraordinary that in under three years I had gone from working in a showroom to captaining bomber aircraft. When I look back on those years, from call-up to operational flying, I feel that in that time I reached the maturity of manhood.

It can be argued that your age helped you. You have already spoken about not fully appreciating danger at that age, and that must have helped you during your operational flying.
It certainly did. I couldn't see or appreciate the dangers that the even more mature captains could recognise. For the most part, each operation was an adventure to me. I had no real fear of going on them. A prime example was the occasion of my eighth operation when, on the 15th-16th of November 1944, one of my engines wouldn't start. I couldn't go with the rest of the squadron to Mergui, in Burma, but W/Cdr Blackburn gave me until two in the afternoon to take off. I kept nagging the ground crew to get my plane airworthy so I could join in on the action. Most pilots would have been happy that their aircraft suffered a mechanical fault, as it meant that they wouldn't

have to take the risks that came with bombing a target, but I was desperate to get up in the air. I just wasn't scared.

I can't say I ever really did develop that sense of danger. I think a big part of it was the fact that I just loved flying so much. All I wanted to do was to get up in the air, and that love of flying largely overshadowed any fears I might have had. Of course, there were moments of fear, such as when under attack by Japanese naval ships after bombing a Bangkok target on the night of the 2nd-3rd of November 1944, but, by and large, those instances were rare.

Looking back, some of the things I did were mad, and sometimes I can't believe I did them. Like the journey to meet Laurie, my friend from our troopship voyage to South Africa in 1942, when I put the Dakota on autopilot and played cards with my crew in the back. No one was keeping a lookout in the cockpit, as all of us were in the rear of the aircraft. The only reason I went into the cockpit every so often was to check on an oil leak. I should have remained there to keep a lookout for things like other aircraft, to make sure that everything was working and to be at the controls in case a response to a sudden problem was needed. It's hard to comprehend that I did other mad things like beating up airfields, coming in so low to land and hopping over trees at the last second. I'm certain that I did those things because, at my age, I did not appreciate the element of risk. Happy days!

Looking back, what are your thoughts on the operations themselves?
The tour of operations itself turned out a lot easier than I anticipated, with a few exceptions. Going into the tour, I expected to come under a lot more anti-aircraft fire during our flights. However, by the beginning of my tour of operations with 159 Squadron the focus of the Japanese was more heavily aimed towards the vast Pacific Ocean area than to the Burma region. As a result, the Japanese military forces in the Far East were stretched thinner.

Having said all that, 159 Squadron lost three Liberators during my twenty-three-operation tour, and I witnessed two of them shot down, one each during my seventh and seventeenth operations. Either loss might very well have been my aircraft and my crew –

such was the fickle nature of flying combat operations, and being in the wrong place at the wrong time.

The third 159 Squadron Liberator lost during my time at Digri was on the night of the 10th-11th of November 1944. This Liberator disappeared on its one-aircraft C Flight special operation, with the loss of the entire crew, so we never knew if it suffered mechanical or weather-related problems, or if the Japanese were responsible.

Two more 159 Squadron Liberators were downed by enemy fighters early in October 1944, the month I arrived on 159 Squadron. Another, captained by Gerald Schroeder, whom I had screened on my nineteenth operation, was shot down in flames by anti-aircraft fire thirteen days after my twenty-third and final operation.

Then there was the C Flight Liberator from 159 Squadron named WOTTAWITCH!!, which disappeared over Burma on its radar-snooping operation on the 31st of January-1st of February 1945, just four nights after I finished my tour. It was learned, eventually, that four of the six captured crew were tortured and beheaded by the Japanese.

However, I survived my tour of operations on 159 Squadron, and my mind and body were intact. W/Cdr Blackburn survived a total of 200 operations flown, over Europe, North Africa, and Southeast Asia. Intact. Five operational tours! Completing my own tour made me feel that I had achieved what I had been trained for and what I had spent years working towards. Flying my own Liberator at the age of twenty, I can't get over that. I'll forever feel a sense of satisfaction and accomplishment at having completed a full tour of operations as a Liberator captain at such a young age.

Which operations are you most proud of?

The three raids on Penang Harbour are achievements that I am really proud of. This is largely because everyone believed that it wasn't possible, and we proved them all wrong. Also, at least on the first occasion, we took the Japanese by complete surprise. They were not expecting it at all, resulting in the operation being a huge success. It's amazing that we flew for up to nineteen hours non-stop.

The occasion when we dropped napalm bombs in Bangkok on the 2nd-3rd of December 1944 leaves me with a strong sense of achievement, because we completely wiped out an essential Japanese supply depot. Also, it took a week of training to prepare for that one raid, because the target was in quite a concentrated area. The single napalm bomb, along with the incendiary and conventional bomb load of each Liberator, had to be dropped in a precise way to avoid unnecessary damage to the area surrounding the target. It was also the only occasion that I, as the pilot, released bombs myself; this sticks out in my mind because the aiming and dropping of bombs, or mines, was never before, and never again, my responsibility.

Your operations seem to have generally been a resounding success, with 159 Squadron working like a well-oiled machine. How much of that do you think was down to W/Cdr Blackburn?
W/Cdr Blackburn had an uncanny way of organising quite unusual raids. The Penang and napalm raids, as examples, would never have happened without him. I found that if I was flying my own plane to a target and I knew that he was also on the same target, then I felt safe, and that everything was going to be okay. What it boiled down to was that he inspired confidence in people.

As I have already mentioned, when I met up with him in Malta after the war, he admitted regret in allowing me to go late to the target, Mergui in Burma, on the 15th-16th of November 1944. If you recall, he gave me a two in the afternoon deadline for taking off, following an engine change, and I met the deadline with seven minutes to spare. He claimed that not only was he worried about me, but also that if anything had happened to me then the obvious question in the inquiry would have been how he could have allowed a twenty-year-old to carry out such an operation entirely on his own. W/Cdr Blackburn had made a calculated command decision, and thankfully – for him and for myself and my crew – I brought my Liberator and crew home unscathed. I admired his courage in allowing me to go, as I knew he was aware of my age.

I was fortunate to have him as my CO, especially at that time in my life and under those circumstances. During my career with the RAF I had a good number of COs, but he was by far the most competent. He was excellent.

How did the war change you?

I matured far more quickly than had I not gained such broad-ranging experiences. When war was declared I had not long left school, but with all the men I was working with soon called up into the armed forces, I had to fill their shoes and take on their responsibilities. Adolescents had to grow up fast. In a short time I had progressed from sweeping the floors of the showrooms to taking on jobs that came with real responsibilities, and that was before the RAF came into the picture.

The training I received in the RAF was excellent. The standard of training provided by the RAF was indisputable, I acquired so many new skills that I never would have learnt otherwise.

Fortunately, my new-found confidence and acceptance of responsibility served me well, in that I quickly adjusted to the fact that as captain I was responsible for not only my own life but also for the lives of my crew, in the sense that I was flying the aircraft and had to keep it in the air. As captain, I was in the position to give orders. My duties were quite a lot to take on, especially given that I was only twenty years old.

From the time when you were a boy, key decisions have altered the course of your life. For example, whether to go into the Air Defence Cadet Corps – soon to be renamed the Air Training Corps – or the Sea Cadets, and whether to re-enlist with the RAF. With all this in mind, do you have any regrets?

I wish it had been possible for me to join the Sea Cadets. I love the sea, I really do. For example, aboard the troopship SS *Rangitiki*, transporting me from the UK to South Africa in December 1942 and January 1943, most of the others grew bored and sick of the voyage. On the other hand, I loved every minute of it, I really did. I looked forward to each day and spent as much time out on the upper deck as possible.

I believe I would have been well-suited to the navy. I remember that when I was twelve, I joined a choir outing to Chatham, in Kent, where we went on board a battleship. I soon separated from the group in order to explore everywhere possible. I investigated the gangways, I walked up and down steps and I just took in as much as I could. I was eventually found. Even then I loved ships and the sea.

What about W/Cdr Blackburn's offer to meet him in Marseille?
Yes. Looking back I also regret signing on with the RAF for another year in 1946, while at Swannington, because if I had not then I would have been able to accept W/Cdr Blackburn's sailing offer. It wasn't so much being with W/Cdr Blackburn that was so enticing as it was the pulling power of the sea. The idea of being out at sea on a yacht for extended periods of time really appealed to me. If the two options of signing on for another year with the RAF or taking W/Cdr Blackburn up on his offer had both arisen at the same time, then I would have been off to Marseille in a flash, no doubt about it.

Is there anything you regret not doing?
That's a tricky one. I suppose it goes back to not being able to join the Sea Cadets and then the navy. I also regret not being able to go to Hong Kong in late 1955 when the potential for a posting there arose while I was converting onto Shackletons at Kinloss, Scotland. I liked the idea of going somewhere new, and I was looking forward to the opportunity to fly the Sunderland flying boat out of Hong Kong, but I simply lost the posting to an officer with seniority over me.

What are your total flying hours?
According to my log book, I flew 3543 hours as a pilot or co-pilot. However, I'm certain that the total is actually more than that, as I know that on a few other occasions I didn't enter flights into my log book. Out of the 3543 recorded hours, 2172 were on Lancasters, 362 were on Liberators and the rest were on various other aircraft. I was also a passenger for 450 hours. My log book, then, indicates that I spent 3993 hours in the air.

How many different aircraft did you fly in total?
I piloted thirteen aircraft and was a passenger in an additional six, as can be seen in the Addendum following this chapter.

Out of all the aircraft you flew, which one did you like the most?
The Lancaster was my favourite, because it was so highly manoeuvrable, as I demonstrated against a Vampire jet in the 'Battle of Britain' display over Gibraltar in September 1951.

However, the Liberator was certainly more advanced than the Lancaster. For example, many things within the cockpit of a Lancaster were controlled by levers, which could be a job to operate, while the Liberator had switches which one just flicked. Also, in typical American style, the Liberator was built for comfort, with padded seats and other luxuries. There was even armoured plating behind the pilot's seat to protect him from behind. W/Cdr Blackburn had it removed for the Penang raids to reduce the overall weight and, thus, to help achieve the range needed to reach the target and to return, a distance of just over 3,000 miles. Nevertheless, even though the Lancaster had cushions instead of padded seats and was less advanced than the Liberator in many ways, it was still my favourite aircraft.

Your flying involved taking many risks, especially on operations. Did what you went through have any effect on your religious views?

I have always believed in God, right from early childhood. I told you how my second foster father had died on the 8th of December 1943. I believed that he had passed on in order to become my guardian angel, to keep me safe, a conviction I still hold to this day.

Also, while I was stationed at St Mawgan in the 1950s I became friendly with the Methodist minister of the area and attended his service every Sunday, if flying duties permitted. To this day, I still say my prayers every night before going to sleep.

What are your thoughts when you look back and see how much Britain has changed in your lifetime?

One immediate thought is that British society has lost most of its authoritarian element, and what is left is virtually powerless. The respect that figures like policemen and teachers used to have has fallen a lot. Such figures once commanded automatic respect, whereas now people snub their noses at them, for lack of a better saying. In short, authority has largely lost its grip. Before the war, gun and knife crime hardly existed, unlike now, where it is so often in the news.

I'm sure that when you stepped foot onto the SS *Rangitiki* in December 1942, you had all these hopes and dreams for what the future might hold. Did you achieve your dreams?

For the most part, yes. I thoroughly enjoyed all the different adventures I experienced and all the travelling that came with it. I visited so many of the places I had read about, and in particular, India; I was especially attracted to India. I remember in school when the geography master asked me to trace the flow of the river Ganges, and there I was, years later, flying over the Ganges. Flying and especially earning my wings were other dreams that were realised.

Not receiving the DFC because of a change of CO on 159 Squadron was very unfortunate. It was an award that W/Cdr Blackburn had personally recommended for both Frizzy and me.

Is there anything else that you would like to add?

Looking back, I am rather surprised at how quickly the time went by, bearing in mind that I was in the Air Training Corps and its predecessor, the Air Defence Cadet Corps, and then the Royal Air Force, including the reserves, from October 1940 up until July 1961.

Thank you for your time, Denis.

Thank you for your time.

AIRCRAFT IN WHICH DENIS FLEW WHILE IN THE RAF

(All are British-built except where noted.)
(Total hours flown as pilot or co-pilot: 3543)

Aircraft type	Hours flown
Airspeed Oxford (Twin engine trainer)	157
Comments: It wasn't an aircraft I particularly liked, but at the same time I didn't dislike it. It wasn't difficult to handle, but one had to be careful when landing so as not to land nose first, as the propellers could make contact with the ground.	
Avro Anson (Twin engine multi-purpose plane)	2
Comments: Like with the Proctor, it's difficult for me to comment on the Anson. It is the plane I was briefly tested on for my private pilot's licence.	
Avro Lancaster (Four engine heavy bomber)	2172
Comments: My favourite plane. It handled so well. It had comfortable seating and didn't provide me with any problems when taking off or landing. It was highly manoeuvrable too.	

Aircraft type	Hours flown
Avro Shackleton (Four-engine transport & maritime patrol aircraft)	297

Comments: It was the plane I liked the least out of all those that I flew. Though it was a powerful aircraft, it was very noisy, and it vibrated. In my opinion, its handling didn't match that of the Lancaster.

Aircraft type	Hours flown
Consolidated B-24 Liberator (American four-engine heavy bomber)	362

Comments: A truly lovely plane, which handled very well. The crew positions were well thought out. The pilot's seat was luxurious, and it even had armrests. It was great to handle, and the autopilot was very good, which helped on long-distance operations.

Aircraft type	Hours flown
de Havilland Canada **Chipmunk** (Single-engine trainer)	6

Comments: It was a little difficult for me to adjust to the Chipmunk at a time when I was primarily flying Lancasters. Once I had adjusted, however, the Chipmunk was easy to handle. I sometimes performed aerobatics when I was flying it.

Aircraft type	Hours flown
de Havilland Tiger Moth (Single-engine trainer)	77

Comments: It was an excellent training plane, and easy to fly. I learnt to perform many acrobatics in it. Its one weakness was that if one performed a three-point landing, then the tail skid risked breaking.

Aircraft type	Hours flown
Douglas Dakota (American twin-engine passenger & transport plane)	224

Comments: The Dakota was a marvellous plane, and well ahead of its time. It was claimed that it could fly on one engine with a 5,000-pound load. I have never heard one word said against the Dakota. It handled very well and was a joy to fly.

Fairchild Argus (American single-engine light transport & passenger plane)	5

Comments: Like the Sentinel, it was easy to handle. To me, it was quite similar to the Sentinel.

Percival Proctor (Single-engine trainer)	1

Comments: There isn't much I can say about the Proctor, as I only flew it for part of one hour.

Stinson Sentinel (American single-engine light liason, air ambulance & observation plane)	37

Comments: A light aircraft that I found easy to fly with all the experience I had built up by the time I flew it. Its claim to fame was that it could land in very small spaces. It was easy to handle.

Aircraft type	Hours flown
Vickers Warwick (Twin-engine passenger & transport plane)	96

Comments: A plane that I didn't like. After the Liberator, the Warwick seemed rather cumbersome. Handling-wise, it was average.

Aircraft type	Hours flown
Vickers Wellington (Twin-engine bomber)	107

Comments: A wonderful plane to handle, and the Wellington was my first feeling of real power. It seemed to easily push its way through the air.

Aircraft in which Denis flew as a passenger while in the RAF*:

Avro Anson
Avro Lancaster
Beechcraft Expeditor
*Bristol Blenheim
de Havilland Comet
de Havilland Tiger Moth
Douglas Dakota
Handley Page Hastings
**Imperial Airways flying boat: 'Caledonia'
Short Sunderland
Vickers Valetta

Total hours flown as a passenger: 450

*Denis made one flight before joining the RAF: aboard a Blenheim when he was an ATC cadet.

**This flying boat was flown by Imperial Airways, not the RAF

Printed in Great Britain
by Amazon

67958299R00173